ASSAM ADVENTURE

ASSAM ADVENTURE

F. KINGDON WARD

GYAN

Published by

Gyan Publishing House
5, Ansari Road
Daryaganj, New Delhi-110002
Phone: 011-47034999, 9811692060
E-mail: books@gyanbooks.com

Distribution Network
gyanbooks.com
India, USA, Canada, UK, Australia

ISBN: 978-93-7447-512-6 (PB)

First Published, 1941

2nd Impression 2026

Printed at: Gyan Press, Delhi.

ASSAM ADVENTURE
Author: F. KINGDON WARD

ASSAM ADVENTURE

ASSAM ADVENTURE

by

F. KINGDON WARD

B.A. (Cantab), F.R.G.S., F.L.S.

(Founder's Medal, Royal Geographical Society, Livingstone Medal, Royal Scottish Geographical Society, Veitchian Medal and Victoria Medal of Honour, Royal Horticultural Society, George Robert White Medal, Massachusetts Horticultural Society)

JONATHAN CAPE
THIRTY BEDFORD SQUARE
LONDON

CONTENTS

ILLUSTRATIONS

ILLUSTRATIONS

FOREWORD

TIBET has always exercised a fascination over the minds of men, and it does so no less to-day than it did a century ago, when it was still but a name to the West. Its aloofness, its sublime heights, its well-guarded and remote approaches, above all the strange culture and religious fervour of its people, all tend to make it even in these days a land of mystery.

For a generation which will enjoy the sight of many Tibetan plants growing in English and American gardens, and perhaps have the opportunity to solve some of the problems here discussed, I have written this book.

I am told that nowadays the competition to be first with the news is so keen that an explorer ought to write his travel book before he sets out on his travels. This gives his publisher a flying start.

My publisher is more patient. I am afraid I have let the grass grow under my feet for five years, owing to continuous journeys of exploration between 1937 and 1939. Meanwhile I have profited by the intervening years of travel and study to write more fully and accurately of the flora than would have been possible had I published a book immediately on my return from Tibet while the exploit was 'hot news'.

About a quarter of it was written while I was actually travelling in the Assam Himalayas in 1938. Another quarter was written at the 'Blue House', Hamilton Farm, Gladstone, the beautiful New Jersey home of Mr. and Mrs. Charles Suydam Cutting, with whom I stayed in the summer of 1939. The remaining half was written in London during the war, in 1939-40.

My sincere thanks are due to all those who helped me directly and indirectly, consciously or perhaps unconsciously, in the work, especially in ensuring some temporary degree of accuracy in names, whether of places, plants, or animals, sufficient to make them identifiable by the present generation.

FOREWORD

I would especially thank Dr. J. Ramsbottom, Keeper of Botany, Natural History Museum. Dr. George Taylor and Miss Nancy Lindsay for much useful help and advice; Mr. J. E. Dandy of the Natural History Museum; Sir George Reid, Governor of Assam; Mr. J. P. Mills, I.C.S.; Mr. A. C. Tunstall of the Tocklai Tea Research Station; Captain G. C. Lightfoot, Political Officer, Charduar; Captain and Mrs. Whitehead of the Assam Rifles; Dr. N. L. Bor, Indian Forest Service, and Mrs. Bor; Mr. F. Ludlow; Captain George Sherriff; Sir William Wright Smith, Regius Professor of Botany, Edinburgh; and not least Mr. and Mrs. C. Suydam Cutting of New Jersey. I am also indebted to Mr. Jonathan Cape, for his patience, tact, and understanding.

Others also have helped, who, if I have omitted their names in an endeavour to avoid compiling a directory, are not forgotten in my heart.

F. K. W.

London 1940

To

My Daughter

PLEIONE

ASSAM ADVENTURE

CHAPTER I

THE WORLD WELL LOST

THE travel story which I am about to tell is the story of my Tibetan journey in 1935, but most of the observations on the Balipara Frontier Tract, its flowers, its people and its geography, I made three years later on my second visit.

The village of Shergaon is a collection of chalet-like houses built partly of stone, partly of timber, and partly of bamboo matting. Several small streams, gathered from the crumpled hills, converge on this green bowl and flow north-eastwards towards the Bhareli in a larger valley. Shergaon stands on a curved terrace lining the bowl, and overlooking the river. Surrounding it is a forest of green oaks, blue pines and scarlet rhododendrons.

The first building in Shergaon to catch the eye is a small white-walled temple—one can hardly call it a monastery; it is a place of worship rather than of residence. It contains graven images. A little balcony juts out above the massive wooden door, and each morning and evening a red-robed monk stands there, blowing on a conch shell. Prayer flags flutter from every house, and prayer drums, run by hydro, but not hydro-electric power, revolve on every stream.

We pitched camp just outside the village in an open space. By 'we' is meant Tashi Thondup, Pemba and myself. Tashi and Pemba, two Sherpas from Darjeeling, had met me in Calcutta. Tashi was with me in Tibet in 1933 as 'third man,' and had proved so staunch and invaluable that I had promoted him to Sirdar by 1935. He was an ex-Everest coolie, who on one of the earlier attempts on the mountain had carried a load to over 25,000 feet. He had been rather a joke in 1933, and was undoubtedly a numskull. Short, deep-chested rather than broad as befits a mountaineer, with a round, corroded face, and long ragged hair like dusky seaweed matching a pair of unfathomably dark eyes and a weathered nose, he gave little hint of the iron strength of heart and purpose within. He was a natural rock climber, and had been taught ice-craft on Mount Everest. The high windy plateau of Tibet, where he could squat round a yak-dung fire and talk, was his natural milieu. He was not clean or tidy or intelligent, but he had a natural dignity, honesty and loyalty.

Pemba was more of a live wire. He had none of Tashi's magnificent record, nor had he been with me before. He was Tashi's younger cousin, a short stocky little man, of some education; he spoke excellent Hindustani—which Tashi never mastered—and had even learnt to write a little English. He had a round, pleasant but expressionless face, a soothing voice, and endless patience. Rarely did he have a grievance, but when he did he aired it thoroughly. Pemba was a find, the more so because he and Tashi were complementary one to the other.

It was in such good company that I was to cross southern Tibet.

My first visitor at Shergaon was Wangia, a well-known inebriate and a great man. He is not only headman of Shergaon, but one of the 'Seven Kings of Rupa'—the ruling families of the Sherchokpa. Wangia, now in his sixties or seventies, is a somewhat lachrymose old man with red-rimmed eyes not solely due to the intensity of the light outside or to the darkness within doors. His lank white locks are greasy, his brownish skin wrinkled like a dried apple. He had dressed himself for the occasion in the greatest finery his limited wardrobe could provide— a faded Tibetan *chupa*, gaudy coloured cloth boots, and purple skull cap. He welcomed me fervently. Behind him came several servants bringing presents of rice, walnuts, chillies, and other local produce.

He was well pleased when I gave him two bottles of Indian

country spirit. He must have tried them immediately to make certain that they were beyond proof, since I did not see him again for two days; I was told he had met with an accident, and was still insensible.

A greater than Wangia was in Sheragon that May day; none other than Geshi Ishi Dorje, High Priest of Mönyul. Ishi Dorje is a rotund man with little pig eyes in his creased full-moon face, and he is going bald. He speaks slowly, in a thick soupy voice pitched low. His expression is benign, for he is a kindly man, a great favourite amongst the people whom he has been shepherding for a generation. He put on his canonical robes for me, that I might take his photograph, and an impressive figure he made. Perhaps the chief attraction was his hat, a gorgeous wooden steeple, lacquered and gilded. In the west the Roman church has always aimed at increasing the stature and dignity of the theocracy by crowning them with high hats, such as the mitre. In the east the Tibetan church is not far behind. And so Ishi Dorje perched on his half bald head a miniature golden pagoda, which ended in a red glass ball. It all screwed together neatly and in fact it took him some time to assemble the parts. He thrust his fat legs into vivid scarlet and green cloth boots, with snub toes, covered his ample torso in a monkish robe of dull red edged with silver braid, and throwing a brightly coloured wrap over one shoulder, appeared before me.

Ishi Dorje is an important official, both lay and clerical.

I asked him if I might go into Tibet, and he looked very wise and promised to consult the omens about it and give a considered reply later. Meanwhile, he requested me to write two letters, one to himself and one to the Tsöna Dzongpön, formally stating my request in writing. I wrote the letters, of course in English. Ishi Dorje said he would send my letter on to Tsöna Dzong, and he expected a reply in about a fortnight. It would, he said, be a favourable reply. I was very pleased at the delay which gave me an opportunity to botanize in this rich region. I gave Ishi several presents, including a really good noisy alarm clock. He sent me a sheep, which ran along with us a fortnight before we had to butcher it.

Between Shergaon and Dirang Dzong are three ranges of hills, all parallel to the main Himalayan range; and the streams between flow eastwards to the Bhareli river. Leaving Shergaon, we crossed the first range, covered as usual with oak and pine forest, and descended to a wretched little village called Dumko, in a beautiful valley. I spent two days here, for all the forest trees were lathered with flowers, laurels and maples and rhododendrons and oaks, and called aloud to the botanist. Pottering along by the stream I noticed that the rocky bank was covered with a small flowered and by no means conspicuous primula. But as a botanist, I happened to be interested in primulas, and though at the time I had no inkling of what a treasure I had found, I nevertheless collected and put into the press a good many specimens. Discovered by that distinguished botanist, Dr. Griffith (whose death at the early age of thirty-two was a great loss to Natural Science) a century ago, *Primula filipes* had never been met with since, and was very imperfectly known. It had long puzzled botanists interested in this aristocratic genus. Though its large oval leaves of curiously thin texture are attractive, it has the tiniest pinky mauve flowers, and not many of them, hence it has no claims on the rock gardener.

Beyond Dumkho we crossed another range of pine-clad hills, and descended to the larger Mönba village of Phutang, at an altitude of over 7000 feet. The houses cling together on the steep slope as though they were afraid of sliding down it if they did not clasp one another tightly. I spent a few days at Phutang also, not so much because I wanted to botanize here, as because a bout of fever had laid me low on the road, shortly after leaving Dumko. It was with difficulty that I completed the march, almost 'passing out' on one occasion.

On May 19th we crossed a high range by the Manda La, a pass of 10,000 feet, descending into a deep dry valley. On the Manda La we were amongst silver firs and big tree rhododen-

drons for the first time. There were many flowers: the curious little yellow flowered *Bryocarpum himalayense*, a plant of shady forest, and the blue *Primula Whitei*, its clustered flowers looking like a turquoise in the heart of a brussels sprout. Another primula which grows here on the banks is *P. austrolisteri*. It has small rose pink flowers, and is not much more showy than *P. filipes*.

Rhododendrons were many. The bushy *R. megeratum*, with flat cream-white flowers and tiny leaves like box, grows perched on trees. Here and there the blood-red bells of *R. neriiflorum* were conspicuous, and the large gaping flowers of *R. bullatum*, white with a flush of pink on the outside, and a yellow flame mark on the inside, which also grows on trees. It was surprising to see *R. neriiflorum* here, for it has hitherto been found only in China and was not known to occur anywhere in the Himalayas. It is quite common just east of the Bhutan frontier. Not less common was *R. Lindleyi*.

It is a long and steep descent from the Manda La to Dirang Dzong which is only 5250 feet above sea-level, considerably lower than any village we had passed through since crossing the Pankim La. It stands on the right bank of a fair sized river from the west, one of the sources of the Bhareli. Here I spent several days, living in an empty two-roomed barn-like house, built to accommodate travellers.

CHAPTER II

THE 'YELLOW CAP' MONK

DIRANG DZONG, like Phutang, is a Mönba village. The Mönbas are a mild people. One might almost use the word gentle to describe them. They do not beat their wives or run amok. They rarely get drunk, except on infrequent feast days and at funerals; and then the only effect is to make them merry and anxious for you to join in the fun. The women are necessarily sluts: but industrious sluts. Their sluttishness is of mother earth, not of the slums.

I stayed five days at Dirang Dzong, and made friends with the Jongpen, a rather saturnine Tibetan, who lived a blameless domestic life in the big white dzong. He did nothing, and did it very well. It was pleasant to see how Mönyul ran itself. I could imagine it being run by a British official—the files full of reports, returns, assessments, settlements, cases, all that ranting, roaring, clanking machinery of government. The fact is we get a great deal too much government in the West. The secret of good government is probably to let people alone, and they will learn to govern themselves.

I wanted transport for my destination, the Ze La. The Jongpen promised it should be there.

The morning of May 26th arrived, but no transport. We got up, breakfasted, packed the loads and waited. I was fuming. Tashi went off to the dzong to expostulate and to find out what had happened. Nothing had happened; they had forgotten. What on earth did it matter! Why make a fuss? Wasn't there a to-morrow?

The Jongpen himself arrived on the scene in a state of indifference and undress; it was early in the morning for him to be abroad. He had forgotten his garters and his long cloth boots sagged below his knees. A Tibetan without his garters is rather like an Englishman without a tie.

After some acrimony the transport appeared, men and ponies. That morning we marched to Liu, a village almost as large as Dirang Dzong, a few miles to the east. The valley suddenly widens out into terraced rice fields beside the river — a rare sight in Mönyul. A little monastery perched above the village commands a fine view of the Zela range across the valley.

We passed a hot spring in the river bed. My nose led me to it, for it smelt strongly of rotten eggs, and the water quickly blackened a silver rupee. It did not feel particularly warm — until I dipped my hand in the icy river for comparison! All the same I should have hated to bathe in that hot spring. When the river rises the spring is submerged; but the smell remains. An enterprising people would surely have constructed a bath here, and cured all the local diseases; or drunk the sulphurous water. But the Mönbas are not enterprising.

It is more astonishing to find the Church blind to such an opportunity. Here surely is a heaven-sent chance to emphasize the power and influence of the lamas; nothing less than a new Lourdes! The gushing of water from the solid rock is in itself a miracle, and it would lose nothing in the telling. A miraculous cure — and the fame of the Tibetan Church would resound throughout the Eastern Himalayas! But the fact is, the grip of the Tibetan Church is so sure that it can afford to neglect the bodily needs of man. Its mission is to the spirit. Besides, the Tibetan Church does not want to raise the status of mankind. It might become vocal, and critical, and foment schism.

From Liu we descended to the river now rushing through a gorge and crossed it where it is no more than a boisterous mountain torrent. Then we climbed flight after flight of stone steps. This side of the valley catches the full blaze of the afternoon sun, and is thinly wooded with oak and scarlet flowered rhododendrons, like a park. In June the steep slope is pale blue with irises (*I. decora*) but the flowers are fugitive. Even more gorgeous are the tall white lilies (*L. Wallichianum*) which lean over the rocks in August.

Turning north into a side valley, now high above converging torrents, we reached a large Mönba village called Nyukmadong. Here the influence of the Church is strong and lamas dominate the scene. It is too cold to grow maize; but there are fields of buckwheat and in early summer, barley. Paper is manufactured under the direction of the lamas; for the Church uses a lot of paper. Its manufacture is in fact a Church monopoly.

At Nyukmadong, rhododendrons begin to appear in some variety. The lovely and sweet-scented *R. polyandrum*, with long white trumpet flowers, the blood-red *R. neriiflorum* and *R. bullatum*: for we are now on the flank of the high Zela range. Across a deep gulley and over a thousand feet above us we see Senge Dzong, a white dot astride the spur which leads to the pass; behind it an array of blue mountains. From airy Nyukmadong we go down to the bottom of this deep ravine where no sunshine ever penetrates; it is cool and moist, filled with lush evergreen forest. Now in early June, on the bank of the torrent there was flowering the finest bush of *R. rhabdotum* I have ever seen. It was covered with enormous lily-like flowers. This shrub, though not quite hardy in England, is a great favourite with connoisseurs. I do not admire it. Remarkable as the great trumpet flowers white banded with red are, there is something more than a little absurd in that military red stripe down each of its five trouser legs. How capricious was this shrub. Three years and two months later, in August 1938, I passed this way again and there was *R. rhabdotum* in the same spot, unchanged. Indeed it did not appear to have grown an inch, although it must have done so. It was not, of course, in flower in mid-August, as it had been in June 1935; but the point is, it had not borne any flowers at all this year. Not one! On the other hand it was covered with fat flower buds, and would be a magnificent spectacle in June 1939. Evidently one good flowering, followed by the long ripening of its great woody fruits, exhausts it, and it needs a year of complete rest in which to build up its strength. Thus it flowers in alternate years. In England one would pick off the little fruits after flowering — 'dead head' it, as the term is, so as to conserve its strength. But there is no one to do that service here.

Though *R. rhabdotum* was not in flower when I crossed this glen in August 1938, many other plants were; notably a big rough-leafed begonia (*B. Josephi*) bearing aloft on a long branching stem a shower of little white blossoms, like hailstones; and a Didymocarpus, with dark clouds of clustering purple flowers.

From this torrent to the Ze La is a continuous ascent of 6000 feet.

Presently we came to an open grassy ridge, where cattle grazed. At the far end of the ridge stood Senge Dzong, consisting of a little square stone fort on a rocky eminence, a small village, and a charming monastery. The village was in two parts with the dzong in the middle, each part compressed along the narrow ridge. Aloof at the top end, where the forest began, was the monastery in the woods.

And what a magic wood it was. Larch and hemlock spruce now appear for the first time at about 9000 feet altitude, and the tall hemlocks, with their well-combed branches spreading out fanwise like green coral, rise above a surging ocean of rhododendrons of all colours, and all in full bloom. Most brilliant was *R. Keysii*, hung with countless clusters of glowing red hot tubes each rimmed with yellow, like fairy lamps — for *R. Keysii* does not, like most species of rhododendron, bear its flowers only at the ends of the shoots, but all along the branches.

At the monastery I found Ishi Dorje arrived ahead of me. He and his clerk were counting *tankas*, the thin silver coins used in Tibet, and worth about twopence each. Seated cross-legged on the floor in his flowing robes, letting the metal discs run through his fat fingers and fall in a heap, with a continuous metallic clinking, he reminded me of the Merchant of Venice.

I asked Ishi Dorje for an answer to my request that he give me permission to go into Tibet, and after some further consultations with the Powers of Light and Darkness, he said I might go. I wanted his permission in writing. Ishi's reply was as disingenuous as it was dignified. He said: 'You are a distinguished foreigner, so what need is there for me to give you a letter of recommendation to my countrymen, who will welcome you as a guest? I too am a person of importance. My word carries weight, my blessing is beneficent. Mention the name of the Geshi Ishi Dorje, and men's hearts will open to you.' In other words, Ishi Dorje was too shrewd to put anything in writing, and I was simple enough to go without it. He had lived up to the highest traditions of a Tibetan gentleman and granted a request made in person.

It was my desire to cross the great snow range on to the Tibetan plateau and see something of what lay behind that mighty barrier which is clearly visible from Kohima in the Naga Hills, two hundred miles distant. I did not, however, want to go to Tawang, which is the main road, but by a more difficult though direct route which would take me through the district of Mago. Thence, crossing two passes, over 17,000 feet high, in quick succession, I should reach Tibet. By either route I had, of course, first to cross the Ze La, about 14,000 feet high.

On June 3rd we started from Senge Dzong with twenty-five coolies. They carried all my baggage, and that of my two men, and food for themselves for four days.

Above 12,000 feet, in the silver fir forest, the rhododendrons were a magnificent sight, most beautiful of all being *R. concatenans*, a slender pyramidal shrub, its branches arched and dropping with countless carillons of crystal orange bells. The sunlight shining through these played strange tricks, and being in part refracted, the bells glowed as though they had been heated in a forge, shining now red, now yellow, with waves of salmon, apricot, and orange playing over them. The leaves of

this shrub are small, of a delicate glaucous green, and do not interfere with the display of the flowers.

Here and there the ridge narrowed to an isthmus connecting one hump with the next, where we walked under a pleached roof of rhododendron branches. Most of these trees were certainly upwards of a century old. They stood thirty or forty feet high, their stout limbs grown gnarled in the age-long strife, and formed a solid wall of foliage on either side. Yet their broad leathery leaves, silver or bronze plated beneath, and enormous bunches of white, sulphur, or old rose flowers, were as gay as though they had not a care in the world, and everything they needed – food, sunlight, summer warmth and a winter blanket of snow – came to them as they desired it. At this season, at least, they showed no trace of what must be a fierce struggle for life. Year after year they pour forth their generous stream of beauty, and all the birds of the hills flock to the honey feast. A rhododendron forest in the Himalayan spring is a wonderful aviary, in which sibias, tits, honey suckers, laughing thrushes, and many other small birds gather.

We climbed another thousand feet, and everything changed once more. The forest of silver fir remained, but a fresh tide of rhododendron was flowing. Now came into view the tubby, round-leafed *R. campylocarpum*, whose innocent pale primrose-yellow bells one can imagine giving out a silvery tinkle, in contrast to the metallic clang, reminiscent of the forge, emitted by the red hot bells of *R. Thomsonii*. Mixed with these was *R. fulgens*, its flowers clenched into solid balls of an even more vivid crimson than those of *R. Thomsonii*. The oval sea-green leaves of *R. fulgens* in their first year are padded beneath with white plush, but this slowly turns tobacco-coloured as it ages. There is a larger yellow flowered shrub too, almost a small tree, with long, narrow, dully-gilt leaves, and bunches of sulphur flowers finely freckled inside with crimson. This is *R. Wightii*, a beautiful shrub, shy of flowering until it has attained a considerable age and size.

Before we reached the pass it had begun to drizzle, and as we climbed higher cloud and rain came sweeping up over the alps, chilling and blinding us. It was a wet black-out. So we trudged up the rough stone causeway which clings to the mountain flank and, rounding a shoulder, reached the Ze La, a gap between high peaks. Just over the pass are two glacier lakes (but no glaciers). The Tawang road skirts these to the left, going north-east; but we turned aside, diverging to the right. The country was quite open, bare of trees, and the rocky ground dabbled with the crimson heads of the little aromatic leafed *R. anthopogon* and the crushed-strawberry of *R. fragariflorum*, on which we walked as on a springy carpet. Presently the descent became steeper, and we were scrambling down the rocky bed of a torrent lined with crimson and yellow flowered scrub rhododendron, too large to walk over, and too resistant to push through, though it grew only knee high. So we kept to the bed of the torrent while our boots filled with icy water. We descended a long way, and reached a side valley, up which we turned.

It was not an ideal camping ground; a patch of gravel in the midst of a wilderness of boulders in a sunless alpine valley, flanked by grim screes. But it was the best available. The altitude was about 13,000 feet. The rain was now coming down in sheets and we were all wet to the skin. It takes a long time to make a fire of rhododendron branches, but once you do get this tough wood alight, it keeps on burning.

So for three days we travelled north, or sometimes north-east, climbing over a succession of rocky spurs by narrow awkward passes. We crossed also a succession of valleys, whose stream flowed westwards towards Bhutan. The heads of these valleys were wide, shallow and basin-shaped, but they narrowed and steepened rapidly till presently the stream plunged into a gorge to leap over tremendous cliffs into the main valley far below. It was clear that all the upper half of this range had once been scored by glaciers. Not a vestige of ice remained, but it had impressed itself indelibly on the rocks, and on the shapes of the mountains.

Crossing the heads of the valleys, we walked over carpets of brilliant alpine flowers. Once we sat down to lunch amidst a field of mauve mop-headed primulas (*P. atrodentata*) – very like the well known *P. denticulata.*

On June 5th we reached a valley which it was just possible to descend. It was a breakneck sort of path, but we all came down the 3000 feet safely, to find ourselves in a much bigger valley through which foamed an angry grey snow-fed torrent, the Lugathang river or Lungdang Chu. Large as it was we were close to its source. Crossing it by a wooden bridge, we turned upstream. The river was shut in between walls of *Rhodendron campanulatum*, all in full bloom. The colour of the flowers is pale blush purple with a hint of lavender or mauve in it, giving them an almost ethereal quality.

As we approached the head of the valley, frowned on by rocky peaks, we left the river, and climbed several hundred feet up the steep slope by a rough track, till presently the village of Lugathang came into view – half a dozen wooden houses, huddled together for warmth; a rabbit warren of dark cabins. It was a cheerless spot. Not a single domesticated plant grew round these dismal buildings. Not a single domesticated animal either welcomed or challenged our approach. No smoke rose from the roofs: the village appeared to be deserted.

Such was Lugathang, the first Drokpa village. Later we found an old, old woman, half blind, with wrinkled skin and bony hands, who invited us into a house – a den rather, for it was pitch dark. The inhabitants, she explained, had already migrated with their flocks and herds to the higher pastures: and we stayed here two days while a messenger went for them. They returned on the second day, bringing a team of yak.

There also arrived a messenger from Tsöna Dzong, bringing an official-looking letter, which he handed to me one evening with all ceremony. I unfolded it, and saw half a dozen lines written in a clear hand, and an official seal at the bottom. Evidently it was in reply to mine, written at Ishi Dorje's request. With a sinking heart I called upon Pemba to read it to me. But luckily Pemba could not read it, and said we could find somebody at Karta to read it. We never did, because I lost it, and did not find it again until we got back to India. This was providential because it was unfavourable, and my conscience would hardly have let me go on, had I known it was forbidden.

Lugathang is peculiarly isolated. It stands close to the bare treeless head of the valley at a height of about 12,000 feet. We had come up the valley, but it is impossible to go *down* it, beyond the point where we had crossed the river. Only by crossing the mountains the way we had come, or the still higher mountains to Mago, can one get out of the valley.

So while it rained and rained, I botanized round Lugathang.

CHAPTER III

APPROACH TO A FRONTIER

It was still raining when on June 7th we left Lugathang. The sky had that queer unfathomable look which suggests that it will rain for ever. And the mountain tops were buried in grey mist.

The Lugathang river rises, as I have said, quite close, in the Zela range which we had just crossed; or partly crossed, for already we were climbing towards another pass. Presently we entered an alpine valley; the ground covered with soft spongy turf, sprinkled with flowers. We reached the Drokpa camp, and the kindly people, shapeless in their padding of sheep's wool or yak hair, which still retained all its original grease so that the rain fantastically spangled them with thousands of twinkling dewdrops, came out to greet us.

Above the pastures, we threaded our way amongst bare granite towers, gurgling streams, and sandy flats, to the knife-edge ridge of the Trukya La, where a crust of snow was frozen to the rocks. From the ridge we descended over smoother ice-worn slabs. The altitude of the Trukya La is about 15,000 feet. A grey swirling mist made it impossible to see anything clearly. I was unaware that we had reached the top, and while we were crossing the range, visibility was reduced to a few yards; I had to keep up with the yak, or I could never have found the way. There is no path.

When at last we emerged from the cloud we saw an alpine valley below us. And the first things that caught my eye were a jade-green glacier lake and several patches, at different levels, of brilliant gamboge, like yellow silk handkerchiefs spread out on the rocks to dry. The first patch, I found, was caused by thousands of clear yellow primulas, each a large hemispherical head of flowers (something like the head of a primrose), on a short fat stalk. So closely did the plants grow that it was impossible to avoid walking on them. In each of these meadows there was a wooden hut, like a gardener's tool shed; you might think someone had been especially cultivating these lovely flowers for the wholesale market. Here were yak pastures, and wherever the tethered yak had trampled and manured the ground, the primulas clustered as eagerly as flies on a piece of stinking raw meat. Its name is *P. strumosa.*

Here then was a problem of deep interest. What was the connection between the yak and the primulas? For this was by no means a solitary example. We shall observe like scenes in Tibet, and with other species of primula. On the Bhutan frontier, not far west of Dirang Dzong, I came upon an acre of boggy pasture reddened with myriads of the fairy *P. Kingii.* It bears claret coloured bells, two or three of them swinging freely from the top of a slender stem not more than four inches high. Every other flower, and they were not a few, was swamped beneath this inundation of tiny primulas. The marsh, surrounded by a forest of silver fir, lined with rhododendron bushes which in June made a band of brilliant colour, crimson, sulphur, scarlet and mauve, was also a yak pasture. But the yak had gone up the mountain to higher pastures, leaving the primulas untrampled. So I too climbed to the alps. And when I reached the tree line at about 13,000 feet, I found the wet spongy pastures invaded by millions of primulas. But again they were of a totally different species. The mountain landscape was sheeted with shrill yellow — not the yellow of *P. strumosa* (though that also grew here, mostly under trees) but the dilute yellow of *P. Dickieana*, a very different plant.

I observed closely the yak grazing, and although they could not move through the pasture without trampling on this primula and breaking off the stems — for the plants grew so closely that often they were touching one another — yet they deliberately avoided eating it. They would eat the flowers of

polygonum and potentilla, and carex and ranunculus, yet they would not touch *Primula Dickieana*!

Now it is impossible not to recognize some connection between the cattle and the primulas, which are not merely dominant in the pastures, but overwhelming. Elsewhere they are absent, or at least rare. There seems to be one fairly obvious connection.

All plants need nitrogen, some in considerable quantity, because nitrogen is an essential ingredient of protoplasm, the stuff of which living matter is made. And although nitrogen is so abundant in nature that four-fifths of the air we breathe is composed of it, yet in this form it is not generally available to plants. Only in the form of soluble salts can plants acquire nitrogen, by means of their roots, from the soil. And it so happens that it is in the soil that there is a serious shortage of nitrogen. Nearly all soils are poor in nitrates. Most of our fertilizers consist of nitrates. Our crops wring every available atom of nitrogen from the soil, which becomes so impoverished that if we did not return it in some form, nothing more could be grown until, by the slow processes of nature, the balance had been restored. Only in the East is an adequate quantity put back into the soil in the form of human excrement. The West is killing Agriculture with sanitation, although to offset this millions of tons of nitrogen salts are made annually by fixing atmospheric nitrogen. A few plants have circumvented these hard facts, but they are quite exceptional. It is not too much to say that the whole vegetable kingdom suffers from nitrogen starvation; and in the alpine region this starvation probably reaches a maximum. But yak dung may be relied on to supply nitrogen compounds in a form suitable for assimilation by plants; and several species of primula, it would seem, are able to profit by this, to the greater glory of the alps, though to the ultimate ruin of the pastures as pastures. That is another aspect of the matter which is not without a certain grim humour.

In this wet climate with its abundant summer rain, forest

covers the mountains. There is nothing comparable with the steppe land of Russia or the prairies of the middle western United States. Pasture and grassland is the exception. Even above the tree line, we still find woody plants, rhododendron mostly, forming a thick scrub. But the growth of grass can be encouraged by cutting down and burning the forest, especially in places where trees have some difficulty in growing, as on an exposed ridge. This is what the herds do, making artificial clearings for their cattle. Up comes the grass, also many alpine flowers. Presently a primula comes in, and multiplies fast. These plants are apparently better adapted than any others to make the most of the new situation. Thus they gradually drive out the grass, and since the yak will not eat them, the herds have to destroy more and more forest in order to get grass, while gradually a few species come to dominate the alpine scene.

We camped in one of the saffron meadows above the jade-green glacier lake I had seen from above. The sun came out, and the mountains were lacquered with many colours.

Next day we descended a steep and narrow ravine through which the water from the lake tumbled to the valley. At the bottom we reached a river foaming swiftly between thickets of rhododendron which were a mass of blossom. This river, the Gorjo Chu, like the Lugathang river, flows westwards. It rises amongst the glaciers of Gori Chen, a snow peak on the crest line of the great Himalayan range. Surely, I thought, we were now at the foot of the main range. One more climb over one pass and we should be in Tibet. Already, since leaving the Assam plain, we had crossed nine passes.

However, no sooner had we reached this torrent, swollen by rain and melting snow, than we crossed it by a timber bridge and began climbing the mountain on the other side by a slanting track. The slope was mauve with countless thousands of *Primula atrodentata*. We reached yet another pass, the Chera La, and looked down into a valley, two thousand feet deep, in which another snow-fed river, the Dungma Chu, rushed westwards. But across this valley rose a mountain range which in the distance looked like a dark wall whose top was protected by white china and glass. It was the Great Himalayan range at last; and behind it lay mysterious Tibet!

The Chera La is about 13,000 feet, and over the summit rolled a ruffled sea of pink and purple scrub rhododendron. Millions of primulas danced in the breeze. We began to go down; the steep and stony path zigzagged through a forest of silver fir and rhododendron, and below was bordered with red and yellow primulas. Presently, peeping through the trees, we could see a Drokpa village, in the district of Mago. We reached the bottom of the wide stony valley, crossed the river, and half an hour later arrived at Nyuri, which consists of a few log cabins.

There is no cultivation. Rank weeds with ugly flowers such as *Scoparia lurida*, born of the sour mud, surge round the village. But beyond is the clean forest. All the open valley was ablaze with rhododendrons, the delicious shell-pink form of *R. lanatum* – the typical form has yellow flowers – and the fierce salmon, cinnabar and apricot hues of *R. concatenans*. On the cliffs I noticed the lurid magenta of *R. Baileyi*.

At this point the Dungma Chu is joined by another equally big stream from the north, the Goshu Chu. Nyuri stands on a cliff in the angle between the two rivers. Opposite to it, across the Goshu Chu is another similar village, called Dyuri. The two villages together are often called Mago, which is also the name of the district.

Immediately below the confluence of the Goshu and Dungma rivers, a stark granite cliff, many hundred feet high, fronts the village, and forces the river into a gorge. A mile or two lower down, the Gorjo Chu, which we had crossed earlier, joins in and henceforth the river is called the Mago Chu. There is no path down it.

Most of the inhabitants of Nyuri had gone up the valley with the cattle, leaving only a few crones to hold the village. So I stayed here three days, living in a curious little timber loft, reached by a ladder, while I waited for transport. They were days well spent, for the district of Mago is worth exploring. The altitude of Nyuri is about 11,000 feet.

The forest consists chiefly of fir trees, both *Picea likiangensis* and the silver fir *Abies Delavayi*, with an undergrowth of rhododendron and other shrubs. Above the village on the open grassy slopes one may find the grossly-inflated chocolate, red-and-yellow striped bags of the Tibetan slipper orchid, *Cypripedium tibeticum*, a hardy plant here, though it does not take kindly to our English damp.

Near the village is a hot spring, but it is not exploited by the local inhabitants. So hot is the water, that it is impossible to hold one's hand in it. A rough sort of rock pool has been constructed round the vent; and in spite of an extensive entanglement of gelatinous blue-green algae, and other lowly aquatic life which thrives in it, I had an enjoyable bath, wallowing in a foot of hot silt at the bottom. An old Tibetan came along for his periodical treatment. He fished up a pebble from the bottom as though he were snatching a plum from a snapdragon and pressed it to his eyes, informing me that it was a sovereign remedy for eye complaints — which in Tibet generally means cataract.

Looking north up the valley of the Dungma Chu I could see snow peaks on the main Himalayan range. The passes, therefore, were not very far distant.

The naturalists, Mr. Frank Lublow and Captain George Sherriff had been in Mago the previous year, crossing the passes from Bhutan. They were collecting birds. Later I learnt that they had not found the valley so rich in species as they had hoped.

At last on June 11th, the yak appeared. A bargain was soon struck; the Drokpa would take me to Karta on the north side of the Great Himalayan range in four days: and on June 12th we started up the valley of the Dungma Chu.

CHAPTER IV

OVER THE HIMALAYAS

THE next four days (June 12th to 15th) proved to be the hardest travelling I had ever done. The actual distance we marched was less than forty miles. But we crossed two passes over 17,000 feet high, and camped two nights at about 15,000 feet. The weather was beastly.

June 12th began fine, but after midday, by which time we were out of the forest, it turned very wet.

Above the hot spring the dark fir forest was illuminated by bushes of *Rhododendron campanulatum* covered with purplish-mauve bloom. No two were quite the same shade, and the sombre background threw the flowers into fantastic relief. They looked like phosphorescent waves breaking amongst black basalt rocks.

Colonies of primulas bordered the path, the violet-flowered *P. Roylei* down below, the yellow-flowered *P. strumosa* above. They often grow together side by side; but they hardly ever cross and when they do the result is not a success. I noticed a very few hybrids, with washy *café-au-lait* flowers.

In the middle of the afternoon we reached Chunak, that is to say Blackwater, so called from the colour of a stream which rises amidst mountains of coal black shale. It is a herd village comprising a few scattered stone houses, occupied only during the summer. There was a pleasant pasture, like a golf green. We stopped only long enough to add a yak-load of firewood to our little caravan, and went on for another hour, camping under a cliff in the mouth of the gulley, above the last trees. The altitude was about 13,000 feet. All night a cold draught off the snows poured down the gulley; we could not get shelter from the wind.

At this height there is no forest, but the south slope of the Himalayas is well covered with scrub, amongst which rhododendrons bulk large, although now reduced to a few species. By the stream, mixed with willow, barberry, honeysuckle and dog rose, grew the yellow-flowered *Rhododendron Wightii* and the crimson or purple-freckled *R. aganniphum.* A more gorgeous display was made by two dwarf species, *R. anthopogon* and *R. nivale,* which covered the exposed flank of the valley, and flowed in a broad foam of crimson-rose and heather-purple down the rugged slope. *R. nivale* is a brushwood plant with very small purple flowers borne in tight little heads at the ends of the interlacing twigs, amongst the tiny nickel-plated-looking leaves. There were marmots here, popping in and out of their holes, and whistling to each other; but birds were scarce. The commonest was a babbler, or laughing thrush, of a dark rifleman green with black head and white tabs behind the ears and under the eyes. It was as big as a song thrush, and its haunting plaintive cry fitted the melancholy of these wild mountains.

Thrilled as I was at the prospect of crossing the Assam Himalayas, the weather, fair or foul, always affects my spirits; and being cold as well as wet I felt a black depression coming on.

The sky, gloomy from the start, now began to threaten, and soon the rain was driving down in sheets. Visibility was bad, and under the conditions it was difficult to collect plants, or even to see them. We reached the junction of two grey stony valleys, and followed the torrent to the east; there was still a lot of water in it, and I began to realize that we were a long way from the pass. After going about a mile, the torrent divided again, and once more we turned north. Even the scrub carpet was threadbare and at a height of about 15,000 feet it petered out altogether. A wilderness of broken rocks cracked off the high cliffs above us, and piled up in huge cone-shaped screes, barred the way.

We were in a long grim-looking valley in the cold heart of the Himalaya. The path was steep and rough; already I was feeling the strain. Hour after hour the yak plodded on, and I, stopping to collect unfamiliar plants, dropped farther and farther behind. By two o'clock I was exhausted, and also very hungry; I began to wonder whether the yak were ever going to stop! They went on like slow relentless machines, and the valley seemed interminable. We were still mounting steeply. Men and yak disappeared from view, and I felt utterly lost amidst these tremendous mountains.

At last I came up with the caravan, halted. We had now reached a height of 16,000 feet. It was still raining, but not so heavily, and I sat down under a rock for half an hour's rest, ate a snack, and drank some hot tea out of my thermos flask. The valley had broadened, and the stream wandered in several channels. We were approaching the glaciers at its head. Snowcock cried harshly and warningly from high up on the screes.

Resuming the climb from near the foot of the glacier, we followed a track which slanted obliquely up a thousand feet of soft, almost pulverized, slate towards a gap in the ridge. Snow peaks shone dimly through the clouds to our right front. We might have been on the moon, so harsh and bitter was the landscape. Not a blade of green did I observe until we were close to the top. Yet I noticed that the deep hoof-prints of the yak quickly filled with water. There was in fact no shortage of underground water at the base of the screes, although the surface was dry.

Suddenly I caught sight of a clump of short woolly leafed stems with spikes of dazzling sapphire-blue flowers crouched under the lee of a big boulder. It seemed astonishing that anything so lovely could survive in such a howling wilderness. This plant was *Veronica lanuginosa*, a rare Himalayan species related to our common blue speedwell (*V. arvensis*), though so different in appearance.

At this moment the sun came out for the first time, and shortly afterwards we reached the top. We were above the clouds. The Trulung La, 17,250 feet, is just a gap in the ridge between lofty towers, and we looked down into an arid valley about 2000 feet below. That was all the view there was. The tall shadows cast by the mountains were lengthening, and presently the sun disappeared behind a range. Ahead of us, beckoning me on, a pane of glassy blue sky gleamed like a church window.

The north side was very steep, and snow lay in drifts. We stumbled down a stony path, and reached a place where many vegetable cushions grew amongst the boulders. Every cushion was sprinkled with starry flowers, some white (arenaria), some yellow (potentilla), but most of them forget-me-not blue. This last, *Chionocharis Hookeri*, the Himalayan forget-me-not, is one of the most heavenly of all alpine plants. It bulged up out of the hard hungry earth, glistening silver-grey, each rug-headed, cushion encrusted with large turquoise-blue jewels, shimmering like stars in the lilac dusk. Imagine a dome of coral, with a turquoise set in every pore, the whole forming a mosaic of blue and silver amongst the pewter-grey micaceous stones. That will give you some idea of *C. Hookeri*. These cushions grow very slowly. I think many of them must have been a century old.

The valley below was boggy where water trickled out at the base of the hills, but as hard as a rock where it didn't. The wet places were freckled rose with the minute *Primula tibetica* mixed with a dwarf form of *P. sikkimensis*, the gold buttons of *Oxygraphis*, sewn tightly to the earth, and other plants. There was no firewood, but we had brought our own.

The night was cold, the temperature in my tent dropping to 34° F. before dawn on the 14th. We were enveloped in mist, and snow was falling. Down the valley yak were grazing, and on the slopes sheep and goats nibbled at patches of thorny scrub which snuggled into sheltered hollows; but we met no man.

Soon after re-starting, we reached a ridge and as we turned the corner the north wind off the Tibetan plateau smote us full in the face. My eyes watered till I was half blinded. At the head of this valley we could see glaciers and snow peaks. Since crossing the Trulung La we had not dropped below 15,000 feet, so we had not far to climb on the next pass. At this altitude, and in the teeth of a freezing wind, even a thousand feet was exhausting. I had not completely recovered from my malaria attack and I made heavy weather of this march. However, about the middle of the afternoon the slope eased off and we stood on a bare rolling ridge. Even here one could find a few alpine flowers hiding under the shelter of boulders. I noticed *Primula atrodentata*, its mauve mop heads flush with the crown of pale leaves and without any visible stem at all, yet happy in desolation. It is significant that the flowers are not asked to make any sacrifice for the general welfare. Stems are telescoped, leaves are stunted; but the flowers are as large and numerous as those of plants growing 5000 feet lower down.

During the ascent to the pass a mushroom-shaped black cloud had been gathering ominously round the snow peaks, and now the storm burst without further warning. The hail came down like a fluttering white curtain, quickly glazing the rocks with ice. The blizzard had struck us full in the face just as somewhat exhausted we reached the top of the Pen La, 17,350 feet above sea level. Lightning ripped through the whirling veil in vivid streaks, to be followed instantly by loud explosions. Flash followed flash, and the thunder echoes rolling back and forth amongst the mountains made a drum-fire of noise. We wrapped our scarves round our heads, and to the accompaniment of this Wagnerian music crossed the Great Himalayan range.

It was an impressive moment. India lay behind us, simmering three vertical miles below. In front was the plateau of Tibet. We were across the mightiest rampart nature has ever raised between man and his neighbour. It was but a step to the Roof of the World. But neither southwards from the Trulung La, nor northwards from the Pen La, twin passes separated by a valley, was there much of a view.

We went down the screes, past a half-frozen lake, as fast as we could. In an hour we were out of the storm which was moving rapidly across our front; at the end of another half-hour the sun was shining, but only for a short time before it sank behind the line of jagged peaks. We came to a gravel terrace above the stream; there was a herd's tent in sight, and yak were grazing farther down the valley. Once more we were approaching inhabited country. So we camped just before it grew dark. It was our first night in Tibet.

The wooden tent pegs could not be driven into the solid ground, and we tied the guy ropes to boulders.

The June sky was cloudless when I awoke next morning. There was a sharp nip in the air, yet so dry was it, one could barely see the sparkle of the thin frost crust on the grey stones. The pink and white flowers of a cushion plant, *Androsace Delavayi*, were frozen as brittle as spun glass, but when the sun had thawed them out they looked none the worse. Inside my tent the temperature went down to 28° F., and outside the water in the buckets was frozen solid. Pemba picked up a blackened rupee. He said it must have been dropped by the naturalists, Ludlow and Sherriff, who had probably camped at this very spot in 1934.

Shortly after starting down the valley we met with willow scrub by the stream, and a mile or two farther on came to dense buckthorn scrub. It was barely ten inches high, but the tough little plants grew close, and the long thorns were as hard and sharp as needles, and pierced our ankles painfully. This seems to be just a dwarf form of the widely spread buckthorn, *Hippophäe rhamnoides*, which at lower altitudes forms a sturdy gnarled tree in dry Tibet. I do not know whether, under favourable conditions this undershrub would grow into a tree. The dwarf form appears to be fixed, and, if so, would make a beautiful rock garden shrub. Covered with orange berries, smattered amongst the pewter-coloured leaves, it is lovely. Mixed with it were berberis, *Rosa sericea*, and two species of lonicera, one with amethyst flowers like *L. syringantha*. These tiny leafed thorny undershrubs are 'specially selected' to withstand a hard climate, 14,000 feet above sea-level. On both sides of the stream were high cliffs of consolidated gravel, with deep gashes cut in them by sudden spates such as might have been caused by the previous day's storm. But the torrent beds were dry now. On these barren cliffs I noticed an extraordinary plant, one mass of large white sweet scented flowers, like night stock, surrounded by a broad collar of narrow downy leaves. It suggested a bleached sea-anemone, waving its tentacles slowly in the current. But although I climbed up the cliff and spent some time taking a photograph of the plant, I have never been able to discover what it was, because I forgot to collect a specimen. And curiously enough I never met it again. A strange lapse! In October, when we recrossed the Pen La, most of the plants had died right down to ground level, leaving only the enormous rootstock to persist through the long hard winter. This type of plant, living perhaps for half a century, growing with extreme slowness and producing annually leaves and flowers from the crown of its scarcely visible rootstock, is characteristic of the cold dry plateau of southern Tibet. Of the strange Crucifer, therefore, I secured only a few leaves, a long slender fruit (silique) like that of a wallflower, and half a dozen seeds; all of which shed little further light on its identity!

Many high alpine plants adopt one or other of two special forms, namely the cushion habit and the subterranean. Certain plants like *Ephedra Geraldiana* and *Dicranostigma lactucoides* have, like Europe, sought shelter from air raids by digging. In the former, an immense unsuspected stem lies beneath the surface of the ground, little more than the current year's green shoots showing. The people depend largely on the underground trunks of Ephedra for fuel. They are a little better off than the plateau dwellers farther west who have no wood at all and are forced to burn yak dung only.

We now entered a defile; and although we were still some

14,000 feet above sea-level, from the dark cliffs fluttered the pale violet flowers and fine fern-like foliage of the graceful *Paraquilegia grandiflora*, a strange member of the ranunculus family. It always surprises me to see so delicate-looking a plant amidst such brutal surroundings. I suppose it is tough inside.

We emerged into the open again, the valley widening out. Another wide stony valley from the west joined in here. There is a path up it and crossing the high Shangshang La the traveller reaches Tsöna Dzong in three days. And now, not only were the sides of the mountains covered once more with scrub, but there was a tree; and not only was there a tree, but a house. The tree was a poplar, and it grew of course beside the water, as do all trees in arid Tibet. The village is called Goshu. It was surprising to find cultivation here; it must be a hardy and early-ripening variety of barley they cultivate. Barley is the only cereal which can mature in less than four months in this rigorous climate. It was the first cultivation we had seen since leaving Senge Dzong, almost a fortnight ago.

Now that the valley had become residential, it did not take us long to reach a small village of mud houses called Cha. The Mönbas untied the loads. They refused to go any farther because there was no grazing in this valley, so Tashi went in search of the headman to ask for fresh transport. The headman, to gain time, invited us to stay the night, saying that his people were all out working in the fields. But we were only a few miles from Karta, an important village, and I felt it would be wise to press on as fast as possible, at least for the first few days in Tibet. Tashi therefore urged the headman, and he sent out children to call the people in. They came, bringing two or three saddled ponies, the sorriest looking nags imaginable; and an hour later we resumed our journey.

While we were waiting a black cloud appeared from nowhere, like an Arabian Nights jinn, and a thunder-storm broke over us without further notice. In an hour it was all over, and the sky cleared like magic; but the rain was torrential while it lasted, and it gave me some notion of the way it can tear up a steep country which is completely without the protection afforded by vegetation. Yet scarcely had the sun come out than the ground was dry.

The valley took on a more and more lived-in appearance, with occasional scattered trees, and even groves. It was double, a valley within a valley. The outer one was wider, higher, and cultivated: the inner was a deep narrow bed for the stream. Some very old specimens of *Hippophäe rhamnoides* reached a large size. There were cultivated fields and wayside shrines. The road left the stream, and mounted the cliff by a flight of cultivated terraces. Alongside the road ran an aqueduct bringing water to the high level fields. Wherever possible a channel is contoured round the hillside, but sometimes the water has to be carried across a ravine in wooden gutters supported by trestles. At each flight of terraces water is drawn off and distributed through a network of ditches to the fields; women armed with wooden spades splash it on to the crops. These irrigation works stand between the people of dry Tibet and starvation. Most of the inhabitants of the valley looked as though they never had enough to eat. The women in particular are small and wizened. The population may originally have come from south of the Himalayas; their ancestors were probably slaves.

It was a beautiful sunny evening, the sky a deep turquoise-blue, and the bare mountains stained yellow and smouldering red. With every mile the valley grew more fertile, the fields greener. There is not much wrong with the soil, in spite of its hard famished look. Wherever water flowed, and there was shelter from the wind, large shrubs such as buddleia grew vigorously. I can imagine no better country for raising fruit.

We came to irises growing beside the aqueduct; at first scattered plants, then clumps, finally large colonies. But they were not in flower. Then we turned the corner, and abruptly Karta flashed into view like a sheet of flame. The village stands on a sloping triangular terrace between two deeply eroded valleys; there are a score of houses, besides the gompa, but all I saw at the moment was this sheet of brilliant yellow. The rapeseed, an important crop in dry Tibet, was in full flower.

The first view of Karta was startling. I did not know that anything in this severe land could be so beautiful. The cold blaze of yellow in its emerald green setting, under a blue sky, hit one right between the eyes. Presently I noticed also two separate groves of trees; closer inspection showed that they were both protected from wind and irrigated.

Masses of *Clematis orientalis* were in bloom. Rarely did it find adequate support, but it seemed quite content to sprawl over the rocks, without climbing. The flowers are dusky, often chocolate, but a gayer form has deep golden yellow flowers, contrasting with the sage-green leaves.

Solid white houses, which looked like castles, very tall and stately, with rectilinear lines, were scattered about the terrace. Beside each stood a ruined tower like a broken factory chimney, and an earlier house. These houses are built of mud and have very thick walls. When they fall down they are not repaired; the owner builds a new one. To build a house is a meritorious act. But they do not often fall down; they crumble. Occasionally one sees a brand new house standing by the ruins of another, which in turn is standing by the ruins of a really historical mass of debris; like an imago contemplating several earlier metamorphoses. One house stood in a grove of poplar trees out in the middle of the highest terrace, the whole garden surrounded by a wall. Half a mile distant, at the apex of the fan, a white stupa, or *chorten*, peeped out from the midst of another grove. Trees are as rare in this part of Tibet as nuts in May. Yet, given water and protection from wind, it is surprising what trees will grow, including elm, willow, poplar, buddleia, cypress, buckthorn, and perhaps almost any hardy tree. But it must be hardy, for the temperature here falls below zero!

So we reached the yellow fields, and found the ditches thickly lined with irises and other flowers. Now the irises were in bloom, an enchanting sight. The standards are pale violet, the falls primrose-yellow, delicately feathered with violet. It is a dwarf rhizomatous plant, named *Iris lactea*, formerly known, wrongly, as *I. ensata*, which is quite a different species. In dry southern Tibet, *I. lactea* grows like a weed, but some forms are better than others, the Karta form being perhaps best of all. Farther down the valley, at about 12,000 feet altitude, it grows so thickly as to form meadows in the sandy river bed.

After a zigzag walk across the fields we came to the villa in the grove. A mud wall four feet high enclosed this oasis, which was about fifty yards square; but the only gate was locked. Presently someone brought the key and admitted us. The ground inside was blue with irises, and a most pleasant and secluded retreat it looked. It was the Karta Country Club, where young people came to spend the day under the trees; a sanctuary. I was given a comfortable, if bare room on the roof of the club house, which was used as a granary; Tashi and Pemba installed themselves in the caretaker's cottage close by. Meanwhile a crowd had gathered to see the stranger from the other side of the Himalayas. The arrival of a white man is not an everyday event in Karta; the last one had passed through about twelve years before, and although it had caused comment at the time, the excitement had now died down.

The next day, June 16th, being full moon, was a public holiday, and a number of people from the village visited the club. They really came to see me, and to ask for medicine. In Tibet the white men of the south are the equivalent of the wise men of the east of an earlier and more picturesque age. They are popularly believed to know all about mechanics, medicine, and other mysterious branches of learning. Thus the arrival of a white man is the signal for everybody to bring cheap clocks, musical boxes, and their own bodies for alterations and repairs.

After receiving visitors, I went out to collect plants and made for the flume, which I followed right round the head of the terrace gardens. This flume brings water all the way from Cha, four miles up the valley, to irrigate the crops. *Primula sikkimensis* was mixed with *Iris lactea* along the ditches, and I found also ranunculus, pedicularis, vicia, euphorbia and thalictrum, all very English-looking, though not identical with any English species. A Karta plant which owes nothing to irrigation is *Dicranostigma lactucoides*. The terrace is truncated towards the apex and ends in a gravel cliff about two hundred feet high where converging streams from the north (Tak Chu) and north-east (Loro Nakpo Chu) have trimmed it. It was on these bare crumbling cliffs that I first noticed the fluttering yellow poppy flowers and strap-shaped glaucous leaves of Dicranostigma. But as with icebergs, the visible part was only a fraction of the hidden part. For these solid gravel cliffs are not like the loose-textured screes, damp just below the surface. Either water runs off them, or it cuts ravines in them. Plants, to live here, need immensely long tap roots, which can probe deep. They bore for water. It almost needs a charge of blasting powder to dislodge the rootstock of this plant from its stony bed. It seems to be welded to the rock.

Another curious plant is a species of asparagus with long whip-like stems and feathery leaves. It wants to climb, but there is nothing for it to climb up. I can hardly imagine any part of this green leathery looking asparagus being edible.

Strange also is a corydalis with big underground rhizome, producing annually a fine shower of small yellow flowers in the midst of a crop of delicate sea-green fern-like leaves. Several shrubs grew along the flume, notably a gnarled buddleia with flannelly leaves, *Berberis kartanica* and *Lonicera quinquilocularis*.

The day was fine, but the raging Tibetan wind which reached its climax about four o'clock, and gradually snuffed out at sunset, was nerve shaking.

I wanted to spend one day at Karta, but not more; speed was the essence of the contract. Yet it was pleasant at the Karta Country Club, in the poplar grove, amidst the sea of irises.

The poplar trees were about 25 feet high, and owed their preservation to the four-foot wall which had protected them from the wind when they were very young, and to watering. Under the peacock-blue vault of the Tibetan sky, surrounded by mountains, bare but fantastically carved by wind and water, I revelled in the grandeur of Tibet. All day the sun shone on the chrome yellow fields. All day the wind roared down the valley, tossing the branches of the poplars, and displaying the silver whiteness of the leaves which trembled from dawn to dusk. And then suddenly darkness and silence – and peace.

I had crossed the Assam Himalayas, and the first part of my task was done. But now I was curious to know what sort of flora grew *behind* the Great Himalayan range. I wanted to go on just a little farther.

CHAPTER V

CHAYUL DZONG AND THE SOURCES OF THE SUBANSIRI

KARTA, the first village in Tibet where there was a resident magistrate, was the crisis of my journey. If permission to proceed were refused me here, we were immobilized. If he ordered the villagers to supply me with transport, they would do so unhesitatingly; if he forbade them to help, they would be deaf to my entreaties. On the other hand, if I were given magisterial permission to proceed one more stage, the next village at which I arrived would accept me and pass me on automatically. I would be part of the system. So it would continue, nobody stopping to ask awkward questions, at least not to begin with. Hence my decision to move swiftly during the early days. How far Ishi Dorje's unwritten writ ran, I did not know; but I suspect not very far.

I estimated the population of Karta at two hundred and fifty to three hundred persons, or three hundred and fifty to four hundred, counting the outlying villages up the valley. Most of the population live in the tenements round the stupa, which is known as the labrang, literally, the dwelling-place of the chief Lama. In accordance with Tibetan custom two magistrates divide the not very arduous work of administration between them. One of them is called the Sandu Purang Dzongpön, the other the Labrang Dzongpön. Karta lies within the orbit of Tsöna Dzong, a small but important village about fifty miles to the west. It was to the Jongpen of Tsöna that I had written a note at Ishi Dorje's behest; and it was from the Jongpen of Tsöna that I had received a reply by special messenger when we were at Lugathang.

At Karta I was able to replenish my dwindling supplies,

Tashi after a look round, returning with flour, eggs, spinach (probably turnip leaves), and cooking oil. His conversation with the Lamas however was less promising. He had been to the monastery to ask for transport; he told me there was a hitch. The Lamas, it seemed, were in doubt. Who was I? Whence had I come? Whither bound? What was I doing in their country? They were not hostile, only perplexed. These questions, of course, could be easily answered; but would the answers satisfy the Tibetans? Tashi, most tactful of ambassadors, whom nothing ever discouraged, was quite confident that all would be well. Patience was required; and patience was rewarded. He returned that evening with a favourable answer to my request. The Lamas would give me transport to Chayul Dzong, two days' march distant, in the main valley of the Loro Chu; we could start next day. At last I felt I was securely launched on my Tibetan travels.

Next morning, June 17th, the minimum temperature was down to 46° F., but the day promised to be fair. Soon after eight o'clock we were on our way down the valley, marching north. But first I went across the fields to see the monastery and the beautiful white *chorten* in its nest of trees. The monastery stands close to the edge of the cliff, between the two rivers, a small and picturesquely coloured building, with a courtyard in front.

We descended the cliff and crossed the Tak Chu; no sooner were we shut in between the high gravel cliffs at the bottom of the valley than groves of trees appeared, poplar (*Populus szechuanica*), willow, and *Hippophäe rhamnoides*, sharp green against the sable mountains. There were many prickly shrubs. Most notable, because gregarious, is *Sophora Moorcroftiana*, growing on the toughest and driest terraces, or sometimes partly buried under sand, although it is more characteristic of solid ground than of the dunes. The hard orange-brown seeds, like large ants' eggs, lie all the winter under the bushes, and are easily picked up; in fact to collect these is the best way to be sure of getting ripe seed. The plant can be found in flower from May onwards, and I have picked up ripe seed in September. *Sophora Moorcroftiana*, which bears masses of violet and white flowers, should grow well in the Mediterranean region, not too close to the sea. Also in bloom were *Spiraea canescens*, the spur twigs ending in spines, and *Cotoneaster racemiflora*, both attractive shrubs when lathered with their cream-white flowers. Under drought conditions they grow very compact, wasting no substance but knitting themselves together. The pale ashy-white foliage, due to a covering of silky hairs, is very different from the deep leaf-green typical of a wet climate. Nearly all the undershrubs which grow on the arid plateau, e.g. Berberis, Caragana, Rosa, Hippophäe, and Sophora, are thorny, while such normally inoffensive plants as Cotoneaster, spiraea, Leptodermis, Ceratostigma, and Wikstroemia, not to be outdone, develop a spiny habit. Even the honeysuckles are spiny. But of course these are tight little shrubs, not the twining plant we know as honeysuckle in England. Although most shrubs are either thorny, or spiny, and the leaves look as unappetizing as chewing-gum, goats eat them just the same. In a softer climate with richer soil and adequate shelter many of them grow larger, looser, and less hairy. These characters then are not fixed, but are imposed afresh on each generation by the climate; the natural tendency of the plant is to grow tall, and loose limbed and green — not ashy-grey.

It was a pleasant surprise later in the day to see the common white-flowered fragrant jasmine of our garden walls (*Jasminum officinale*) in full bloom on the hillside. Had one not known that Asia gave it to us, one might have believed it had been introduced into Tibet from English gardens.

In this tough soil, herbaceous plants find small comfort, but I saw the astonishing *Incarvillea lutea*, a tropical looking member of a tropical family, at home. Never did a plant look more of a foreigner, adapted though it is to this bitter land. The big yellow gloxinia-like flowers up to a score in number are borne in a tall spire, a foot or eighteen inches long. In very exposed places the stem is stunted and the flowers crowded into a head, but under normal conditions the spire tapers out. Unfortunately the flowers are in undertones of yellow, due to a sprinkling of brown spots, and they have a foetid smell. Thus it is not such a good plant as the dwarf *I. brevipes* or *I. grandiflora*, the latter also found in Tibet. Though by no means rare, *I. lutea* is scattered and apt to be solitary, rarely forming colonies of a few plants, although it sets plenty of viable seed in its hard pointed wooden capsules. It produces a long spongy tap root, the juice from which is said to be used to stain wood black.

On the gravel cliffs *Onosma Hookeri Wardii* had opened its bearded croziers of rich violet tubular flowers, crimson tipped. This, one of the finest of the Onosmas, which I introduced to England in 1925, has lately been lost to cultivation.

Passing through a gorge, we crossed to the right bank of the torrent by a timber bridge, and reached a village called Shio. There are several well-built houses here with clean whitewashed walls, standing amongst groves of poplar. A minor official, or *depa*, lives at Shio, but fortunately he was away. When I met him several months later, on my way back, he was curt and inclined to be obstructive. His *locum tenens* made no difficulty about finding me fresh transport.

Below Shio we recrossed to the left bank, and now the more gently sloping sides of the valley flared out like a funnel. The path along the hillside became easier. We passed several ruined villages, each marked by its four-sided watch tower. At one point I noticed a tree growing out of the hillside where there was a spring. It appeared to have two kinds of leaves, but closer inspection showed that a willow and a poplar had fused near the base of the trunk to form a natural graft. The effect was certainly surprising.

About three o'clock in the afternoon we reached the confluence of the Loro Nakpo Chu ('Black Loro river') with the Loro Karpo Chu ('White Loro river'), having marched fifteen miles. Opposite us, on the left bank of the completed Loro river, stood Trashi Tongme, conspicuous for an imposing gompa, or monastery, perched on a rock, with a cluster of poor houses and green trees clinging closely about it like a ragged skirt. We walked across the Loro Karpo Chu, its valley terraced with barley fields, and I hardly noticed it was a river at all; much of the water was being drawn off above to irrigate the crops at Trashi Tongme. And yet the valley continues westwards for thirty miles, growing ever wider and stonier; for a few months in the summer there must be more water in it.

The Loro Chu flows eastwards, parallel to and north of the Assam Himalayas, and at Trashi Tongme we changed direction from north to east. At the confluence of the 'white' and 'black' streams the former expands in a wide gravel delta, six hundred yards or more across. The mountains are quite bare, but the lower rubble slopes are striped with deep chines as though they had been ripped open by sharp claws. Although the howling winds have flayed the very flesh from the face of the mountains, the country is nevertheless beauty spotted with oases which look the greener by contrast with the wilderness.

The people of Trashi Tongme are almost unbelievably dirty, even when allowance is made for the cold and the lack of water. The squat featureless women varnish their faces, so that they seem to peer at you through black dominoes. The object of this unlovely cosmetic is to protect the skin against the ravage of the climate; but prevention looks worse than the disease.

I set up my tent in the mud-walled monastery garden, overlooking the river, and a flight of terraces green with barley. About 4 p.m. the wind began to blow strongly, and continued till long after dark. The temperature dropped to 49° F. inside my tent.

Below Trashi Tongme the valley of the Loro Chu is well cultivated for several miles. Village succeeds village, and there are groves of trees wherever shelter, natural or artificial, is to be found. I was much impressed by the contrast between the large size of the valley which is both broad and deep, and the small size of the river which is neither, though it is certainly swift. Farther west, the valleys of the outer plateau grow still wider as the rivers shrink; till the size of the river is in inverse proportion to the size of its valley. In 1925 when marching south from Tsetang on the Tsangpo, near Lhasa, to Tsöna Dzong, I crossed another headwater of the Subansiri; and though it was mid-winter and the stream consequently at its lowest ebb, it quite obviously bore no relation to the size of its valley. It was but a brook flowing in a broad rift. Formerly the valley of the Loro Chu must have been filled with gravel to a depth of several hundred feet, and a series of sharply defined terraces indicates the former size of the river, which has been gradually drying up as the glaciers disappear. The large size of the rounded boulders on the terraces is a further proof that there was once much more water in the river than there is to-day; the present Loro Chu could scarcely move them.

On June 18th we turned east and reached Tre Shika in an hour; here we changed transport. On the way we passed a large white stupa, something like a certain type of Burmese pagoda. From the stupa I had a magnificent view of the Assam Himalayas, now almost due south of me, a cluster of snow peaks grouped round Takpa Shiri, a peak nearly 22,000 feet high. The alignment of the range is here definitely north-east to south-west, and within a distance of forty-five miles are eighteen peaks of over 20,000 feet high, four of them being over 22,000 feet, and two of them over 23,000 feet. If ever a mountain range looked like a great divide, surely this tremendous snow barrier does. Yet the Loro Chu on the north side joins the waters which flow down the south side of it to form the Subansiri — in other words, all those snow peaks give birth to one river, and to one only — the Subansiri.

After marching seven or eight miles through a wide dry valley we crossed to the right bank by a wooden bridge, where the sundered streams unite; and these expanses of gravel are seen no more. Passing Takpa Shiri, the Loro Chu breaks into violent rapids, lashing itself into a fury of foam amongst the boulders. We changed transport for the second time and at 2.30 p.m. reached a castle-like house at the mouth of the ravine, where we halted for the night, having marched twelve miles. An extensive system of flumes irrigates the fields, which are cut out at different levels amongst the rocks and boulders above the river; and here I found a considerable flora. *Primula sikkimensis* lined the brook, and along the field paths grew plants like *Veronica Anagallis*, *Pedicularis ornata*, Thalictrum, and Corydalis. Amongst shrubs I noticed *Leptodermis pilosa*, *Lonicera spinosa*, *Ceratostigma Griffithii*, Wikstroemia, salix with woolly leaves, and all those previously seen higher up the valley. I also found a curious species of Codonopsis. The altitude of Hordoryu, as the house is named (Hor means Turki), is over 12,000 feet, which is both too high and too low for maximum vegetation on the outer plateau; too high for the warmer valley flora, too low for the moister alpine flora. Below Trashi Tongme the vegetation is of the same type as at Karta, that is to say, thorn scrub, although it is slightly richer in species; but it is far poorer than it is in the Tsangpo valley, 2000 feet lower. On the other hand, if one were to climb 2000 feet up the mountain towards the snows, one would find a varied alpine flora.

The houses in the Loro valley are well built and the mud plaster is washed a dark slate grey. Beside almost every house as usual, haunting it like its shadow, stand the ruins of another house. We also passed more abandoned villages — abandoned I suspect because of the increasing difficulty of irrigation. One gets the idea of a population perpetually on the move, within well defined limits. Perhaps there was once a larger population. The people provided me with food, shelter, and transport willingly enough. We used ponies, donkeys, and coolies.

On June 19th we crossed to the left bank of the river seven miles below Hordoryu, and reached Chayul Dzong, another three miles, in less than four hours. The valley was still com-

paratively well cultivated with small scattered villages, some high up, others low down. At one spot there is a strip of cultivation in the river bed. Some distance down the valley I caught sight of a high isolated sugar loaf peak, bearing 51°; but there was no snow visible.

Chayul Dzong, or Chadze as it is sometimes called, is a squalid village in an arid valley, harassed by a ceaseless wind. The monastery is worthy of a better background. The dzong itself is a rabbit warren of living quarters, stables, store rooms, dungeons, and nameless black holes all with flat mud roofs. Outside the walls is a collection of hovels where the very poorest people live in squalor. The population must be considerably less than a hundred persons, of whom twenty or thirty would be monks, although I never saw more than a dozen present together. Most of them had gone on missions to the Drokpa.

So this was to be my base for botanical exploration! Here I was, behind the Assam Himalayas, my goal reached. Yet I felt already that I had been duped. Either I had come too far, or I had not gone far enough. Forward or back it must be. But who ever went back!

CHAPTER VI

WIND, CLOUD AND STARS

At Chayul I took up my headquarters in a small upstairs room off one of the courtyards of the dzong. The Jongpen was away; it was said he had left for Lhasa the day before I arrived. However he was expecting me and had sent me a chunk of butter with a scarf, which stood for felicitations. I rather suspected he had not gone away at all, but was simply, in the accepted social sense, common the world over, 'Not at home'. My sudden arrival had perhaps embarrassed him; it meant doing something, and that is just what a provincial Tibetan official abhors.

I had now to decide on my next move. Should I keep to my original plan, make Chayul Dzong general headquarters, and explore the Assam Himalayas from the north?

From the Assam side it is quite impracticable to reach the passes to the north-east of Gori Chen. But here I was within two or three days' easy march of them. Such a chance might never recur, which strengthened the case for staying.

But there was an alternative. If my credit stretched thus far, why not use it to the utmost? Why not go on and discover more unknown country? The Loro Chu was as dry and lifeless as the Suez Canal. But within a week's march was the district of Tsari, famous in Tibetan legend for its flowers. Why not go to Tsari? Straightaway I made up my mind. I would stay a few days at Chayul Dzong, long enough to inspire the Jongpen (who, I was convinced, was only in temporary retreat) with confidence in me, but not long enough to arm him with authority to stop me. Without orders from his superior, to stop me meant taking a big responsibility. I doubted whether he would shoulder it.

Below Chayul Dzong, the Loro valley becomes a waterworn gorge buttressed by steep overlapping spurs. Every day I saw to the east a menacing cloud bank which hung over the gorge within a few miles of us. Five miles away it was raining hard; over Chayul Dzong the sun shone, and the blistering wind roared. Sometimes the wind, dropping suddenly at midday, had brought a sprinkle of rain to moisten the parched earth; but that was rare in June. So long as the wind blew, though it might tear off the ragged fringes of the cloud, no rain fell; the dry air dissolved the cloud as the white cloud from a railway engine is dissolved. When the wind dropped then only was it sure to rain. Wind and rain were mutually exclusive. This almost incessant wind gave me violent headaches. Yet I usually enjoy a blustering wind on the heights. A gale braces me.

Temperatures were moderate. On June 20th the minimum was 56° F. and on the 23rd, 54° F. The shade maxima on the same days being 68.5° and 69°. During five days towards the end of September, similar temperatures prevailed; but the winters are severe. The chief factor making for high temperatures is the comparatively low latitude of Chayul Dzong, which is about 28½°; that is to say, Chayul Dzong is south of Suez, Jacksonville, Fla., and Shanghai. Factors favouring low temperatures are altitude, which is 11,450 feet, the proximity of snow peaks, the absence of vegetation to screen the naked rock, the absence of water to retain heat and, in a lesser degree, the coldness of the river, and the clearness of the skies. But temperature is, on the whole, much less significant to plant life than is moisture.

In order to obtain some idea of the dryness of the air, I took a number of observations with a 'wet' and 'dry' bulb swing thermometer, from which the relative humidity can be calculated. Saturation point for any temperature is of course 100%. Thus on June 20th at 7 a.m. the relative humidity was 61% of saturation, and at 5 p.m. 37%. On June 22nd at 10 a.m. it was 43% and on September 25th at 2 p.m. 27%, the lowest recorded. It is important to remember that these figures refer, not to the *absolute* amount of water vapour present in the air, but only the *relative* humidity, which varies with the temperature for the same amount of water vapour. But while accurate instrumental measurements are essential for the advancement of exact knowledge, observation by the senses told me the same thing. I knew just as surely as I did from reading the thermometers that the air was dry because my photographic plates dried in three hours instead of three days, and my sliding wooden camera legs opened and shut easily, without jamming, and because my hair crackled when brushed, and my lips cracked. The absence of trees, except in a few favoured damp spots, told the same story. Such rough observations of natural everyday events are the first to impress themselves on us. The next step is to construct an instrument which will *measure* the dryness on a standard scale. When this has been done, it becomes possible to compare the dryness of Chayul Dzong with the dryness of say, Salt Lake City, or Cairo. From comparisons of the fauna and flora in dry places generally, the scientist then draws his conclusions, the truth or falsity of which can be tested. These are the methods of science, and in this way a body of accurate knowledge, which can be applied so as to make the world a jollier place to live in, has been built up.

In the river bed at Chayul Dzong a broad strip of gravel and sand was exposed on which grew thickets, dense or open, of buckthorn. Some of the trees were perhaps upwards of a century old. Here I spent several enjoyable hours collecting plants and watching birds. There was more life by the river than I should have expected. The dividing line between the abundant life of the river gorge country to the east and the sterility of the lofty plateau to the west is a thin one, and a slight bias will turn the scale. Tibet is a thirsty land, and cold. The soil is thirsty; the very air we breathe is thirsty. Thirst is the overmastering appetite. Man has made the soil yield by irrigation. But man cannot moisten dry air, and the amount of water vapour present in the air is just as important to vegetation as the amount of water present in the soil. In dry Tibet a moist habitat, as in bogs, is not uncommon. In the river gorge region farther east where the atmosphere is damper, dry well-drained soils as on scree slopes, are not uncommon. Anything more utterly different than the vegetation of the two habitats for the same altitude it would be difficult to imagine. The trouble in Tibet is wind. There is always a wind blowing, often with gale force, for days on end, or regularly each day between certain hours. It is the wind which is hostile to plant life. This is well illustrated in an arid gorge, such as the Loro Chu. Given water, many plants grow easily at Chayul Dzong – (of course a much greater number would grow than do in fact grow there). With very few exceptions they are herbaceous plants, annuals or perennials rarely above a foot or eighteen inches tall. I found that wherever the ground is always moist, as in bogs, it is green, at least throughout the summer, and covered with plants such as *Primula tibetica*, the vivid gamboge *Pedicularis ornata*, ranunculus, potentilla, *Veronica Anagallis*, while the irrigation channels are lined with a lush growth of lucerne, trefoil (*Medicago lupulina*), several potentillas, carum, *Rubia cordifolia*, plantago, elder (*Sambucus adnata*), and others. Moisture in the soil, however, will not of itself ensure the growth of trees and shrubs, because their aspiring height brings them into conflict with the wind and the evaporating surface of their leaves is so large that they lose water above ground through the leaves faster than it can be replaced by the roots from below. Thus no amount of irrigation would greatly increase the number of trees which can withstand the Tibetan wind, although a comparatively slight increase of atmospheric humidity is all that is needed to promote forest. Looking eastwards down the gorge I could see forested mountains, muffled in cloud, within a very few miles.

Trees at Chayul Dzong are rare and of few species; most of them have been planted. Just below the dzong is a grove of walnut and poplar trees, while peach and pear certainly, and poplar (*Populus alba* and *P. szechuanica*) and willow (*Salix cheilophila*) probably, have been planted. There is a small walled garden by the river, where the Jongpen's ponies graze and yawn beneath willows and poplars. In fact trees in the wild mountainous valley of the Loro Chu are much rarer than they are in the crowded built up cities of western Europe.

The only truly wild tree appears to be *Hippophäe rhamnoides*, which is gregarious, thus affording shelter to a number of plants of which the most conspicuous were white jasmine in full bloom, and *Clematis orientalis* which was in fruit, its innumerable silver powder puffs hanging in long cascades over the trees. In flower it must have been a wonderful sight. The flowers are thimble-shaped, of a rather bitter yellow, or even chocolate.

Just above the strip of uncovered gravel, which was rarely flooded, a flight of small terraces revetted with stone walls and irrigated by a brook, had been built; niggling little bits of land stolen for civilization from the barbaric landscape. Irrigation is always difficult in the big valleys, and so most of the villages are situated in the smaller valleys at a much higher altitude. There is a far larger population living at 13,000 feet in dry Tibet than at 11,000 feet.

At one point a stone wall, about three feet high and a hundred yards long, had been built to hold back the river, and had become a home for voles, several of which I caught. This creature proved to be *Cricetulus lama*. It picked up a living in a large bed of *Iris lactea*, which a month earlier must have been a brave sight with hundreds of blooms, though it was now over. Some of the clumps were a yard through and bore six or eight flowering stems. One day I saw a black hare. Apart from a few curs of low degree, and razor-backed pigs which foraged disconsolately round the village muck heap, these were the only local mammals.

The most interesting bird was a laughing thrush (*Trochalopteron henrici*) which was common here in September, living mainly on the ground and feeding on hippophäe berries. In England, no bird will touch these fruits, which contain a very acrid juice; but the trochalopterons did — there was not much else for them to eat. Other birds I noticed were hoopoes, black and white magpie, chough, rock pigeons, rose finch, wagtails, sparrows, and in September, the common English kingfisher. On June 20th I glimpsed two partridges (probably *Perdix hodgsoniae*); but though I combed the thicket day after day, I never saw them again.

A stagnant pool contained a number of small frogs (*Altirana Parkeri*); and when I returned here in September, the same pool was black with tadpoles.

Naturally in this flowerless land there was not much insect life, but on September 25th I saw two species of butterfly battling breathlessly with the breeze. Houseflies at any rate were far from rare; but there was not a single blood-sucking insect, except of course the ubiquitous flea.

I had thought that after the rains, in July and August, even Chayul Dzong would freshen up and look quite green, especially as I noticed several plants not yet in flower in the fields. Yet when I returned in September, the vegetation looked rather scrappier than it did in June – and much more raddled! A few plants did flower during the intervening months; but those I had already noticed.

A considerable proportion of the local flora owes its presence to cultivation, and but for that could not exist here. Such plants are part of the human scene, and are present not only because where there are crops there is moisture, but also because where there is cultivation there is humus; and that means nitrogen. The coarse gravels of Tibet are extremely poor in nitrogen salts and the scraggy array of dwarfed shrubs is largely the result of nitrogen starvation. The green fodder plants already mentioned, and such weeds as burdock (Arctium), dandelion, species of potentilla, Capsella, Sambucus, *Cynoglossum amabile*, and malva owe their presence to cultivation.

An interesting plant of the dry stony slopes I noticed here for the first time was *Mirabilis himalaica* (formerly called *Oxybaphus*), remarkable for the fact that it is the sole Asiatic representative of a tropical American genus. Why it should grow native in Tibet of all places is a mystery. There were also a few scattered tufted grasses, but nothing approaching pasture.

The most useful and certainly the most heroic plants are those which boldly colonize the gravel spits thrown up by the river, and destined one day perhaps to become permanent land not subject to flooding. They are hippophäe and oxytropis, and sometimes rosa. These plants may be submerged from time to time, and are frequently torn from their anchorage, and left to perish on the beach. They are bombarded and raked with gravel during floods, their roots are undermined, their foliage flayed alive. But they persist. The final result is a thorn thicket in which twenty or thirty species of plants may flourish, the outstanding ones being *Clematis orientalis*, *Jasminum officinale* and *Iris lactea*.

I could buy no eggs or chickens in Chayul Dzong; water boils at so low a temperature at 12,000 feet (189° F. instead of 212°) that you cannot cook an egg; the albumen will not coagulate at this temperature. So what is the use of keeping chickens? Apparently they will not live in dry Tibet anyhow. Perhaps there is not enough food for them. My sheep, slain on June 1st, had lasted a fortnight, though it was becoming rather high towards the end.

The owner of the house where I stayed came to me the morning after my arrival, and asked if I could do anything for him. I had not seen him because he was drunk the day I arrived. I now understood why. The whole of one side of his face was inflated like a child's balloon, the result of an abscess. The poor man had been like that for a long time, and was always in great pain. Beyond giving him a sleeping draught I could do nothing to help him.

I was not the only inmate of the dzong. Walking over the flat roofs, one could see into little courtyards where people worked outside rooms no larger than kennels. Here they lived, slept and cooked. There was a woman, weaving a woollen rug, and a man in a long grey smock, wearing a wide circular wooden collar round his neck. He was a big man, with a disarming smile, a ready word, and tousled hair. But his small eyes were shifty, and too close together. He was a felon, caught in some paltry misdemeanour. This man had been sentenced to wear the heavy wooden collar, or 'cangue', for a term of years. It is more familiar in China, whence it was introduced into Tibet. In many of the hill villages in Assam, small pigs are condemned to wear a triangular 'cangue'; it prevents them from breaking through the hedges and getting into the crops. My felon wandered about a free, if branded man. He made boots – he was a cobbler by trade. He was always cheerful, and was very grateful for some cigarettes I gave him.

I had arrived in Chayul Dzong with twenty-five loads and I now began to make preparations for departure, it being my intention to be away a month. One can cover a lot of ground in a month if one travels fast; and the secret of travelling fast is to travel light. I cut down my transport by more than half, and after much thought, packed twelve loads – first line transport, not an excessive amount for myself and two servants for a month's travel, collecting plants all the while.

On June 23rd a small cloud appeared on the horizon of my contentment; the acting Jongpen – the number one really had gone to Lhasa it seemed, leaving his deputy in charge – returned from a tour and requested me to call on him. He had recovered his poise, it seemed, and was ready to make a decision. But Tashi quickly reassured me.

'That is good, Sahib. The Jongpen wishes to see you.'

'It is unfortunate, Tashi. He may refuse me permission to travel.'

'In India it may be so, Sahib, but not in our country. The Tibetan magistrates are very polite to strangers. If you ask for something, they will not refuse. I will request him to let you go to Charme, and he will say yes, do not fear.'

And it all turned out as Tashi predicted. I found the magistrate in a pleasant room above a clean courtyard. He was sitting by a glass window, while outside were boxes filled with scarlet pelargoniums and purple stocks – an amiable young man dressed in a long red robe, with a saffron-yellow collar, to which he had added the inevitable Homburg felt hat. He lamented that most of his flowers which he had brought from Lhasa had died in the winter. In the courtyard he kept a wolf – the golden wolf of Tibet, *Lupus tibetanus* – in a cage; it had been caught in the hills and, though quite young, looked vicious. The Tibetan word is *chang-ku*, written *spyang-ku*.

After a short talk, in the course of which the Jongpen asked me a few questions, he said I might go to Sanga Chöling.

CHAPTER VII

THE PAINTED MONASTERY

JUNE 24th, a hot sunny day, found us marching eastwards down the Loro Chu. Half a mile below Chayul at the confluence of the Nye river, we crossed to the right bank by a good timber bridge and came to a village called Kap. Here were the same irrigated crops, but more trees, mostly willows. As we continued down the south bank of the river, the flora gradually increased, but the open slopes were still covered with thorn scrub. In the gullies, crimson roses (*Rosa Moyesii*), jasmine, and mock orange or syringa (*Philadelphus*) were in bloom, with pink flowered deutzia, spiraea, and other shrubs. On the drier slopes grew thickets of box (*Buxus sempervirens*), *Wikstroemia canescens*, juniper, and a lot of small flowers, notably irises (*I. kumaonensis*), columbine, the weedy washy *Campanula colorata*, and sedum. A thousand feet above the river were dark patches of picea forest. The change from plateau vegetation to a moist Himalayan type begins just below Chayul Dzong. For the next twenty or thirty miles while the climate grows gradually wetter, we are in a transition zone. But there is no change in the appearance of the valley, except that it now begins to grow more and more gloomy.

After halting for lunch under a grove of trees and changing our ponies for coolies, we recrossed to the left bank of the river by a sagging broken-down bridge. Suddenly things became more difficult.

At this point the Loro Chu enters a savage looking gorge, and begins to break through the Himalayas. So far the path had been reasonably good. Now it became rougher and after ascending a flight of crazy steps, narrowed to a ledge cut in the face of the cliff. Presently the ledge became a bracket, no path at all, just flag stones laid across wooden stakes wedged into cracks in the cliff a couple of hundred feet above the dark river. The bracket sloped upwards and disappeared round a corner; and the flags wobbled as I stepped on them! It ended abruptly at the foot of a vertical ladder thirty feet high. I had lagged behind to botanize. By the time I had sidled with faltering steps dizzily to the foot of the ladder, where the two-foot-wide ledge petered out, there was only just room to stand. Tashi, Mount Everest hero, stood waiting for me; but his presence did singularly little to restore my composure. The last coolie had gone up and disappeared out of sight, like Jack on the Beanstalk. I went up five steps, and clung there almost overhanging the river, too frightened to go another step. So I came down again feeling sick with terror. Tashi shouted up to the coolies, and a man raced down like a jolly tar. He offered to carry me up on his back, like one of my own loads, and started putting his leather rope round me to carry out his threat. Whether I was more stung by the indignity of such an inglorious ascent, or scared stiff at the prospect, I don't know. However the audacity of the proposal gave me an idea. I tied the rope round my body, gave the man the other end and told him to go slowly, keeping just ahead of me, and not to pull on the rope. I followed him, keeping my eyes on the ladder, not daring to look down. Thus we went to the top, as though cliff climbing. I found the other coolies sitting on the brink of the precipice and spitting into space. They grinned when I arrived; I could afford to laugh at myself now; and did.

The path improved. We descended more gradually to the river again, crossed it for the third time and reached Trön at sunset. We had marched about sixteen miles, though it seemed longer. The difficult rock-climb through the gorge confines traffic between Chayul and Trön to man power. Formerly there was a pony trail at the foot of the cliffs, but that required crossing the river several times and all the bridges were in ruins. There had been a trade slump, so nobody had troubled to repair them.

Trön is the last Tibetan village on the Loro Chu, and a penal settlement. On the brink of a precipice stands a square white-washed tower. They unlocked the heavy wooden door, and I found myself inside a dark dungeon. We went up a ladder to the flat roof, from which murderers used to be flung over the precipice. They say swift retribution is no longer inflicted even on murderers in Tibet. We came back to the tower and I saw a large square stone in the floor, with an iron ring in it. The guide lifted this stone, revealing an underground cell, hewn out of the living rock. It was twelve feet deep, and black as hell. There was nobody in it; nobody alive at any rate. I shivered.

I spent June 25th at Trön. I wanted to go another day's march down the valley to the first Lopa village, where forest begins, but the Tibetans refused to take me. The Lopas apparently are quarrelsome folks, always fighting. So people living in a state of nature hate each other too! But they don't fight with the Tibetans; they know better. It seems unlikely however that the Church – always in the van of Tibetan colonization – will penetrate much farther in this direction.

These Lopas dwell in the jungle, far down the valley, south of the Great Himalayan range. They are the people whom on the Assam side, we call Daphlas, or Akas, or possibly Abors – imprecise labels. But to the Tibetans, they are all alike, Lopas, or Chachu,[1] that is to say, savages. In the Loro valley and beyond they are economically dependent on the Tibetans, from whom they obtain that most necessary substance, salt. In the summer they cross the eastern Himalayan passes to work in the fields of Kongbo, and help to gather in the harvest. In the winter they come up the river valleys which pierce the main range as traders, to buy salt in exchange for the produce of their own jungles – animal skins, musk, rice, chillies, star anise,

[1] The Tibetans distinguish between Chachu Or who visit Sanga Chöling, and Chachu Kung who go to Chayul Dzong. They are probably different clans of one tribe.

which is the dry fruit of illicium, an aromatic condiment, and cane. They make silver ear-rings, and tobacco pipes, and cover bamboo drinking vessels with a thin sheath of woven bamboo. They also weave cloth.

I had hoped to spend part of the summer going down the Loro Chu into the Lopa country, until I reached a point where all the other tributaries which rise north of the Himalayas had joined in, and the combined river was really and truly the Subansiri of Assam. Then I would work up stream, westwards again, following one of the other branches, back into Tsari. By this means I might descend the valley so low as 7000 feet, or even 6000 feet, and reach the subtropical jungle, surely a botanist's paradise!

That plan was quickly nipped in the bud because the Tibetans refused to go. I had to think of another plan; and I decided to make straight for Tsari by the direct route over the Drichung La, a high pass immediately north of Trön. The Tibetans were willing to take me over the range to Charme; we would start on the 26th.

Meanwhile I had walked a mile or two down the valley below Trön, until presently I could see snow ahead on the next spur and dark fir forest. There are trees in a deep sheltered gully at Trön, notably *Picea likiangensis*, and a pine. The only rhododendron at the bottom of the valley is the little pink flowered *R. virgatum*. But higher up, where forest begins, there are several species.

Next day we crossed the river once more. I noticed that the colour of the water had changed overnight from slate grey to dirty yellow, indicating heavy rain in the Nye Chu valley. It is interesting to be able to tell where it is raining by the colour of the river.

We climbed a steep path to upper Trön, a village more than a thousand feet above the river, where yak transport awaited. Potatoes are grown here and the houses are shaded by green trees – weeping willow, maple, peach, walnut, and poplar.

The air too is noticeably damper, and the cloud ceiling at night had hitherto just hidden the village from view.

Above Trön we continued to climb steeply, the path aiming towards a sharp ridge. There were large clumps of paeony in the hollows, and a few big golden globe flowers survived to proclaim the plant *Paeonia lutea.* We were on a dry south slope, so that it was not till we had reached about 12,000 feet that the air was damp enough to support a different type of vegetation. Up to there it was just shrubs and more shrubs: *Potentilla fruticosa,* cotoneaster, berberis, *Rosa sericea,* and a small flowered form of *Clematis montana* which was in full bloom. Quite suddenly, while we were still some way from the ridge, the slope came alive with myriads of flowers, at first scattered, then in colonies, soon in solid masses: *Primula pulchelloides, Adonis brevistyla, Stellera chamaejasme,* anemones, two species of Androsace, and the large ruddy brown slipper orchid, *Cypripedium tibeticum* were a few I noticed. Then came tuffets of heather-like cassiope, *Rhododendron lepidotum,* and a lovely glaucous leafed berberis; and from this point onwards the mountain was in glorious flower. As soon as we reached the ridge, we halted for lunch, and I threw myself down in a grassy dell amidst bushes of yellow and crimson flowered rhododendrons – *R. Wardii* and *R. aganniphum,* and a form of *R. lanatum* with straw-yellow flowers thickly peppered with crimson spots. More dramatic was a heavy cloud of amethyst purple in a gully; it proved to be a single bush of *R. oreotrephes* in marvellous bloom, the only one I found. It was clear that the poverty of plants in the valley of the Loro Chu is due to local conditions; to heat, drought and wind. The real flora of southern Tibet was here, spread at my feet. We were in fact at the meeting point of *two* floras, that of the river gorge region and that of the outer plateau. The river gorge flora has to ascend in order to find sufficient moisture – and loses some of its variety in consequence of the cold; the hardy outer plateau flora creeps into the dry upper gorges, and gains in wealth of species, thanks to the warmth.

We continued up the ridge but had not gone a mile when the Tibetans said we must camp, as there was no water higher up. The altitude was about 14,000 feet, my tent being pitched in a grassy dell amongst rhododendron bushes, most of them in bloom. Besides the big bushes mentioned there were two dwarf species, one aromatic leafed, with pink flowers, *R. kongboense*, the other, *R. nivale*, with tiny purple flowers. But the most interesting of all was *R. lanatum*, because it is one of the few economic rhododendron species in Tibet. The under leaf surface is covered with a thick shaggy coat of foxy red hairs. This pelt can be stripped off whole with the thumbnail, leaving the leaf uninjured; but it requires knack. The pelt is then twisted and used as wick in oil lamps. The only other species which is put to any use in Tibet, so far as I know, is *R. kongboense*, the aromatic leaves of which are burnt in the daily religious ceremonies of rich householders in Kongbo. It surprises me that the timber of the tree rhododendrons is not used for cups, of which great numbers are turned in Tibet.

I spent the rest of the afternoon botanizing. A beautiful primula, like a large scented grape hyacinth, grew scattered in the pasture, amongst the bushes, and sometimes under them. Leaves, stem, and inflorescence are powdered with snow white meal, and the flowers smell deliciously of hyacinth, hence the name — *Primula hyacinthina*. But its likeness to *P. bellidifolia* is undeniable. Other alpine flowers were *Nomcharis nana*, trollius, morina, lloydia, polygonum, vaccinium, scabious, and colonies of a dwarf form of *Primula sikkimensis*.

The pastures were rustling with grasshoppers.

The morning had been fine and I was hoping for a grand view of the Himalayas across the deep chasm of the Loro Chu. But the Himalayas remained obstinately muffled in cloud, and towards evening rain began to fall.

To the west I noticed a small glacier on the range which separates the Loro Chu — Nye Chu from the Char Chu — that is to say the range on which we now were. It was in the direction of the Le La, where there is a group of snow peaks, clearly visible from above Sanga Chöling.

That night the temperature dropped to 41° F. I slept uneasily because I was so anxious for a clear dawn. Almost every hour I awoke to see the stars shining mistily through a veil of cloud. There was no view in any direction when I got up; but a cuckoo was calling lustily.

At first the going along the knife edge-ridge was good enough. The east side was precipitous, crumbling, and without much vegetation on cliffs and screes – although what plants there were might have been interesting. The crest was hacked like a handsaw, rocky and bare, too. Only the westward slant, with its pastures and patches of scrub, afforded a way, but the path kept as close up to the crest as it could. There was a deep wooded valley below us, and beyond that another ridge, like the one we were on.

We heard snowcock calling all round us, and caught a glimpse of several; but they were very wary. Millions of flowers spread a carpet of ever changing colour at our feet; wine-red pools of *Primula Roylei*, changing to pale cream waves of *P. sikkimensis*, not typical yet not distinct enough to warrant another name. At about 16,000 feet, the number of flowers and the number of species had fallen to a low ebb. We were in the midst of a stony wilderness; and the last 1000 or 1500 feet up a scree sloping at 60° to the jagged crest was troublesome. I would never have guessed that there was a pass here, as I squeezed between two rocks in the toothed ridge and pitched down the scree on the other side. Then a squall of hail hit us, and it all was cold and cheerless. We were hardly over the top – about 17,000 feet – when I noticed in crevices of the cliff a perfect gem of a primula with big-eyed mauve flowers, two or three clustered together at the end of a mealy stalk. The leaves are spoon-shaped, and powdered snow white beneath. The plants were numerous, but I could not get them out of the cracks. Lower down the valley we came upon a colony of this *P. consocia*, growing on a scree; it looked quite a different plant here, much bigger, with an enomous bunch of fine roots anchoring it in the half fluid soil. It is closely allied to *P. Caveana.* Though well able to take care of itself three miles above sea-level, it might hate Sussex.

In this valley north of the Drichung La are unmistakable signs of glacial action, the first I had seen since crossing the Pen La.

However we did not stick long to the valley, which narrowed and steepened until it was just a forested ravine. We kept to the open, and climbing again, marched at the base of snow-covered peaks. The gorge of the Char Chu was now directly below us, and across it, farther north, I could see snow on the mountains of Tsari. We were still pretty high up, walking over hassocks of dwarf rhododendron (*R. nivale* and *R. fragariflorum*), and an occasional plant of the sky blue *Meconopsis bella*, and many another rare alpine flower.

This country is terrific; but we were so close up against the snow peaks we couldn't see them – only the ruts between, where the rivers have sawed their way 5000 feet below. Now we were plunging down the slope straight towards the river of Charme, taking almost any line we pleased. Over it spread an intermittent crimson crust of *Androsace tibetica*, an invasive cushion plant, tough but handsome. On our left was a deep valley, where a stream from the Le La (a pass west of the Drichung La) flowed in. Towards the bottom we passed through a sheltered glen where small trees and shrubs grew thickly. It was like a plantation, only the trees – larch and fir, with birch, willow and rhododendron undergrowth – would never grow much taller.

It was five o'clock when at last we reached the Charme river. The rain had stopped, and it was warm; my clothes were nearly dry.

Charme proved to be a poor little village, most of the houses in ruins. Tashi had found us quarters for the night in a small house standing on the ruins of a mansion, and I was impressed with our welcome. A raven croaked dismally from an empty window frame, while a tortoiseshell cat slept peacefully on a beam which supported nothing else.

Exhausted after a ten hours' march, I slept soundly, and awoke to hear the song of birds. Then the housewife lit a bunch of juniper in the holy oven, and presently a column of aromatic smoke was cleansing the somewhat rancid atmosphere of the dark house.

After breakfast we started up the valley for Sanga Chöling, about eight miles distant. The vegetation was again scanty and xerophytic, and became more so as we travelled westwards; but only down at the bottom of the valley. On the rocks were hundreds of pearl-grey gasteropod shells, squat little spirals; and, more conspicuous, ugly black lizards up to a foot in length. These scuttered up the rocks with great agility, but did not get under cover unless they thought themselves in immediate peril. About half way we crossed to the left bank of the river, and came to houses and cultivation again. Along the irrigation channels grew *Primula sikkimensis* in its typical form. It has been stated that this charming plant does not grow in Tibet. There were trees in every village, shading every solitary house, for the Tibetans love to have trees around; elm, and willow and peach, the latter much disfigured by leaf curl. Broad beans and potatoes are grown in some quantity.

We turned a corner, and suddenly Sanga Chöling burst into view, like a challenge. The white monastery, clapped on to a narrow ridge, looked like the superstructure of a battleship in dry dock. We walked along the stone flagged quayside where crooked houses, with window boxes, suggested a Georgian English seaport; passed a stone-flagged bridge, and reached the entrance to the main monastery. Outside is a *mendong* or religious wall, a hundred yards long. We went through into the big courtyard, and I felt rather as though we were in the Piazza at Venice looking at a cruder St. Mark's. In the centre stood a flagstaff about 120 feet high, but rather cock-eyed; on its summit was perched what might have been either a fancy rocket or a ballet dancer.

Three sides of the square are occupied by residential quarters – including the public inn – with stables underneath. A wooden gallery runs lopsidedly round the buildings, and gives entrance to the cell-like rooms. I was conducted to a room in the corner, and it was a tight fit. From the gallery I looked straight across the courtyard to the great temple; small wonder it fairly took my breath away. The high façade was white, with the many deep and narrow embrasures picked out in slate-grey. A flight of high narrow steps led up to the massive timber doors, which were studded with iron nails. At the top of the building, just beneath the roof, a broad band of faggots formed a sort of dado; and to this were attached heraldic designs in gold on a blue ground; ornaments which looked as though they might have come out of a large cracker. One was like an Irish harp; another was like a scythe, and that of course suggested Father Time. Sombre black curtains, tattered and dingy, draped part of the façade, hanging from a wooden gallery, but a gay note was added by the window boxes full of bright flowers.

The gaudiest part of this notable building is the flashing golden roof, its corners curled up in the best Chinese tradition. It is shaped like a motor car bonnet, with a golden radiator, and has eight cylinders, or may be seven.

Here undoubtedly Sanga Chöling parts company with St. Mark's, but it has a piercing and sombre magnificence of its own. The village seems to be all monasteries; two of them are large, and the view of the perpendicular architecture from the other side of the river is uplifting. A closer view reminds one that here too splendour and squalor live side by side, while the many window boxes in temple and hovel suggest a sort of everlasting harvest festival. I found Sanga Chöling an Arabian Nights palace, and the monks having greeted me as a friend, I was quite ready to stay over a day, or over a month.

A monk known as the Depa visited me. He was a pleasant-voiced, mild-looking Lama, about fifty years of age, dressed in a fine red robe braided with silver. I was a little surprised to find that he had no religious scruples against drinking alcohol. He lapped up some gin, of which I had half a bottle, and ambrosia could not have irradiated him more. He told me that in ten days' time there would be a big festival, and I might come and take photographs if I liked; but he offered no objections to my going to Tsari. It hardly seemed worth while to come back so soon, it would probably be raining, and I could not take photographs if it rained. I decided to go to Tsari, nor did I return to Sanga Chöling till September 15th.

The monastery had its permanent beggar, a blind man with a ragged cloak, a staff and a wooden cup, and no other visible property in the world. All day he sat in the courtyard, in the sun if there was any; at night he slept just anywhere on the stones, with or without a roof over his head. Children mocked him, adults shunned him. But he just went on existing, sometimes tapping his way from one side of the courtyard to the other. He excited in his fellow men derision rather than pity; for Tibet is a hard land, where survival is to the fittest, physically. He must have eaten sometimes, but his bowl set on his lap always appeared to be empty.

Tashi gathered some information about the circuit of the holy mountain Tsa-ri, and I felt inclined to make the pilgrimage, which would take twelve or fourteen days. But meanwhile a more ambitious plan was beginning to formulate itself. Why not go north until I reached the Tsangpo, thus linking my present route to that of 1924?

CHAPTER VIII

PASTORAL

On June 30th we turned north again, following a rough track up a stream which entered the river just below the village. I had hardly noticed it the day we arrived, it was so exactly like scores of other streams; but this one was important, not only as an exit from the valley, but also as the source of Sanga Chöling's water supply.

For the first mile the cliffs were as dry and bare as the main valley, and wriggling with lizards.

Above the first steep gorge, which every torrent must make for itself before it can reach the main river, the arid slopes were covered with scattered thorn shrubs, now wreathed in the smiling pink blossoms of *Clematis montana*. The tiny flowers are borne very close together, and the long branches make floral chains linking bush to bush indissolubly. I think that this beautiful climber would grow well in the Atlantic States of North America, including even New York itself.

Other dry zone plants in flower on these rather inhospitable looking slopes were the stiff and stately *Incarvillea lutea* and two rosette plants, *Didissandra lanuginosa*, and *Androsace strigillosa*. One would expect to find succulents plentiful, but xerophytism has slanted in another direction, and neither succulents nor bulbous plants are common in Tibet. This may be due to the hard winters; after all, we were more than 12,000 feet above sea-level!

As we approached higher and cooler levels where the rainfall is heavier, the valley opened out and a much more diversified flora appeared. At one point we passed through a gorge the cliffs shaggy browed with *Picea likiangensis*. The stream itself was lined with bushes, and even small trees, which ask only water and shelter from the wind.

We halted for half an hour on a grassy terrace, having climbed perhaps 1500 or 2000 feet; and here I noticed *Dracocephalum Hemsleyanum* in flower for the first time. It is a perennial herb of bushy habit, attaining a height of two feet, but the weak stems sag, so that it grows more in bulk than in height. The numerous deep gentian blue flowers marked it out as a plant worth putting in English and American gardens. Seeds brought to England germinated quickly. I sowed some in March 1936, and by June plants were flowering. They continued to flower till September. I formed the opinion that *D. Hemsleyanum* would do best treated as an annual, especially in the United States of America. It is now a popular garden plant in Britain.

Looking back down the valley, I caught sight of a fine snow peak, with one large and two small glaciers, across the river from Sanga Chöling and less than twenty miles away. This peak must be 19,000 or 20,000 feet high, and stands somewhere between the Drichung La, which we had just crossed, and the Mo La which I was to cross in September; perhaps near the Le La.

We ourselves were ascending an old glacier valley, and the whole of this range, forming the watershed between Char Chu and Tsari Chu, is glaciated; just as the range to the south, between Char Chu and Nye Chu is glaciated. But the northern range, paradoxically, is moister than the southern range.

In the absence of exact knowledge, it is perhaps futile to speculate as to which is the higher, and I shall confine myself to giving the approximate heights of the passes we actually crossed, or those which are known.

We climbed sharply, through wooded broken country. Amongst naked rocks, in deep shade, mauve flowered *Primula pulchelloides* grew lavishly. I had never held a high opinion of this 'Nivalis' Primula until I saw it so robust and colourful, its sleek washleather leaves green above, snow white beneath. Here also under the bushes a tall almost a rank meadow rue,

Thalictrum diffusiflorum, looked very attractive. The large flowers, trembling on their hair stalks, hover like an arrested shower of amethyst drops over the big green maiden-hair fern leaves.

Approaching the alpine region, common on the turf slopes was *Thermopsis barbata*, a prostrate plant with vetch-like leaves and flowers which would be pretty but for their dull chocolate colour. Here and there slabs of dwarf crimson flowered androsace formed part of the turf crust: and the tall but acidulated *Primula szechuanica* grew beneath scattered rhododendron bushes. The five corolla lobes are bent back till they touch the narrow tube, giving a curiously pinched look to the flowers.

We camped early so as to give the yak – which hate going down into the hot valley – plenty of time to graze. The alpine valley grew wider. Less than a mile above camp it bifurcated; a lot of snow was visible up the north-east branch. I had collected twenty species of plants, so I had work to do in my tent that night.

July 1st was a wet day. We started at 8.30 to cross the Cha La, a pass over the sacred Tsari range, 16,610 feet high. The valley, flanked by wide screes, became stony, but wherever water came to the surface flowers grew, not singly but in drifts. One of the commonest was *Primula sikkimensis*, a dwarf form with few flowers, larger and paler than usual. The pink stars of *P. tibetica* twinkled in bogs, *P. Roylei* crimsoned the pastures. The three species are so different in appearance that perhaps it needs the expert eye to recognize them as all belonging to the same genus. Other alpines were *Phlomis rotata*, its flat cruciform rosettes occurring in thousands; the violet flowered picrorhiza, trollius, fritillaria, *Primula petrocharis*, more widely scattered than most primulas, and *Meconopsis horridula*, the commonest and perhaps the ugliest of the prickly blue poppies. At the very top of the pass, which was a broad saddle, grew *Chionocharis Hookeri*; never before had I seen this cushion plant inside Tibet.

On the pass we met a trader who was on his way to Sanga Chöling: a rather saturnine person who stared disagreeably at me, as though to ask 'What sort of a pilgrim are you!' Looking eastwards, in the direction of Takpa Shiri I could see a lot of snow, but the bulk of the range was hidden in clouds.

After crossing the Cha La, we came down to a wide shallow ice-worn valley where the gathering streams flowed gently. The ground was marshy, and covered with humps and hummocks, on which a species of dwarf rhododendron, like *R. nivale*, grew. The slope above was glazed yellow, violet, and white with a mosaic of anemones.

It proved a long march of ten or twelve miles down the valley to Chösam, a Drokpa village of stone houses without an acre of cultivation. On the way we passed the meeting place of three streams, called Chorten Namu. Up the northern stream is the Kongmo La, which we were to cross in September. The descent had been very gentle, so we had not lost much height even in ten miles; Chösam stands at 14,200 feet and the winters are grim.

The twenty houses which comprise the village are well built, the flat stones carefully fitted together, the wooden roofs solid. Or so it seemed. Inside they were dark and cold, and the roof leaked, as I discovered in the night when it rained.

A bridge, supported on stone piers, spans the torrent, which was still small.

About a month earlier the yak had calved, so there were lots of baby yak around. They are shy little creatures, not yet having developed the insatiable curiosity of their parents. In fact, so sensitive are they that whenever they notice a stranger staring at them, they grunt and run coyly for cover. But they are naughty too, and have to be disciplined. They much prefer mother's milk to grass; but after they are weaned, a prickly bamboo muzzle, shaped something like a gas mask, is fitted over the head. This is enough to make them unpopular with mother, who dislikes being prodded in the udder with a sharp instrument, and kicks the little rebel into the middle of next week.

We were now in the district of Tsari. After a night spent at Chösam we continued down the valley of the Tsari river. The previous day, after crossing the pass, we had changed direction from north to east, thus we were again gradually approaching the Great Himalayan range, which trends in a north-easterly direction. The mountains were hidden in a thick mist, and rain fell steadily. Below Chösam the valley was not only a botanist's paradise, it presented a scene of almost unbelievable beauty, even on a rainy day.

The sheltered side was smothered under rhododendron bushes, most of them in flower. Silver firs appeared, scattered at first, then in groves. The valley narrowed again; and the path scrambled high up the rocky mountain where acres of alpine flowers bloomed between scattered shrubs. Abundant beneath the rhododendron bushes was the silky petaled *Adonis brevistyla*. High up on a bastion I caught sight of the yellow flowered *Primula Barnardoana*; and *P. atrodentata*, in fruit, grew everywhere. Although the path clung dizzily to the cliffs, the valley itself had a gentle tilt, and after a couple of miles we descended again to the stream, and a verdant meadow two or three miles long and half a mile wide, called Senguti. It was marshy, at least in the summer, and it must have once been a lake, which the river had silted up. Towards the lower end of the meadow was a solitary house, called Totsen, standing amidst fenced corn and grazing fields. Now the forceful beauty of the Tsari valley struck me. Across the meadow the mountains were dark with fir, with lighter patches of willow and birch by the river. Tapering tongues of forest licked their way up the sheltered gullies to meet the white tongues of glaciers which crept down out of the mist from invisible snow fields. Somewhere behind that mist lay Takpa Shiri's sacred peak.

The lower half of the meadow itself was a sea of *Primula*

sikkimensis, not the dwarf form, but typical, with dangling clusters of large daffodil yellow bells and long narrow leaves, the blade gradually passing into the indistinct leaf stalk. Mixed with it, but far less numerous, was the grape-juice-purple colour variety of P. *alpicola*. This species has bigger and broader leaves, the oblong blade sharply distinguished from the slender leaf stalk, and puffy with a fine network of raised veins. At first a rarity, *P. alpicola* quickly increased in numbers as we descended the valley, until by the time we reached Chickchar, it was almost as common as *P. sikkimensis*. Meanwhile a third species, having milk-white flowers, *P. Hopeana*, had joined in the pageant, scattered and rare to begin with, presently becoming more abundant, though never so common as *P. alpicola*. Up to within a short distance of Chickchar, the riverside meadows were sunny yellow with huge drifts of *P. sikkimensis*, containing millions of flowers, with a few purple strands of *P. alpicola* and *P. Hopeana* lost like drops of milk in a daffodil sea. Once, where the primulas grew more scattered, I observed all three species forming a single clump, a little triumvirate; but this was exceptional. Generally, small colonies of *P. alpicola*, and separate plants of *P. Hopeana*, were as flotsam in endless rocking seas of *P. sikkimensis*. And for ten miles we waded almost up to our knees through these lush flowery meadows, the damp air heavy with their delicious scent. What a scene in Paradise it was, this silent fairyland of mute bells! Now violet shadowed with irises, now crimson-lit with pedicularis, dappled gold with buttercups, or white on an emerald field with anemones; all familiar friendly flowers though in strange garb. Down the centre of the valley rolled the grey Tsari river, swelling as the glacier streams from the south came tumbling in. And down the valley also, enclosing the Tsari river, danced the shining band of primulas. Between silver fir forest and golden meadow came a border of shrubs and smaller trees, as rhododendron, honeysuckle, barbery, cotoneaster, rowan, cherry and spiraea; and between fir forest and snow field another border of dwarf alpine flowers. The whole valley was a procession of glorious beauty.

Then near Chickchar purple flowered *Primula alpicola* increased in numbers till it formed drifts by itself, great eddies of wine in the daffodil yellow seas. So far as this species is concerned, purple is the dominant colour form in Tsari, nor did I see a single specimen of the violet form, called *P. alpicola* var. *violacea*, although this name is intended to cover the purple. But one is blue, and the other red. The original *P. alpicola* is a *yellow* flowered species, rather paler than *P. sikkimensis*; and that also is absent from Tsari.

One would expect these 'sikkimensis' primulas to cross freely. Perhaps they do; but if so, few of the offspring survive. Amongst the millions of flowers I could rarely distinguish an unmistakable cross. Yet crosses and variations do sometimes occur, and it will be a task for future plant explorers to wander through these alpine valleys and select the finest forms for propagation. There was a form of *P. Hopeana* with flowers inclining to red, which may be a cross with purple *P. alpicola*; but this was very rare. Equally rare was a cross between *P. sikkimensis* and *P. alpicola*, which gave, not beautiful pastel shades but dull or washy colours. A further complication was added by the occasional occurrence of a taller, more robust *P. sikkimensis* with flowers of a deeper yellow. Had it been connected by easy stages with the common form, I should hardly have remarked on it; but it wasn't.

It was a vile day for collecting plants, but not for enjoying flowers. In the bed of a gently flowing stream I found *Primula involucrata yargongensis*, with beautiful heads of lilac-purple flowers. It grows best in shallow alpine stream beds, with a sandy bottom, often wedging itself between flat stones. This charming plant, often called *P. Wardii*, does wonderfully well in Scotland and Ireland; it has a delicious scent, and varies from lilac to purple shades with an occasional pure white. Late in the afternoon we crossed to the right bank of the Tsari river, and climbing over a forested derelict moraine, where myriads of primulas swayed in the breeze, descended to a wide-mouthed bay. Here we turned away from the river, south towards the high peaks; but I still could see no sign of a village. We had marched fifteen miles, and had taken a good many hours to do it; I was dead beat.

This valley, too, was marshy and hummocked with hassocks of dwarf rhododendron, as heather grows in a peat bog. *R. fragariflorum* and *R. paludosum* were the two species, both in flower. At the sides, on drier ground, primulas and irises were massed: above them were shrubs, especially the same two bush rhododendrons that I had seen all the way down the valley from Chösam. Both at Chösam and at Chickchar a bush with large balls of pinkish purple flowers made a good show. *R. Wardii*, sulphur yellow with a crimson flash at the base of the corolla, although scarce at Chösam was now a grand sight, being in full bloom; lower down the valley it was over. On flowering plants of *R. Wardii* the leaf buds were not even breaking in the first week of July; but bushes which were not flowering this year were already fledged with new leaves of verdigris green. In other words, flower buds retard leaf buds (as I have often observed in rhododendron). The reason seems to be that the opening flower draws heavily on the reserve of certain growth promoting substances (hormones) which are present in minute traces; and until a fresh supply is available, the leaf buds remain closed. What determines whether the flower bud shall precede the leaf bud, or vice versa, is bound up with the rhythm of the plant's life. In rhododendron and in many deciduous shrubs and trees, such as forsythia and prunus species, it is the flower bud which opens first. In horse chestnut, some species of magnolia and prunus, and many others, the leaf buds open first. Thus the growing points of plants – leaf bud, flower bud, and probably root-tip – profoundly affect one another, and their activities are synchronized, urged on, or restrained by chemical substances.

In the high valleys of Tsari, a cold wet region, rhododendrons flower later than the same species elsewhere. Growth is delayed by the cold, resulting from the great accumulation of snow in the mountains.

Continuing up the valley, we turned a corner, and half a mile off, Chickchar came into view. Near the village I saw colonies of the wonderful sky blue *Meconopsis betonicifolia*, though it is not common hereabouts. But *M. paniculata* is. The gracious spire of chrome yellow flowers rises like Aphrodite from a sea of meadow. Scattered amongst scrub all down the valley was *M. simplicifolia*; yet I cannot recall seeing a single really blue flower; all were stained a vicious purple. Shortly before we entered the Chickchar valley, however, I had found a poppy which interested me much more than any of the others. It was a small plant, with frilled lace white petals and a broad circle of golden yellow stamens round the style in the centre; nothing more. But its name was *Meconopsis argemonantha*, and it was almost unknown. How then did it come to have a name? It was named from a fragment collected and put in a pocket book by F. M. Bailey. As far as the material allowed, it was described by Sir David Prain many years ago; even its home was uncertain – except that it came from Tibet. Here it was, growing happily on rocky banks, often buried amongst bushes and grass; but it is a rare plant – there was not much of it. Sad thought – it will probably prove just as fugitive in cultivation as *M. lancifolia*. It has the stamp of a weak constitution on it.

The few inhabitants of Chickchar are accustomed to visitors from all parts of Tibet, but we roused a note of interrogation; evidently I was outside their normal experience. We shared part of a house with some traders who had lately arrived from Kongbo, and I was given a large room upstairs to myself. A pretty girl came in and lit a fire in an iron bowl, two feet in diameter, but the pungent smoke which had no obvious means of escape, made my eyes stream. As the smoke refused to leave, I had to, for a time.

Having changed my wet clothes, I was soon comfortably installed drinking hot tea, and taking care of the many treasures I had collected.

The village stands at about 12,700 feet, but even in July it was not warm, the night temperature dropping to under 50° while the rain continued, and to 42° F. when clearer weather came.

Chickchar has more monasteries than houses, but the monasteries are small, and the houses big. It lives by and for the pilgrim traffic; the sacred spots of Tibet are as great a draw to the people as are the beauty spots of more commercialized lands. Although in ordinary years pilgrims are comparatively few, more than fifty passed through during the three days I spent here.

It takes about twelve days to go right round Takpa Shiri. Six mountains of 15,000 feet, or more, have to be crossed, so pilgrimage is a summer sport. Yet though there is a rest house at every stage the catering arrangements hardly suggest a business government. I could buy neither eggs nor chickens at Chickchar, neither meat nor vegetables; they don't exist. But this was an off-season. Every twelfth year there is a special pilgrimage, when people from all over Tibet converge on Tsari. Chickchar then is like Stratford-on-Avon during a Shakespeare Festival. There had been an All-Buddhist Convention four years ago, in 1931; the next was not due till 1943. Meanwhile prices were slashed – and supplies too.

The complete lack of meat ties up with the sanctity of the holy mountain, and a strong disposition to love and let live. Every animal, every bird, every flea, louse, bug and cockroach on the circuit is sacred, and immune from man's interference, whether on scientific or hygienic grounds, or even as a mere matter of foolish prejudice. So life flourishes. You must not kill anything; but there is no law against taking live creatures away with you. Several fleas which had become attached to me, left Chickchar under my protection.

Birds are ridiculously tame round Chickchar. Every morning

a cock Harman's pheasant strutted majestically out of the woods and in full view of the village uttered his harsh aggressive challenge to the world. This magnificent bird, better known as Elwes' horned pheasant (*Crossoptilon harmani*), weighs as much as five pounds. The ground colour is slate-grey. The tail is short, spreading and dark; but the scarlet legs, the eye set in a great scarlet sun, a gold chain round the neck, and other minor accessories touch it up with dramatic emphasis, as lipstick touches up a woman's face. These are the decorative effects which strike one at a glance.

I became almost familiar with the crossoptilon during my short residence here. On July 4th I had the unusual experience, while on a botanical ramble, of running into a whole family of them. There were three full-grown birds and half a dozen chicks. As the parents had their children with them, children hatched a few weeks previously and therefore unsophisticated, they were naturally a little flustered. On the other hand, concern for their offspring more than counterbalanced fear of the human, even when the human was trespassing at some distance from the pilgrims' route. The mother bird, which to my untrained eye differs little from the male, ran about rather hot and bothered, trying to drive the chicks in one direction. But the chicks lost their heads and described circles, which made it difficult. The operation suggested poodles herding rabbits; there was a certain lack of co-operation. I easily caught a chick by hand; it squeaked feebly, and proved an irresistible decoy. One parent kept making advances to me, coming within five feet, then running up hill, and returning to the charge. Throughout these manœuvres the whole family were calling on the Harman wavelength. The mother had two distinct calls, the harsh crossoptilon cry, and a shriller maternal cry, plaintive like that of the chicks. Sometimes I could scarcely distinguish between the chick in my hand, keeping the family posted as to developments, and the answering cry of anguish from the mother a few feet away; it might have been Charlie Macarthy.

The parents' behaviour was exemplary. There was no panic. Of course, they felt they were sacred and safe; but there is always the chance of disillusion.

That same day I heard the unmistakable notes of the Tibetan grosbeak, a beautiful gamboge breasted bird, the size of a hawfinch, which I had come to know well when Lord Cranbrook and I were exploring North Burma in 1931.

To the pastures near the village came flocks of big grey rock pigeons. These were almost as tame as the pigeons outside the Royal Exchange, London.

The Tibetan stag, *Cervus affinis*, lives in Tsari. I saw no signs of it.

However, Tsari is a fine national park with sheep (*Ovis nahura*), musk deer, wolves, foxes and other animals. It is one of the advantages of a Buddhist country that it starts as a game reserve. Christian industrial countries, on the other hand, think of sanctuaries too late, although we may all end in the jungle. In Tibet, the game reserve is even extended to include domestic dogs, which being insufficiently fed, are encouraged to earn their own living, preferably at the expense of strangers. A large shaggy animal walked into my room one evening just as I was going to bed, without so much as a bark of warning, sniffed around, looked at me, sized up the situation, and marched out, very dignified. He called again about 2 a.m., and went off with a butter tin which he licked bright. Luckily butter and milk were plentiful.

There are only three or four houses in Chickchar, all of them two storied, the upper floor, and of course the roof, being of timber. I was surprised to see a trellis of bamboo over the window frame, and numerous wooden utensils and woven bamboo baskets emphasized the fact that we were again in a forest climate. It is curious that the Tsari valley should be so moist. Located between the same meridians as the Loro Chu below Trön, and separated from it by a range of snow peaks, it ought to be drier.

The Tsari valley owes its shape to glacier action, while the Loro valley below Chayul Dzong appears to be entirely water worn. Thus it is tempting to argue that the glaciers ploughed a wide furrow through the main Himalayan range here, and that the winds took advantage of this to blow up through the Tsari valley, rather than through the narrower Loro valley, bringing with them the moist air of Assam. But this theory is untenable. The same moist winds must have been blowing when the glaciers existed, to nourish them and keep them moving forwards. Exactly why Tsari should be wetter than Chayul and the Loro Chu is not clear; but Chayul derives some of its dryness from nestling close under the shadow of the greatest rain screen in the world.

The rain continued on and off till July 4th, but July 5th was brilliant fine and I walked down the valley to the river and enjoyed a magnificent view, south to the snow peaks and glaciers which overhang Chickchar, and eastwards down the valley of the Tsari river. Almost due east was a cluster of high rocky peaks, and beyond that a snow-covered peak. Yet these could have been no more than footstools as it were at the throne of the gods. Still farther round, about east by south, was another snow peak from which flowed a glacier. All these peaks were probably on the main Himalayan range, and twenty or twenty-five miles distant. However, looking down the valley, I did not get the impression of a river carving its way through a great mountain range.

Almost due south of Chickchar and within a mile or two of the village are two rock pyramids with several small glaciers. These constitute first check to the pilgrim's progress; he crosses the range by the Drölmo La, at the east end, though the pass is not visible from Chickchar. The view of these peaks, with the flowery meadow and emerald pasture in the foreground, running out into thin forests, the forests passing into scrub and alp, and the alps into bare rock and ice, was enchanting.

From the foot of these peaks to the Tsari river, a distance of about two miles, is the most luscious grazing imaginable. Although interrupted by rhododendron bogs, and lagoons of primulas laced with irises (*I. chrysographes*), many ponies were grazing here; but the yak had departed for higher altitudes.

In order that I might see something of the wonderful scenery I decided to remain at Chickchar until the weather improved. I also resisted the temptation to join a happy band of pilgrims who had just arrived, for that meant abandoning the march to the Tsangpo. I felt certain that success lay in going on; once turn back, and I might have to stay back. Two of the pilgrims looked tough; a third was an oldish white-haired man, who could do nobody any harm; and a fourth was a jovial little Puck, with a quick smile which spoke louder than words.

In the house where I stayed lived a Lama, who visited me from time to time. He was a tall aristocratic-looking fellow, over seventy years of age, according to his reckoning, although his beard was quite black. He had visited India, spoke a little Hindustani, and knew something of the Hindu religion, which he found attractive. He even claimed to be a Saddhu, though on no grounds that I could ascertain. This Lama mentioned a sacred lake in the mountains to the east. Many legends are told of it, and pilgrims visit it. From the description it sounded something which the sightseer simply could not afford to miss; besides there might be some interesting plants there, so possibly the botanist could not afford to miss it either. I decided to visit it before resuming my journey to the Tsangpo.

CHAPTER IX

THE SACRED LAKE

JULY 6th was fine and I set out down the valley of Tsari with a light heart. Several pilgrims were also visiting the lake, so we did not lack for company. A heavy dew had refreshed the meadows, after yesterday's sunshine, and the air was spiced with the rich scent of flowers and aromatic leaves.

The Chickchar stream drops abruptly to the Tsari river, the lateral valley overhanging the main valley, a familiar glacial effect. No sooner had we reached the river than we crossed to the left bank by a wooden bridge. Already we were in mixed forest, with patches of open meadow, all ablaze with primulas. Where the path climbed over a cliff, I found another patch of *Meconopsis argemonantha*, this at a height of about 11,000 feet. It is one of the daintiest alpine plants, and its absence from our gardens leaves a real gap.

The Tsari valley below Chickchar is narrow, steep and thickly forested, enclosed by high mountains. After two miles we reached a large stream from the north; at the confluence stood a single house called Podzo Sümdo, with some cultivation. From this point the river, swollen by rain and melting ice, plunges over huge rocks in headlong rapids. The noise is terrific. It is as though the bottom had suddenly fallen out of the valley and the river were being sucked down into the bowels of the earth.

This physical change is accompanied by a change of vegetation. Hitherto rhododendrons, although plentiful, had been of few species. Suddenly they became much more varied, and crowded with gnarled and stunted trees form an impenetrable barrier. None of them was in flower. I recognized *R. neriiflorum*, *R. grande*, *R. triflorum*, *R. niphargum* and other species, by their appearance, but two were new to me. Then in an open meadow, on a large boulder I found a rhododendron in bloom. It had yellowish butterfly shaped flowers, spotted green, and curiously shaggy pedicels; the leaves are deciduous like an azalea. It was like a more heavily bearded *R. trichocladum*.

The path was so rough and steep now that it would be difficult even for yak. We dropped from rock to rock, waded through mud holes up to our knees. Presently we crossed over to the right bank because of an impassable cliff, returned to the left bank lower down, and stayed there. Now we were in cool temperate forest, mostly conifers above, with broad-leafed trees by the river. The conifers were: silver fir, hemlock, and juniper, with an occasional larch. Broad-leafed trees included maples, oaks, birch, ilex, prunus, *Pieris formosa*, with flowering shrubs, such as deutzia, euonymus, rhododendron, viburnum, rosa, and philadelphus (the syringa of our gardens). This forest was nothing so varied as at like altitudes on the southern slopes of the Assam Himalaya – at Senge Dzong, for example. Below Migyitun it rapidly grows richer in species, as the valley grows warmer and wetter. There was at least one epiphytic rhododendron here – odious little yellow-flowered *R. micromeres*.

We took seven hours to reach Migyitun (twelve miles), where the gorge widened out again, and there were barley fields. We had descended 3000 feet and the climate was warm enough for tobacco, Job's tears, potatoes and possibly maize. Fallow fields were crowded with aster and euphorbia. Sub-tropical forest carnivores such as Temminck's golden cat (*Profelis temmincki*) and a leopard cat (*Prionailurus benghalensis trevelyani*) are found here. Skins of both these were brought to me.

Fifteen coolies and pilgrims had accompanied us from Chickchar and when I saw the guest house at Migyitun, I wondered where they would all park themselves. However, these folk seem to have the power to condense, like mist.

The guest house comprised a square courtyard surrounded by low kennel-like buildings, with rooms opening off three sides.

The best rooms were of mud, and the walls at some period had been plastered, and even painted. A seedy-looking monk and a comely but undersized and sluttish girl were in charge. This curiously monastic inn, and half a dozen scattered timber huts, was all there was of Migyitun, the last Tibetan village in the Tsari valley.

Now I wanted to continue down the river as many days' journey as would be required to pass right through the Himalayas. But who could say we were not already on the other side? Or more likely, in the middle of them. Between Chickchar and Migyitun the Tsari river had certainly passed through some bulky object. Yet, the distance was too short for it to be the width even of the core of the Himalayas; more likely it was one of the lesser ranges. If I could follow the Tsari river southwards as far as its confluence with the Loro Chu, I must surely be well over on the south side of the great range.

But the local inhabitants shook their heads. There was no path. The Lopas were unfriendly — this was true. We were approaching a sub-tropical region in the height of the rainy season, and it was certain that we should encounter leeches, if nothing worse. The inhabitants of Migyitun retain a *cordon sanitaire* between themselves and their surly neighbours, the Lopas; and the first Lopa villages were six days' journey away. Anyhow, what clearly emerged from the discussion was, that the coolies did not want to go.

I therefore abandoned the idea with no great reluctance, and again turned my attention to the sacred lake. It was said to be a long day's march into the mountains; and some of the pilgrims volunteered to carry our kit.

At Migyitun there is cultivation on both banks of the river, which is spanned by a timber bridge. It was fascinating to stand on this bridge and watch the muddy water sweeping beneath with irresistible force. After a little time, one's head began to spin and the bridge itself seemed to be moving in a universal deluge. The air vibrated with the clatter of rocks, and the grey water snatched hungrily at the banks and trees as it rushed by. The gradient here is far less than it is in the gorge we had just descended; but it is quite steep enough to drive the river headlong forward. I could see only a short way down the valley because the river turns a corner to flow southwards.

Just below the inn, a turbulent glacier torrent comes roaring in from the north-east, and several miles farther down stream another glacier torrent comes in. Both these torrents rise amongst the snow peaks which guard the sacred lake, the second of them having its source in the lake itself. By crossing three passes, and the heads of three minor valleys, one reaches the lake, without ever touching the valley into which it discharges.

July 7th was fine and sunny, although the high peaks were clouded. Crossing the big glacier torrent which flows through the village, we turned up stream, and entered the forest. Soon we reached the first clearings. This lower forest (9000-11,000 feet) consisted mostly of broad-leafed trees amongst which *Quercus Ilex* and maples were conspicuous. In another hour we had reached the level of silver fir and tree rhododendron, *R. grande*. On the cliff bush rhododendrons formed dense thickets where the gorgeous *R. cerasinum* still dangled a few loose clusters of crimson-cerise flowers. Few rhododendrons are so easily recognized in fruit as is *R. cerasinum*. It is unique. The flowers are completely pendent, the fruits as usual stand erect. This, however, is not achieved by the straightening up of the long thin pedicel, which remains pendent, but by its extreme tip turning upwards through 180°, so that the ripe capsule is parallel to it, its apex level with the point from which the pedicel springs.

Climbing straight up a slippery grass face, we reached the first pass, called Na La,[1] which is just a notch in the spur. *Adonis brevistyla* was common under the bushes, and for the

[1] Na La=Forest Pass. The second pass is called Pang La=Turf Pass, and the third Ja La=Rock Pass, describing the gradual change of vegetation as one climbs from forest to alp — a succession not lost upon the Tibetan mind.

third time, I saw *Meconopsis arnemonantha.* Masses of forget-me-not (*Myosotis sylvatica*) bordered the track at the top.

From the Na La a steep short descent led to a good-sized valley, and although it was only noon, we stopped at an empty herds' hut for a quick lunch. The tall yellow spires of *Meconopsis paniculata* surrounded the hut. Across the valley rose a brilliant emerald green slope and I learnt to my dismay that when we reached the top of that we should be half way to Tsogar. The slope was moist with boggy hollows, and spangled with/millions of flowers of all colours. There were solid golden carpets of *Caltha palustris*, drifts of white or violet anemone, crimson, yellow and pink pedicularis, *Nomocharis nana* and crowded colonies of sulphur yellow *Primula alpicola*. More exciting was a primula I had never seen before. Although it was of the 'Sikkimensis' type, it looked so different from *P. sikkimensis* I felt sure it must be a new species. It formed tight clumps from each of which arose six or eight short stems, bearing heads of dangling milk-white blooms faintly flushed with mauve; the deeply-cut leaves gave it an original look. Much shorter than ordinary *P. sikkimensis*, the scapes more condensed, with flowers of a different colour and leaves of a different form, I was deceived into thinking it a new species; it proved to be only a new variety, *P. sikkimensis*, var. *subpinnatifida.*

As we worked round the shoulder of the spur, we passed from moist pasture to drier ground where tuffets of cassiope and the dainty dwarf pink flowered *Rhododendron pumilum* overlapped from the rocks above. Then came thickets of crimson *R. anthopogon*, and presently a prize, no less than a delightful new primula. To the plant explorer in Tibet to find a new primula is an event. This plant *P. flabellifera* grew moss-like on the rocks, and had tiny but exquisitely shaped violet flowers, borne singly on thread-like stems. They shone like stars at dusk. Some day we shall solve the problem of how to grow the 'Amethystina' primulas, as they are called—plants like *P. Kingii*, and *P. Wattii*, and have little trays of living jewels sparkling on our tables. At present, although several of them have actually been brought, with pain and anxiety, to the point of flowering – once, they are amongst the rarest of the rare – museum pieces, so to speak; nor can such sporadic successes give any idea of these alpine jewels scattered carelessly over square miles of rock and turf in their native land.

The steep path now skirted the cliffs to a high spot, the Pang La, and slanted down the far side of the spur, still hugging the cliffs, to a wide funnel-shaped valley. We had not to descend very far to reach the stream; but it was annoying to have to go down at all. We had climbed quite 5000 feet, for the loss of 1000 feet, and now found ourselves at the foot of a formidable moraine. Just ahead of us, and to one side, a glacier tumbled down from a sugar-loaf peak over 18,000 feet high. The valley was jammed with rocks, gravel, sand, all the breakages of a mountain ground by ice. There were few plants, because if they grew on top, their roots could not reach the soil, and if they grew below their stems could not reach the daylight. A few plants of *P. involucrata* bordered the stream. I would have been content to halt here for the night, but the coolies were ahead, clambering up towards the third pass; we had reckoned on reaching Tsogar before nightfall.

After a rough-and-tumble with the moraine, we passed the glacier foot and got on to rock, then on to hard snow. Alpine plants shrank under cover, and there were cushion and mat plants, including the crisp crimson flowered *P. dryadifolia* with ace-of-spades shaped leaves silver-white beneath, saxifrage, woolly-white saussurea, and *Eriophyton Wallichianum*, whose beautiful pinkish flowers are almost hidden beneath crowded cowl-shaped dead-nettle leaves. Finally, after an exhausting climb which brought us almost to the limit of flowering plants, we reached the third and last pass, called Ja La, over 17,000 feet high. Unlike the two minor passes we had just crossed, the Ja La is away up amongst the main water partings, and a world of snow peaks and glaciers would have leapt into view, only to my disappointment I looked down only into a cauldron of yeasty cloud.

It was now about five o'clock and daylight was waning. Nevertheless, I set up my camera and waited hopefully behind a rock, sheltered from the cold wind. The Ja La resembles the Drichung La; a gap in a row of rotten teeth, with a steep fall to the valleys on either side.

After waiting twenty minutes in vain for a view of the snow peaks, I followed the coolies down the steep slope. Presently rock gave way to gravel, gravel to turf, and turf to scrub. For the most exalted alpines, revelling in the moist cool summer, it was the height of the short season. On this slope they were far more abundant than on the sheltered slope, where the snow had not yet melted. Here grew a dwarf form of *Primula alpicola*, with pale coloured flowers, sometimes white, sometimes yellow; dwarf yellow *P. sikkimensis*; the tiny mauve *P. glabra*, like a pin-cushion, which I had seen on every pass over 12,000 feet which we had crossed; purple-flowered *Nomocharis nana; Meconopsis simplicifolia* – a really Cambridge blue flowered form of this species at last; lloydia; and fritillaria. The first dwarf rhododendron to appear was *R. fragariflorum.* Lower down masses of the wine-red *Primula Roylei* were in flower.

Just as I reached a grassy alp surrounded by seas of rhododendron in strident bloom, the veil of the cloud was rent, and in a flash there was revealed, a thousand feet below, one of the most beautiful and inspiring sights imaginable. More and more bright grew the scene, like a swift flame, colour and form harmoniously blended. Not that it was tame in peaceful decay, by any means; it was grand without being savage. I was looking straight down on to Tsogar, sacred turquoise lake. The fretted cliffs ran rivers of gleaming ice; the largest glacier reached the edge of the water. On its near side the lake was girdled by an emerald-green arc of rich pasture, dark spotted with yak. There was a smaller lake in front of the main lake, and the stream flowed from one to the other and so away down a valley to the south, to join the Tsari river. In the foreground billows of rose-purple rhododendron blossom tossed in the breeze.

The sun, though well down, fired a parting shaft of light through a gap in the western range, illuminating the scene more brightly. Then the clouds closed in again and all was blotted out. But I was grateful for that one glimpse.

This may sound a strange confession. There is nothing very remarkable, still less mysterious, about Tsogar. It is just an ordinary glacier lake, half silted up; you may see plenty such in Switzerland. Yet this far corner of Asia exercised a fascination over me; I felt spell-bound. Well I knew that no white man had ever set eyes on the sacred lake before. This had something to do with my mood; but not very much. Few of us are completely indifferent to claiming a record; and to be the first white man to do this or that is a form of record breaking. But my business was to find new plants, particularly new garden plants, no matter whether a hundred people had been through the country before me or nobody had; and although I am not a 'superior person', I did not much care about the priority claim. The truth is, such claims are so often without foundation that it would be unwise to make them, were it not that publishers expect it! I get more satisfaction from discovering and introducing a new plant, which thousands can enjoy, than from discovering a new mountain which I can only describe.

The day was drawing swiftly to its end, and I was yet some distance away from our haven for the night. But flowers still detained me. Magnificent plants of *Primula tsariensis*, one of the big cabbage-leafed 'Petiolares' type, had colonized the rich black soil beneath the rhododendron bushes. The thick stems, nestling in a green crater of fat leaves, bear large handsome heads of violet flowers with conspicuous yellow eye.

To get down to the lake we had to descend a sort of rock chute, beneath a dripping cliff. Many beautiful plants nodded like plumes from crevices above our heads, and streamed water at the same time; some of the bunches of *Paraquilegia grandiflora* must have been a quarter of a century old. *Primula Cawdoriana*, another cliff dweller, sticks out two or three inch-long flowers like fringed violet ballet skirts blowing on a doll's clothes line.

This rock chute was really remarkable. In places it was no more than a ledge, so narrow that I had to flatten myself against the cliff beneath cascades of water, in order to get along. Perhaps it is the result of a fault, or perhaps it is merely a softer band in the up-ended slate rock on which the water has acted. When I reached the bottom, I found myself amongst dense thickets of rhododendron, interrupted by patches of boggy meadow. A short walk brought me to a stone house, inhabited by a herd and his wife. Scrambling up a ladder — the ground floor as usual was a stable — I found a corner of the dark room curtained off, my camp bed and table set up, and tea laid. I was thankful for it; it was half-past six, and we had had a long day.

That night my flea bag lived up to its name. I was assaulted by several dozen starving fleas, and sleep was out of the question. The blankets quivered to their dancing and leaping; it was dawn before I snatched an uneasy two hours' sleep. Consequently, I did not feel like starting back immediately. My body resembled a certain rhododendron, white with pink spots. In fact I contemplated spending the day by the lake; but the thought of spending another night in that chamber of horrors stirred me to reluctant activity. Nevertheless I was relieved when the pilgrims asked me to wait till they had circled the holy lake. We agreed to start at noon, and to halt on the other side of the Ja La. Secretly I had rather dreaded the climb up from the lake. But like many unpleasant things, when squarely faced it did not live up to my forebodings.

After breakfast I went for a walk, exploring the lake shore and part of a moraine, where I photographed a colony of *Bolocephalus saussuroides*, a remarkable saussurea-like plant with woolly white globe heads of flowers. Thick clouds were rolling slowly up from the Tsari valley. I do not know the exact altitude of Tsogar, but I should guess it to be over 14,000 feet. The highest peak is called Kang Pemu. One glacier comes right down to the lake. Every hour or so a sérac broke off high up on the mountain and fell with a loud crash, spattering clouds of snow and ice. The glaciers are retreating and the lake is silting up; in the basin itself there is more marsh than water. Although the water had looked blue when seen from above it is not really blue at all, for the glacier streams which pour into it are milky and the fine glacier mud has no time to settle before the water is flowing out down the valley. The pastures are exceedingly rich, but I saw very few cattle here. On the meadow side of the lake is a solitary house or cell of prayer, where a Lama sometimes prays in solitude.

Although it is impossible on the evidence to be certain, I am of opinion that this cluster of peaks really is a part of the Great Himalayan range, that it extends north-eastwards, and that we had, in the course of our ascent from Migyitun been scrambling along the *southern* face of the Himalayas. This opinion was strengthened when next day, from the Pang La, I had a fine view westwards up the Tsari valley in the direction of Chickchar. I could see the whole river on its headlong descent of 3000 feet, and the high peaks on either side, giving the impression of a river breaking through a mountain range; although as I have said before, this gorge is too short to measure the whole thickness of the Himalayas. The next traveller to Tsogar could do useful work by crossing the range somewhere — (I noticed a likely, although unused pass) — and observing whether the streams on the other side flow directly to the Tsangpo, as they appear to do.[1]

The main valley is glaciated almost down to Migyitun, perhaps below, and glaciers reached it from both sides. The Tsari

[1] In 1936 Captain G. Sherriff discovered a pass over the snow range, the Yu La above Migyitun, whence it is possible to reach the source of the Molo Chu which flows directly to the Tsangpo at Lilung.

valley appears to be a cracked anticline, the strata dipping away from the river on the left bank above Migyitun.

It was drizzling when we left Flea Inn, as I called the house. Nor did it take us long to reach the Ja La, whence we descended to the empty herds' hut on the other side. The coolies volunteered to go on, but I wanted a good night's sleep right here, and said so. There was a chance that the next morning might be fine, then I could return to the pass for another bird's-eye view of lake and peaks.

Mindful of my late experience, I pitched my tent and slept in that.

It rained in the night, but the morning broke fine. In my tent the temperature dropped to 41° F. However, there never was any chance of a view, and we marched straight back to Migyitun in three hours.

No sooner had I paid off the coolies, than they settled down to an afternoon's gambling. Their outfit consisted of some dice, a heap of spillikins, and a collection of brass coins, Chinese, Tibetan and Bhutanese, such as you might find in a Whitechapel pawnshop. Every time a player shook the dice, he banged them hard down on the floor – they squatted cross-legged in a ring on the floor – with a loud cry. This was not an oath, or a prayer, but a triumphant challenge to the opposition uttered almost as a threat. Beat that if you dare! it seemed to imply. The party was still going strong, with cries and laughter, when I went to bed, the innkeeper having joined in.

I spent the rest of the afternoon and most of the following day bringing my plant catalogue up to date. As a result of the trip to Tsogar I had added about forty species and a hundred and fifty specimens of alpine plants to my collection. But any botanist who spent a week by the lake might easily add another fifty or sixty species, especially if he was there a month earlier or later.

Tsari is wet and cool, and of course freezing in winter, though little if any snow falls at Migyitun. It is much wetter than

Chayul or Charme to the south, or even than the Tsangpo valley to the north in about the same longitude; the type of forest proves it; the rhododendrons prove it; the primula meadows prove it; and finally plants such as *Rheum nobile*, *Meconopsis simplicifolia*, and *M. paniculata*, *Primula Cawdoriana*, *Gentiana stylophora*, *Adonis brevistyla*, and *Paraquilegia grandiflora*, prove it. But it is not so wet as Pome, or the great gorge of the Tsangpo, or the southern face of the eastern Himalayas; nor was there anything remarkable about the weather we experienced.

On July 11th we resumed our march to the Tsangpo, retracing our steps up the valley as far as Podzo Sümdo.

CHAPTER X

HIDDEN PASS

As my original intention was to return to Chickchar from Migyitun I had left a box of specimens there. I sent Pemba for this on the 10th, while we rested at Migyitun, and he met us at Pozdo Sümdo on the 11th. He reported a fresh influx of pilgrims at Chickchar.

The sky was drizzly with a lot of cloud coming up from the hot valley of the Subansiri. On the way up through the fir forest I collected several ground orchids in flower – *Orchis Chusua*, *Oreorchis foliosa*, and *O. micrantha*, *Didymocarpus aromatica* growing on the cliff, *Berberis Hookeri* with shining silver-plated leaves, *Litsaea*. We halted for lunch at the solitary house of Podzo Sümdo, then turned north up the valley, buried in forests of silver fir and rhododendron. The path was steep and the forest soon began to thin out. After two hours' marching, meadows invaded the dwindling trees, the valley broadened, the stream slackened, and alluvial fans from the cliffs caused some obstruction. There were drifts of primulas, but the commonest was still the purple form of *P. alpicola*, as at Chickchar, with *P. sikkimensis* second. I saw small colonies of *Notholirion campanulatum* and *Meconopsis betonicifolia*, and some dark purple, almost crimson forms of *Primula involucrata* by the torrent. We pitched our tents in lush meadow and it was certainly one of the less satisfactory camping grounds; the evening was wet and we were plagued by sand flies.

It rained all night. The temperature in my tent dropped to 43° F., which was not surprising, because when we woke up all the surrounding mountains were covered with fresh snow. However the rain ceased before we started.

In half an hour we reached the junction of two valleys, which met in a Y. The one from the north-east looked the more interesting, as there appeared to be a glacier or snow bed at its head; but it was up the north-western branch we turned; or rather we climbed the steep face between massive thickets of rhododendron and gradually eased off into the north-west. One of the rhododendrons was a typical 'Lacteum' similar to the one at Chickchar, another was *R. Wardii*, a third, and that a new one, had leaves thickly felted below with cinnamon coloured wool. But none of them were in bloom. In another hour we reached a Drokpa tent and stopped to drink milk.

Traversing round the shoulder of the ridge, still high above the stream, we crossed one or two screes, and finished with a steep climb over the rocks, to a jagged crest line and the Bimbi La, 15,700 feet. Here we found patches of snow. I was feeling thoroughly chilled, but had collected a few plants in the course of the climb. Again the 'Sikkimensis' primulas offered a puzzle to the botanist. *P. alpicola* (purple) and *P. sikkimensis* itself were, as I have said, common in the meadows 3000 feet below. But both stopped at the tree line, and were replaced at the Bimbi La by:

(i) a dwarf *P. sikkimensis* regarded by that great authority, Sir William Wright Smith, as a good species, or sub-species, *P. pudibunda*;

(ii) an equally dwarf plant with narrow leaves and purplish flowers, *P. prionotes*.

To complicate matters further there was also a dwarf white flowered species, which must either be a colour variety of *P. pudibunda*, or a dwarf form of *P. Hopeana*! The hybridist could certainly have fun amongst the primulas in Tibet!

Shortly after we reached the alpine region, I saw a few more plants of the white-flowered *Meconopsis argemonantha*; *M. simplicifolia* also grew here, but it was in unripe fruit. The commonest species was *M. horridula*, which on the north side of the pass had flowers of a deep glossy violet. This is the most widely spread and variable of all species in Tibet. The best forms are quite good, but we generally seem to have the worst forms in English gardens – or else they go bad on us. It is a high altitude plant; and high altitude plants from Tibet either refuse to grow at all, or grow reluctantly at sea-level. But amongst its numerous local races, it should be possible to discover a more adaptable variety for cultivation. On the pass itself, which was a narrow passage between the cliffs, cushion plants grew amongst the clumsily piled rocks; androsace, saxifrage, and spongy masses of pink-flowered *Dispensia himalayana* and crimson *Primula dryadifolia*. On the cliffs *P. Caveana* cowered in crevices, looking as neat and composed as though it were growing in an English garden. It has mauve flowers and resembles *P. consocia*.

I lingered on the pass only long enough to dig up some primulas. The trail led quickly to the rim of a great amphitheatre, bounded by ice-scored rocks, hollowed here and there into small rock basins filled with water. The rocks, arranged in echelon, were scarped on their down sides and it was necessary to pick one's way between them. Here the robust violet-flowered *Primula tsariensis* was quite abundant, and in better shape than at Tsogar. Dwarf rhododendrons appeared as soon as we got amongst the big rock stuff, *R. fragariflorum* and *R. nivale*, both old friends with a considerable range, and the white-flowered *R. temoense* which I had not hitherto met with on this journey. The under leaf surface of the last named is covered with a spongy coat of dark chocolate scales. Hitherto it was the rose-red *R. anthopogon*, an allied species, I had seen associated with *R. fragariflorum* and *R. nivale*.

When we got down to where water was flowing freely, about 14,000 feet, we halted in the sunshine for lunch. A yellow-flowered Cremanthodium grew on the wet sand by the stream, with other moisture-loving alpines; on dry turf slopes the most conspicuous plant was a dwarf form of *Androsace strigillosa*.

We were descending a short and comparatively wide alpine valley, towards a much deeper gorge across which I could see snow peaks. Just as we reached the outposts of the forest –

scattered and heavily scarred junipers and fir trees – we met a small party of traders on their way to Tsari. There were two men, and a woman with a baby on her back. It must be a wonderful experience to be carried about at over 15,000 feet before one has cut one's milk teeth. The traders said they had left the village early in the morning, so we had no hope of getting there that night.

When we reached the big valley, in which a muddy river, the Kyimdong Chu, flowed from the west, we camped. There seemed to be snow peaks all round us, but the visibility was not good. I noticed glaciers to north and east, flowing from lofty ranges which culminated in high hidden peaks. These were all south of the Tsangpo, now only about twenty miles distant.

The Bimbi La is not a much-used pass; but it was surprising to come across only one yak camp between the Tsari river and the Kyimdong river. It can hardly be due to lack of pasture. Across the Kyimdong river was a good pony track and I could see several tell-tale emerald green patches high up on the opposite range, like Irish flags spread out to dry. But this country appears to be very sparsely populated and could certainly support a larger population than it does at present.

We camped amongst bushes on the edge of the marsh. It was a better spot than we had found south of the Bimbi La, but hardly ideal. The altitude was about 13,500 feet.

On July 13th we marched down the narrow valley in a general north-east direction, crossing and re-crossing the river several times. It was obvious from the rather stunted and threadbare forest of birch, juniper and fir, with an occasional emaciated larch, that the rainfall here is not excessive. The valley is semi-arid; but there was a little rhododendron scrub, consisting of *R. vellereum*. It is one of those species which grow in the borderland between the very dry and the very wet country. But whatever the rainfall might be, July 13th at least was a fine day.

As we got lower down the gorge contracted and the forest, instead of increasing, disappeared altogether. It was exactly the reverse of what happened in the Chayul and Tsari valleys. Once you are on the south side of the main Himalayan range, every mile, every thousand feet of descent, brings you into thicker and greener jungle. North of the Himalayas, forest cannot survive in the deep arid valleys, but is confined to the higher slopes where there is less wind and more rain. A glance at the vegetation of this valley told me that when we had crossed the Bimbi La we were north of the Great Himalayan range, whatever Chickchar might be.

Yet there was no lack of flowers under the bushes, and amongst the rocks. As I walked along, I could not help thinking that almost every plant I saw would be a welcome gift to some rock garden enthusiast. Androsace alone displayed three charming species, all of which I had seen frequently before, but never growing so profusely as here. The cushion plant with crimson flowers (*A. tibetica*) was unexpected; and it was interesting to see it growing in association with *A. geraniifolia* (a creeping plant with small white flowers) and *A. strigillosa*. *Dracocephalum Hemsleyanum* was in bloom, and so was my variety of *Onosma Hookeri* which I introduced from Tibet some years ago. *Thalictrum diffusiflorum*, *Primula sikkimensis*, *P. pulchelloides*, a yellow-flowered Sedum, and *Thermopsis barbata* were a few of the species noted, and all were good. Farther down the valley, in grassy patches between the bushes, giant umbelliferae and compositae, species of Bupleurum and Ligularia were plentiful; tall stately plants with voluptuously coarse leaves.

Every now and then we had tantalizing peeps of glaciers at the head of some valley to the north. Twice the road crossed the main river rather than attempt to cross a glacier torrent thundering through a chasm. At the mouth of one such torrent I noticed a big stone house perched high up on a cliff, one of the most isolated and inaccessible residences I have ever seen. Late in the morning the road, now back on the left bank, climbed high up the hillside to a shoulder, whence we looked down into a deep ghyll, and caught sight of another glacier to the north. We crossed this torrent, the road taking us half a mile up stream before we could descend the cliff, and then returning to the main river; the valley opened out; abruptly the scenery became mixed. We were on a wide, gently sloping terrace several hundred feet above the river. There were irrigated stony fields, *mani* pyramids on the road, and just ahead, a small village called Ken, or Sumbatse. The gorge came to an end, and just where the river emerged between dark cliffs there was another scattered village on the far bank. The valley had become drier, and the river below Ken swung about from north-east to north, and then to north-west-by-west. Remarkable features were: a stream from the north-east bringing so great a quantity of water that it had scooped out a wide flood plain, now visible as a glistening pebble bank; a long tapering rock wall, with a very broken crest line, separating the Kyimdong river from an invisible river, the Kama Chu, which flowed behind it. Looking down the main valley one could see where this groin-like ridge tapered off, at the confluence of the two rivers. To the east rose part of the main Himalayan range, with several snow peaks and glaciers visible.

Approaching the village, I found the hard dry earth spotted with the little powder-blue puffs of Erytrichium and the white rigging of *Androsace erecta*. I also saw two hares, which reminded me that one sees few wild mammals in southern Tibet. Still, it is very much easier to see mammals in Tibet than it is in the jungle; there is less cover here, and visibility is good. Yet so much of Tibet is semi-desert that it cannot support large herds of grazing animals. Another creature I saw was a sandy coloured mouse-hare (Ochotona). Whether this was a freak or not I don't know; all the pigmy hares I had seen previously were grey. If it was not a freak it was a creature unknown. The closer we approached the Tsangpo, the drier grew the valley. There were no trees now, except along the streams.

Many flowering herbs grew on the terrace and round the cultivated fields. Grasses, too, were abundant, and in some variety; also rosette plants and succulents, characteristic of arid country.

We slept the night at Ken, and next day reached Kyimdong Dzong inside four hours. First we descended to the river by a steep path. Immediately below Ken the valley which had widened out into a kind of bath-shaped lagoon narrowed again, and the river rushed into a dark, rocky gorge. The path kept close to the river, crossing from the left to the right bank a few miles farther on. It would seem that the vanished glaciers which converged on Ken halted here. The alluvial plain referred to where the two streams unite, is probably the bed of an old glacier lake and marks the limit of the ice advance. The whole country between the Tsari river and the Tsangpo was formerly covered with snow and ice.

Presently we came to a bog filled, not with *Primula sikkimensis* but with *P. Florindae* whose huge heart-shaped leaves and mops of yellow fragrant flowers are now familiar in England. This is nearly its most westerly limit in Tibet. It has the invaluable habit of flowering late, and it keeps on flowering.

We were now marching nearly due west, to meet the Tsangpo which flows east. The Kyimdong river and the Tsangpo meet in almost head on collision. Several other tributaries do the same, notably the Kyi Chu, a fact which has been explained by Sir Sidney Burrard as evidence that the Tsangpo itself originally flowed in the opposite direction, that is, from east to west. Normally, tributaries flow in the same direction as the main river.

A few miles below Ken the tapering rock blade ends in a sharp headland, and the Kama Chu from the east joins the Kyimdong Chu. It rises in the Himalayas to the south-east, and a surprising volume of water comes pouring out of the gorge to swell the Kyimdong river. It was, of course, the height of the rainy season, when the eastern Himalayas are drenched with rain; but I judged that the river is fed by glaciers and snow fields. There is a path up the valley, and by crossing one or two passes Molo can be reached, and also the main Himalayan range. Mr. F. Ludlow, the Tibetan naturalist, explored this route in 1936.

Although there are no trees in the gorge above Kyimdong, the banks of the river are lined with shrubs and bushes. They are hard-leafed and often thorny; a grey, metallic looking vegetation. A species of Euonymus was common; but the only flowering shrub was a Desmodium with long pendent festoons of purple flowers, like a Wisteria. Then Kyimdong Dzong came in sight round a corner; and crossing a large stream from the east, we climbed the high gravel bank to the village. It is a broken-down place which looks as though it had once been more thickly populated; but its position is strategically sound. All these dzongs, or so called forts, on the south bank of the Tsangpo have been placed so as to guard the passes over the eastern Himalayas, and thus control traffic over them. Not that anything so exact as the Himalayan crest line is the recognized frontier between Tibet and the Lopa country. The Tibetans are a realistic people. They do not understand trigonometry. But they have a solid understanding of their own culture, and its natural environment. So while the Indian Government talks high altitude about a natural frontier based on the positions of peaks in relation to one another and to remote astral bodies, the Tibetan walks over the passes and descends the Indian side of the Assam Himalayas until he reaches a point where trees of a certain kind cease, or crops of a certain kind fail, or where the summer temperature is too high for him, or there are too many flies. That, to him, is the natural frontier of Tibet. It is slightly fluid, and vague, and it bears no obvious relation to the stars; but it is practical. There he stops, and marks the spot by building, not a fort, but a monastery to the greater glory of his religion. The Himalayan crest line is by treaty the Indo-Tibetan frontier; but the outposts of Tibetan culture are well down the Indian side of every eastern Himalayan pass which European travellers have crossed.

We were invited to stay at the dzong, which in fact seemed to be the only habitable building in the village. Here I found a cultivated and pleasant official in residence. He was youthful middle-aged, with scholarly features, kind eyes, and a disarming smile. His dress was the rather splendid, casual and unstudied red gown, silk lined, of his caste. It was not new. He wore magnificent leather boots of a kind made only in Kam, and horn-rimmed glasses. His hair was close cropped. He had met the English in Gyantse and liked them, he said, with a slow smile. If he was only being polite he welcomed me none the less warmly.

I was now only a very few miles from the Tsangpo. Looking down the valley, I could see the mountains across the great river; but the Tsangpo itself was invisible. In a couple of hours I could reach it and my outward journey would be finished!

Finished? The thought was unbearable!

Kyimdong stands on a high gravel terrace washed on two sides by rivers. The east river, though small, flows in a big valley. Suddenly I decided to delay seeing the Tsangpo. It had all been too easy; I wanted to enjoy the pleasures of anticipation a little longer. Instead of going five miles down the Kyimdong valley, I would add fifty miles to my journey by crossing the Lang La, and go to Molo and Lilung. I asked permission of the Jongpen and he willingly granted my request; he in turn asked me to deliver a letter personally to the Tsela Dzongpön.

Tsela Dzong is four marches down the Tsangpo valley from Lilung. I had no intention of travelling so far east. Not at first. But here was a letter to be delivered at Tsela Dzong. Then why not go? To be postman to Tsela Dzong however seemed to me rather pointless. After all the letter could be sent by other means. On the other hand, if I went to Tsela, I might perhaps go on from there . . . somewhere. It would be folly to waste time going there and coming back again; I had spent some time at Tsela in 1924 and pillaged it botanically. Yet there were possibilities; I turned the matter over in my mind and agreed to deliver the letter in person to the Tsela Dzongpön.

Before I left next morning the magistrate asked me for a cake of soap. I willingly gave him one, but could ill spare it. I asked him to send a letter to India for me via Sanga Chöling and this he promised to do, the letter going from village to village. It did not reach Sanga Chöling; I never heard whether it reached England or not; it may have gone via Lhasa.

CHAPTER XI

THE GREAT RIVER OF TIBET

WHILE waiting for the coolies I collected a number of dry zone plants, noting the prevalence of shrubs with grey or even white foliage, due to a layer of wax on the leaves, or to a coating of white hairs. Several shrubs have very small leaves, thus reducing the surface; in others the leaves contain an aromatic oil. Thorny shrubs are also typical of the dry zone. The flowers of most of these xerophytes are small and unscented. All the devices mentioned for reducing evaporation, if not direct adaptations to drought, seem to be well suited to the conditions. But no single one has a monopoly. Perhaps the river valleys are growing gradually drier, and the plants are trying out the survival value of each device.

A species of Arisaema with a fleshy bright yellow spathe, like a small yellow arum lily, is abundant on the hard dry slopes where herbaceous plants are rare.

The valley was steep, and quickly grew wider. Above Kyimdong two plants were prominent, *Morina Coulteriana*, a hard thistle-like erect herb with whorls of yellow tubular flowers embraced by a close collar of spiny leaves, and *Codonopsis convolvulacea*. This last has the largest and most handsome flowers of any Codonopsis. They open wide as saucers, instead of pinched bells like most of its relations, and are a deep powder-blue-lavender with crimson centre. I have never seen this plant growing in England and suspect that our summers are not dry or warm enough for it. *Codonopsis convolvulacea* is a child of the sun; New York might suit it better than London – it has nothing to fear from cold.

Towards noon we reached a village called Palangshü, on the left bank of the stream, and halted to change transport. We continued our journey and camped early, close to the last house in the valley. The altitude was about 12,000 feet, where, in the cool dry climate of southern Tibet, so many excellent garden plants have made their homes. There are few trees, but plenty of scrubby bushes, between which were grassy hollows gay with summer flowers, and bogs where primulas grew.. *P. sikkimensis* and *P. Florindae* reappeared. Generally, in the wet valleys of Kongbo, *P. Florindae* and *P. alpicola* take the place of *P. sikkimensis*. But the last named also claims a certain area of southern Tibet, growing along irrigation channels in the not-so-wet region, and just here it overlaps the territory of its allies. It seems to me that yak have a good deal to do with the distribution of these 'Sikkimensis' primulas, but their role is not very clear. However one may be certain that every consolidated primula meadow in Tibet has been grazed by generations of yak. In certain alpine grazing grounds, where temporary encampments have long been established, *Primula sikkimensis* grows so tightly packed one would think that not another plant could be wedged between their ranks.

On both sides of the Lang La, *P. sikkimensis* was in full bloom, and the trembling carpet of daffodil-yellow flowers made a memorable picture. On looking closely, however, I noticed that the plants were not quite touching; in between them grew the flat rosettes of another primula (*P. Roylei*). Even in fruit this species was a couple of inches shorter than its rival; so that by the time *P. sikkimensis* had shaken out its bell clusters, it completely hid the fruiting heads of *P. Roylei*. But about two months earlier, before *P. sikkimensis* had reached its full stature of nine or ten inches, the pasture had been as uniformly wine-red with *P. Roylei* as it now was daffodil yellow with *P. sikkimensis*! Only close observation would have revealed the *P. sikkimensis* plants pushing up between the rosettes of *P. Roylei*, which hid them.

These two primulas shared the field. By their succession, not only did they refrain from interfering with one another, but they kept out all rivals. As soon as one finished, the other took over, a sort of floral Box and Cox. *P. Roylei* asked nothing of *P. sikkimensis* but that it should not bloom prematurely, and spoil the market. *P. sikkimensis* asked nothing of *P. Roylei* except that it should not linger on in flower after its day was done – when, that is to say, pollination had been accomplished. They shared the rain and the sunshine between them; and did not compete with each other for the favour of the somewhat scanty insect population which does the pollinating.

Primulas have a strong social sense. They hate to be alone. On the other hand they loathe all but their own kind. They stand for nationalism, self-determination and intolerance. They are almost as intransigent as men. If they like a place, they want it all; they can brook no rival. But if they don't like a place, they will evacuate it completely, caring nothing for what their rivals do. Dominion or downfall. Once covetous of a place in the sun the noble and haughty race of primula will strive to evict almost every other plant, and themselves cover the landscape. This they sometimes succeed in doing. They are less individualistic than most plants, more clannish. Each primula species stands up for its own rights against every other primula species; but once security is attained, it may merge its particular interest in the general interest of the genus. Then it is primulas against the world; at least the alpine world. On the Lang La, for example, as in Tsari, *P. sikkimensis*, *P. alpicola* and *P. Roylei* were the most successful competitors. In Mönyul I have already described how *P. strumosa* beat all rivals and stained the alps with a patchwork of yellow on green; and earlier in the season *P. atrodentata* was the same. Elsewhere as already recorded the pasture was rapidly becoming consolidated *Primula Dickieana*! By the time no other plant – not even grass – could hold up its head in competition with this primula, the pasture would be useless for grazing. Similarly, at a lower altitude, with *P. Kingii*. These two primulas, *P. Dickieana* and *P. Kingii*, grow in boggy ground; their presence indicates marsh in summer, although the ground dries up and freezes solid in winter. *P. strumosa*, *P. sikkimensis*, and *P. Roylei* prefer drier ground. But *P. Florindae* again is definitely a bog plant and likes running water.

Besides *P. sikkimensis* and *P. Florindae*, the white flowered form of *P. alpicola* was segregated in this valley, as at Chickchar. There was a purple flowered species, but it had narrow leaves without clear distinction between blade and stem, so it could not be referred to *P. alpicola* which has oval or oblong bullate leaves, with distinct petiole. More likely this was *P. Vinosa*, which may be described as a purple flowered *P. sikkimensis*.

July 16th was wet. It took us eight hours to reach the top of the valley, cross the Lang La and descend to a camping ground on the east side; but we covered no more than ten miles. Plant collecting was a penance, but I kept note of the primulas seen.

In three hours we reached an undulating grassy plateau backed by a semi-circle of rocky peaks. There were some tents here, and we called on the herds to drink milk and dry ourselves. The pass was not at the head of the valley, but well to one side. Crossing the screes, we reached the top of the ridge about two o'clock. Ludlow records the altitude of the Lang La as 16,100 feet, which is probably not far out.

The weather was now very thick, and I could not see far. Bearing a little south of east, a range of snow-covered peaks loomed indistinctly through the rain mist. There were several glaciers. This range is a continuation of the snowy range seen above Ken, and it may be connected also with the Tsogar range. If it is not the main Himalayan range itself, it lies close to it. Near the pass I saw *Primula Cawdoriana* and *Meconopsis horridula* with rather washy blue flowers. But by the time we reached the pass I was not feeling so good, and had to content myself with general impressions of the flora.

A finer display of flowers came later. The east valley is moister than the west valley. The forest on the west side ended with junipers; that on the east side began with silver fir. Here were primulas again by the million. A broad swathe of meadow primulas rolled like a golden river between avenues of dark firs; it wound far down the valley, and faded from sight. Their sweet fragrance hung in the air. The dominant species was *P. Florindae*. But amongst purple *P. alpicola*, and white *P. alpicola* there now appeared something rarer and more beautiful than anything I had seen yet; forms of *P. alpicola* in ruby-red, and salmon, and terra cotta shades. These plants were widely scattered, but there was no mistaking them. They shone like beacons in the yellow seas.

As in Tsari, *Iris chrysographes* mingled with the primulas, and late though it was, *Rhododendron Wardii* was in good bloom on the fringe of the forest. We camped in a damp spot at the mouth of a tributary valley, and being tired, dripping wet, and hungry, I was glad to stop anywhere. It was late, and it took a long time to get a fire going, with the wood all soaked. At last I got a cup of foaming hot tea, and certainly tea had never tasted better.

It rained all night. Next morning the weather improved, and while the animals were being collected, I botanized. We were camped in a bush-meadow association where yak do not graze and consequently primulas were by no means in the ascendant. In fact, but for occasional shafts of *P. szechuanica* they were almost entirely absent. So it was possible to see what other plants go to make up the alpine meadow: *Meconopsis betonicifolia*, Phlomis — a tall rather coarse purple-flowered plant; salvia and other Labiatae; *Anemone rivularis*; ranunculus; trollius; Polygonum spp; *Cypripedium tibeticum* and other orchids; Euphorbia; geranium; aster; *Potentilla* spp; Vicia; Morina; iris, and several grasses. The shrubs include willows, spiraea, *Rosa sericea*; Berberis; *Potentilla fruticosa*, and *Juniper*. Probably there is a hidden struggle going on between the shrubby growth and the meadow for supremacy; and in fact, the association of the two is more or less confined to places like this, where the soil is gravelly and well drained. Then shrubs have a chance, and encroach on the meadow, which is at its best where the ground is marshy in summer and unsuited to shrubs. The shrub association in turn is a step towards silver fir-rhododendron forest, which lines the valley on both sides.

Within two miles of camp we crossed another torrent from the north. A derelict house stood on a high mound; it was a lonely spot, several miles from the village. Presently we met half a dozen coolies carrying immense loads of wood for making a red dye. The shrub or tree grows in Pachakshiri, the Tibetan name for the Lopa country on the other side of the Great Himalayan range at the sources of the Syom river. Ludlow and his companion, Dr. K. Lumsden, are the only white men who have ever visited this remote region. The loads were being taken to Kyimdong Dzong via the Lang La, and so up the Tsangpo valley into dry Tibet. We met another caravan, this time comprising mules and ponies, mostly empty. They belonged to a party of traders who were returning to Tsöna Dzong, many days' march to the west. The traders had with them half a dozen pretty little long-haired 'Apso' dogs.

In less than three hours we reached Nepar, a village of large stone-walled wooden-roofed houses, scattered along both banks of a considerable river flowing swiftly from the south-west. The approach to Nepar was decorated with *mani* pyramids, and on the cliffs I saw rock carvings. A certain religious fervour was in the air, for this was holy ground.

On the cliffs opposite Nepar were tuffets of the dwarf *Rhododendron lepidotum*, with cream, white, salmon, cerise, and crimson flowers, *Primula pulchelloides*, and the wonderful *Gentiana Waltonii*, although this last was not in flower yet. More significant were the starfish rosettes of a charming yellow-flowered Briggsia, its leaves covered with henna-coloured hairs. It belongs to the family Gesneraceae, plants which require a very moist climate. The eastern Himalayan region is one of the wettest in Asia, particularly on the Indian side, and we had now travelled so far east, that we were in moist evergreen mixed forest like that of Tsari. By the time the 94th meridian is reached, there is such a concentration of moisture in the eastern Himalayas that a great deal of rain, taking advantage of the low passes, spills over on the Tibetan side, causing thick forest to flourish. There is also an unparalleled development of alpine plants.

Three streams meet at Nepar; the largest comes from the south-west; the next is the one from the Lang La, which we had just descended; a smaller stream flows from the north. At Nepar the river is broad and swift; it is spanned by a cantilever bridge.

We halted for a meal, before continuing eastwards down the valley. In one and a half hours we reached Barong Shiga, a considerable village on both banks of the river. The valley was wide, and there were many flowers, such as blue larkspurs, Thalictrum, and the twining *Codonopsis convolvulacea* again. By streams a purple-flowered 'Sikkimensis' primula grew; and this was true *P. alpicola*. The sides of the valley were covered with shrubs at the base, but there was plenty of forest, the most conspicuous trees being fir and larch. Silver birch was also common, and *Rhododendron Wardii*, still in flower!

Barong Shiga is about a quarter mile from Molo, which is on the Lilung Chu. At Molo, the Nepar Chu from the east joins the much larger Molo Chu from the south. The two rivers subtend a rugged area known as Tsari Sama, crowned by a sacred mountain called Trashi Ka La. Pilgrims march round Trashi Ka La, in five or six days. The route lies up the Molo Chu, over the Trashi La, to the source of the Ne Chu, and so down that river to Tsugang, Nepar, and finally back to Molo. Not many people make the journey, and between January and May the passes are impassable. This region was explored by Ludlow and Sherriff the following year (1936).

I stayed at the headman's house at Barong Shiga, a country mansion in which he had gathered the finest collection of Tibetan arts and crafts I have ever seen. One room was a magnificent museum; there were swords, guns, lances, leather shields, iron gauntlets, bows and arrows, saddlery, and so on. Some of the articles were obviously of Lopa manufacture – for example bamboo *chungs*, for beer, tightly encased in coloured bamboo matting. The Tibetan metal work – iron stirrups, brass tea pots, and other pieces – showed great feeling and craftmanship.

We were now a long day's march from the Tsangpo, the headman told me; and I was determined to get there in a day. There must be no more detours before I reached the Tsangpo. If I deliberately went out of my way a third time, the prize might elude me when it was already within my grasp. A sudden panic seized me that after all my efforts I might not reach my goal. It was not reasonable but it was insistent. I must not delay further said an inner voice; on July 18th I must reach the Tsangpo and finish the journey on which so much effort had been concentrated.

The morning was far from bright, but it was not actually raining. The coolies assembled late, and it was nine o'clock before we got started. Luckily there are no villages in the gorge of the Lilung Chu, between Molo and Lilung; we should not be delayed changing transport. We had to use coolies; ponies could not get through.

In the crowd which assembled to see us off, I noticed an almost pygmy Lopa girl. Since we left Chickchar, I had seen what I judged to be Tibetanized pygmies in almost every village we passed through. Most of them were very short, especially the women. There is a constant drift of peoples northwards from the savage jungles south of the Himalayas, into the pleasanter country of the Tsangpo valley. Formerly the Tibetan overlords raided and captured the Lopas for slaves, but the practice has almost died out, and the Lopas now come over the passes in the summer to work in the fields, and in early winter to trade. Some of them settle down in virtual slavery, but they are not allowed to roam about at will in Tibet. Only certain marts are open to them, and their movements are restricted. There is a good deal of mixed blood in the villages south of the Tsangpo, in Takpo and Tsari. Some of the tribes certainly appear to be pygmies, but not all. The men are almost always several inches taller than the women.

We reached Molo in ten minutes. The village, of several stone houses, stands on the right bank of the Lilung Chu, immediately below the confluence and is connected with the road on the left bank by a stout bridge. Below Molo, the road keeps to the left bank for several miles, and is rough, steep and narrow. It took us four hours to do the first six miles. After an hour's rest, we crossed to the right bank by a bridge. Here the Lilung Chu is thirty yards wide, and six or eight feet deep, the stream swift and turbulent, running at ten or twelve miles an hour. Rarely is the water tranquil. Furious rapids succeed one another at short intervals, the biggest occurring where the slates characteristic of the higher mountains give place to granite as the Tsangpo valley is approached. The coolies now said it would be impossible to reach the Tsangpo that day, and I felt quite upset about it. But we went on, the path getting worse rather than better. By three o'clock we were all rather tired, and I would have given a lot to have been able to camp. I knew that from now on the magnificent scenery of the gorge would be more or less lost upon me, nor could I concentrate any longer on the plants. But still I had that feeling of panic; I must go on, and on, and on: I *dare* not halt.

The gorge of the Lilung Chu — the largest tributary the Tsangpo receives for many miles, and one of the largest on the south bank throughout its entire length — is heavily forested with evergreen trees, which clutch at the almost vertical cliffs, and claw their way right to the topmost visible peaks. At Molo the forest is still predominantly coniferous, composed of Picea and Larix. Gradually broad-leafed trees, including noble specimens of *Quercus Ilex*, also birch and maple, replaced conifers, at least close to the river. On the cliffs below Molo, alpines such as *Meconopsis horridula*, with Cambridge blue flowers, and wet forest plants such as Briggsia grew side by side.

Another gesnerad, *Didissandra lanuginosa,* with deep violet flowers covered the sunnier cliffs. We crossed several large tributaries on either bank and the Lilung river continued to grow, until the volume of water was terrific, and the roar of the rapids filled the gorge. Looking up the narrow ravines to east and west, where one sometimes caught a glimpse of spiked ridges, I realized what a vast area of country still remained to be explored!

Along the path through the forest, and in the patches of open meadow which presently appeared, several species of Thalictrum were in flower. But by this time I was feeling so weary I could not observe anything with precision. The gorge began to widen out, and now the last and greatest transformation took place; the broad-leafed forest began to disappear, and pine forest took its place. We came to a delightful grassy space sheltered by towering cliffs; it was an ideal place for a camp, and I was greatly tempted to tarry. I particularly wanted to botanize at this end of the gorge. But again that frantic urge to push on took possession of me; I could not stop short of the Tsangpo. Besides, we must be very close to Lilung; it seemed weak to give in on the winning post. It was now about five o'clock. At six we were high above the river on a narrow path which clung to the granite cliffs. The gorge ended. The valley was growing rapidly wider; ahead lay open country, the enormous valley of the Tsangpo. The air was balmy, fragrant with the scent of pines, and with the bewitching scent which came from great sheafs of the pink martagon lily (*Lilium Wardii*) which lolled from the cliff. Its flowers were only just open, and their sweet scent in the dry air was delicious. Now the rocks were growing more naked, with twisted pine trees and a few thorny shrubs scattered about.

Dusk had fallen when at last we caught sight of an island about a mile from the Tsangpo. A bridge connects this island with either bank of the Lilung Chu, the village itself being on the far bank.

Cawdor and I had slept at Lilung and crossed this bridge in 1924. So at last I had joined up my two routes.

My tent was pitched close beside a house, in a sort of garden; but it was dark before the last tired coolie arrived, and eight o'clock before I got a cup of tea. But at least I was not shivering with wet and cold; on the contrary, it was pleasantly warm, though the altitude of Lilung is well over 9000 feet.

I had accomplished my object. I had crossed the Assam Himalayas, and southern Tibet, and had reached the Tsangpo. Other things did not seem very important for the time being.

CHAPTER XII

SNOW HORIZON

WHEN I awoke on July 19th I found myself at last by the waters of the Tsangpo. It was twenty-five days since I had left Chayul Dzong. Twice had I turned aside from the direct road to the river in order to pursue my botanical studies and postpone the completion of arrival; for the Tsangpo had always been my goal, if my secret goal. I should have been bitterly disappointed had I failed to arrive.

I had now to decide on the next step; the return journey, and the route I would take. Should I travel westwards up the Tsangpo valley, partly retracing my footsteps of 1924, and then turn south? Or should I – Suddenly I remembered that I had promised to take a letter to Tsela Dzong, forty miles down the valley. A more daring idea began to take shape.

In 1924, Lord Cawdor and I had seen from the hills above Tsela Dzong, a great snowy range, fifty or sixty miles to the north, its white peaks towering up into the blue sky like a fleet of frigates in line ahead. We had made two journeys northwards with the object of locating some of the peaks, which we believed to be 25,000 feet high, and had actually travelled for several days along the southern foot of the range, and finally crossed it at its western end, within a short distance of its culminating peaks, without ever seeing them again. The weather had been thick; and although we had seen the lower ends of many glaciers, we had never again caught even a glimpse of the giant peaks which had so stirred our imaginations. But I had nursed the memory of that glacial barrier glittering in the sunshine away north of the Tsangpo for more than ten years.

Here was I within measurable distance of the lost range.

What a chance! What better could I do than try again? I had to go to Tsela Dzong anyhow. Very well, I would make that the starting point of a new adventure. When I left Chayul Dzong, it was my intention to be away a month. That time was nearly up. No matter. Here was a quest worth while. Forward then!

In spite of our long march the previous day, I was ready for the road on July 19, and we walked down the right bank of the Tsangpo in sunshine, passing through inhabited country, woods, and pasture. Villagers were cutting the corn with sickles, and I saw many Lopas at work; well set up muscular little men with dark skins, not pygmies by any means. Every Lopa wears a round helmet, shaped rather like a British army steel helmet without the brim, on top of his head; from the back of it is suspended a small rectangle of raw hide, which protects his neck from a chance blow. The helmet, which is made of closely woven cane, will stop an arrow, and turn a sword blade: the Lopa carries a short Tibetan sword in his girdle, but that is more for adornment than for use. The Lopa weapon is the long bow.

Below Lilung the Tsangpo valley gets a fairly heavy rainfall, and it is unnecessary to irrigate the crops. Fields of wheat and barley add flashes of vivid green to the glorious landscape of violet-blue hills awash in a sea of foam clouds. The river looks like a sable road winding into eternity. Here and there grey-white sand dunes peep out. A few hundred feet up the mountain side, the sombre olive-green forest begins — *Pinus sinensis*, *Picea likiangensis*, and *Quercus Ilex*, mostly. At Yusum, where we arrived at three o'clock and halted for the night, pines come right down into the valley. There are villages at intervals on both banks, sometimes tucked away in the mouth of a glen, elsewhere perched high up on a terrace. Every village is sheltered by trees, such as pear, crab apple, willow, walnut, and white poplar. In the spring every village is shining with the soft green tresses of weeping willow, through which glimmer white domes of pear blossom, and the red glow of young poplar leaves. One might believe that the Tsangpo valley at 10,000 feet is one of the most delightful spots in the world – and so perhaps it is for six months in the year. But see it in January with a gale raging over miles of sand dunes, the red-rimmed sun peering through a bank of fine yellow dust, and the lead-grey river with its edges frozen to the banks, and one gets quite the opposite impression.

After recrossing the Lilung Chu, a mile from the Tsangpo, we soon came in sight of the great river of Tibet. For several months we had been accustomed to boisterous rivers tumbling over rocks between gaunt cliffs. At sight of the Tsangpo, the Loro Chu at Chayul Dzong, the Char Chu at Sanga Chöling, and the Tsari river all became authentic mountain torrents. Here was a noble river, whose measured roll was the more impressive because no foam flecked its dark surface. From deep down came a sound like the muffled tolling of iron bells, as the water met with rocks in its path, but except for ominous eddies, there was no ruffling of the surface, no hint outside of the awful turmoil within, tearing at the very heartstrings of the river. The Yantze is the only other river in the world which compares with the Tsangpo in majesty at a height of nearly two miles above sea level.

There are few impediments to navigation between Chaksam ferry, which crosses the Tsangpo near Lhasa, and Tsela Dzong, none whatever below Lilung; and it seems strange that the Tibetans have never attempted to make use of their magnificent waterway. Lopas would be available for hauling boats up stream, at least during the high water season. The reason is probably that there is not enough traffic to tempt them to depart from the time honoured land transportation.

Before this vast volume of sand-laden water can spread out over the plain of Assam, it has to drop one and three-quarter miles. It is completely barred from the plains by the Himalayan ranges, which for six weeks we had been painfully crossing.

The Himalayas here strike north-east, and the Tsangpo swings so as to keep parallel to them, rolling along in stately progress towards China. If it flowed on across the continent to the Pacific Ocean, as the Yantgze does, there would be less to wonder at. But it does not. After swelling to a breadth of half a mile near Tsela Dzong, it suddenly begins to contract. Just when you think it is going to develop into a huge but placid stream, which will slide gently down the long eastward slope of Asia, 2000 miles to the Pacific, it springs furiously to life, and batters its way through the Himalayas! Thus it reaches the plains and the Indian Ocean by the shortest route. It is the most dynamic thing in a land of gigantic pressures and forces. Below Tsela Dzong, the Tsangpo enters the great gorge. It emerges from the mountains at Kobo, 400 miles distant, having fallen 9000 feet. That gives a false idea of this amazing break through; for while crossing the Himalayas, it actually falls 6000 feet in one hundred and fifty miles, the maximum fall being 200 feet in a mile.

On July 20th we halted only once to change transport — an indication that the valley is not densely populated. In the afternoon it poured with rain, and I was glad to halt at Tokar earlier than we had intended. It was always miserably cold when it rained. In a narrow lane between high banks covered with shrubs and flowers, we met a Tibetan caravan, with scarcely room for two beasts to pass, and there was a joyful mix up. The yak stampeded the ponies, and the ponies stampeded the mules, and the Tibetan drivers cussed everybody, although they were perfectly good tempered about it.

Later we met a Tibetan official, a magnificent person, wearing army boots and puttees, his gaudy chupa thrown back to expose one shoulder, a large silver ear-ring dangling from his left ear, his black Homburg hat set at a jaunty angle on his head. He seemed a little taken aback at sight of me. But it was an event to meet anyone. Most of the way we had the narrow road all to ourselves; we needed it, being plagued with several foals which insisted on following their dams and whinnying for milk at the wrong moment.

On July 21st we passed through Shoka, a village about half way between Lilung and Tsela Dzong. Below that the valley widens out, and shows unmistakable signs of glacial action. The glaciers probably flowed westwards from the cluster of high peaks round Namcha Barwa. If so, the original Tsangpo must also have flowed *westwards*, as Burrard suggested. This was before the cutting of the gorge through the Himalayas. Glaciers which flowed eastwards down the other side of the range gave rise to the Dihang of Assam. During the final retreat of the ice front, the Dihang cut its way back through the Himalayas so fast that it presently tapped the headwaters of the Tsangpo, and a convenient uplift of the western end of the valley tipped the whole Tsangpo drainage into the Dihang. After that it was easy for the river to complete the gorge. At Paka, where we spent the night, I had the illusion when looking down the valley, that the invisible river really was flowing westwards – now; the valley appeared to slope from east to west, and it gave me a slight shock when presently the river came in sight, apparently flowing up hill. But was it altogether an illusion? It seems probable that the higher part of the valley still retains the original form given to it by the earlier westward flowing Tsangpo.

The farther eastwards we went the more unlike Tibet grew the country. All outward resemblance to a plateau ceased; while trees, shrubs and herbaceous plants rapidly increased in number and variety. Of great interest was the sand dune flora. Several grasses grow in the sand and help to bind it. Once turf gets a start, other plants follow. Typical dune species are the hoary little *Onosma Wallichii* with pale blue tubular flowers which look as though they were made of frosted blue glass, and the silver-leafed *Oxytropsis sericopetala* which bears clubs of purple flowers. The thorny *Sophora Moorcroftiana*, with delightful blue and white flowers, is equally at home on the sand banks, or on stony ground, but will not stand much submergence. Wherever there is turf exquisite tiny plants like *Androsace erecta* and *Eritrichium densiflorum* appear. By streams there is always *Primula Florindae*; in meadows and along the margins of corn fields are Cynoglossum, Thalictrum, *Gentiana detonsa*, Dipsacus, and Impatiens. Many of these Tsangpo valley plants would be suitable for Long Island, or other parts of the Atlantic seaboard of the United States. Here and there one comes across a beautiful oasis, filled with shrubs and climbing plants and even small trees; it was only necessary to go a little way up one of the narrow glacier glens which stripe the north face of the Himalayas, to find a garden of flowers – meadows, marshes and woods in which was coyly hidden many a treasured plant. Of shrubs I saw Euonymus, Spiraea, Rubus, Desmodium, paeony, Cotoneaster, Berberis, *Rhododendron triflorum* and *R. oleifolium*, mulberry, Osiris, and Ceratostigma. In the fields were blue larkspurs, and in the muddy villages masses of domestic weeds like *Scopolia lurida* and *Hyoscyamus niger*. I hailed every additional sign of a more temperate climate with satisfaction, but I knew that by turning aside up any of the tributary valleys I should quickly find myself in forests, with alpine flowers on every hand. And the higher I went, the more flowers there would be. The climate of the gorge country is stratified. At the top it is frigid, at the bottom arid. Between these extremes are temperate layers. As the great river valleys penetrate the Himalayas, below 10,000 feet, the arid climate gradually gives place to a warm temperate, extremely moist climate, as at Migyitun, and presently to a sub-tropical one. There is a marked difference between the coldness of the plateau to north and west, and the coldness of the high peaks above the gorges. The Tsangpo gorge is a region of tremendous precipitation, and frozen precipitation is, of course, snow. The plateau is comparatively free of snow. The converging ranges above the Tsangpo gorge are buried under deep snow for six months in the year; here snow descends lower and lasts much longer than in dry Tibet.

Tibet is a land of extremes. Only a very small part of the country can be described as temperate. Plants which grow in temperate Tibet do well in our gardens — *Meconopsis betonicifolia, Primula Florindae, P. alpicola, Cyananthus lobatus* var. *insignis, Lilium Wardii, Cotoneaster conspicua, Rhododendron leucaspis, Dracocephalum Hemsleyanum, Gaultheria Wardii*, and many more. It is the part of Tibet which has been least explored; assuredly many good garden plants remain to be discovered here.

In the warm and fertile and not too wet Tsangpo valley I saw more birds than I had seen anywhere else, although most of them are probably migrants which cross the Himalayas. It was pleasant to hear ordinary cuckoos and larky birds singing in the cornfields — these last were probably pipits. Then on July 20th I saw green parokeets. Near Tsela Dzong I noticed red-legged choughs, one of the few resident species, and hoopoes, black-and-white magpies, pigeons, and a few duck which I could not identify.

We slept at Paka on the 21st after completing a rather long march. For some time the peak overlooking Tsela Dzong, at the confluence of the Gyamda river, had been in view, and I thought we might reach Tsela that evening. But it was farther off than it looked. We stayed in a large house, and I regretted I had not pitched my tent, for it was a night of minor horrors. To begin with, the house was crowded with unsavoury slaves, who slept several deep in the kitchen, and I was vigorously assailed by fleas. Then all the dogs in the yard started to bark at once — there were at least six of them and they made the welkin ring. In spite of this canine vigilance I finally fell asleep, only to be awakened suddenly by the braying of donkeys. The continual tinkling of mule bells, agitated by restless animals, was bad enough, but this was worse. After that I gave up trying to sleep. When shortly before daylight I dropped off, it was only for a brief spell; before the sun rose the cock crew.

It had rained all night but it ceased soon after sunrise, although the mountains were swaddled in clouds. At the start we had to cross the Paka Chu; there was no bridge, and the flooded stream proved an awkward obstacle. In another hour we reached the Tsangpo ferry and there was a long delay. We crossed in skin boats, as men have crossed rivers for three thousand years. The Tsangpo is wide here, but there are large islands and sand banks even at flood season. In winter more sand than water is visible. After crossing to the north bank we walked through cultivated fields and across pastures to the little village of Tesla Dzong, which stands on the headland where Gyamda Chu meets Tsangpo in a wide network of channels separated by green isles.

The view eastwards down the Tsangpo from Tsela is a memorable one. In the afternoon the tip of Namcha Barwa's 25,000-foot spire peeped out from amongst the curdled clouds, and thrilled by that wonderful sight, so rare in the rainy season, I determined that, come what might, I would go in search of the lost mountains.

The Jongpen, a pleasant and friendly man, welcomed me and bade me put up in the guest house, which he had made ready for me. I gave him the dispatch I had brought from Kyimdong.

Now that I had got so far, and was resolved on my course of action, I determined to rest two or three days at Tsela, before embarking on what was bound to be a difficult undertaking. The Jongpen asked me where I wanted to go, and I replied truthfully I wished to go to Pome; I had a mind to visit Showa, and possibly go as far as Shugden Gompa, before plunging into the tangled maze where I expected to find the snow mountains. It might take me a month to go to Shugden Gompa and back; and I reckoned that by the end of August we should be getting better weather. I wanted clear weather.

But the Jongpen did not encourage this plan. 'There is a good road to Tongkyuk', he said; 'beyond that there is nothing, absolutely nothing.' To him, mountains, rivers, lakes, glaciers, forests, flowers, meant nothing: nor could he understand what

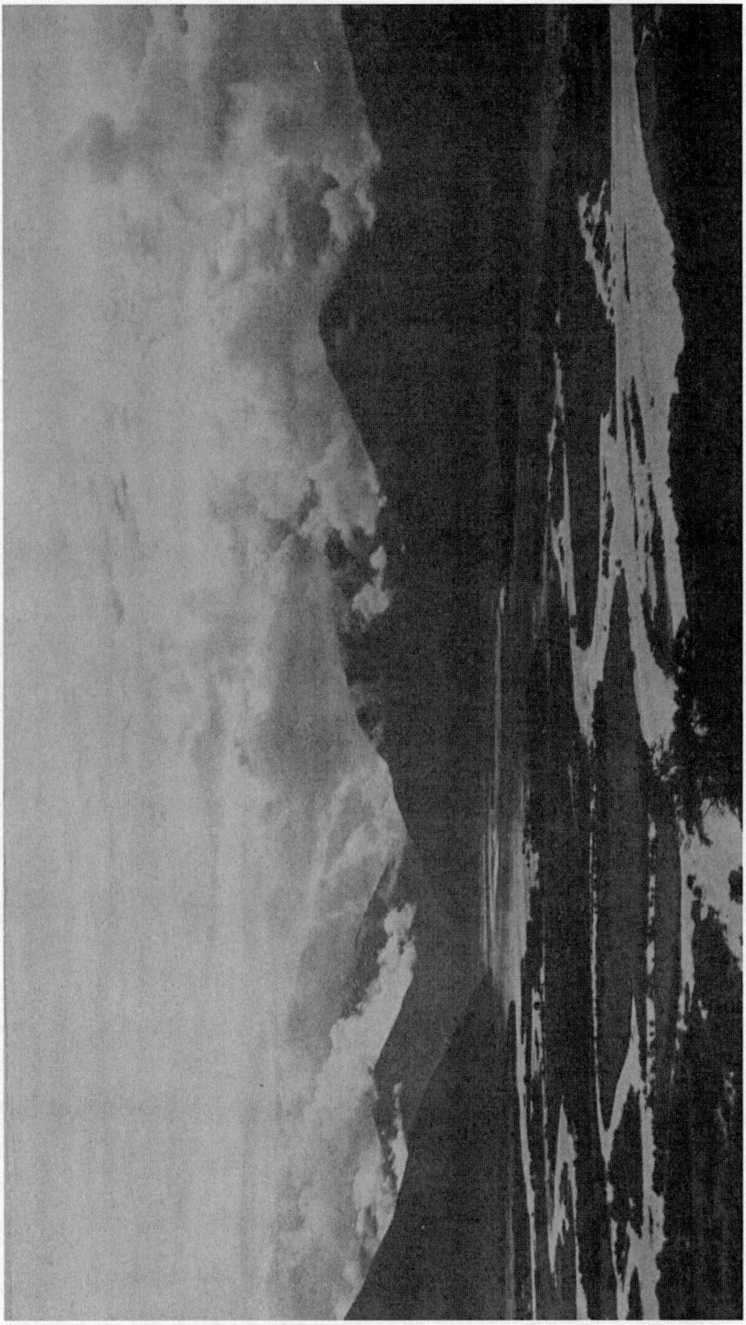

interest they could possibly have for anyone. One mountain was the same as another; I could see plenty all round Tsela. If there were no inhabitants in a country, that country was nothing: people, and taxable people at that, were what counted. They were fair Government game; pay-dirt, as a gold miner would say. Everything else was nothing. Perhaps the Jongpen was right. It was at least a realistic view.

CHAPTER XIII

I MEET THE COLONEL

In May 1924 Cawdor and I had spent three weeks at Tsela Dzong, in the course of what had turned out to be one of the most successful pieces of exploration of my life. Yet now there was something almost melancholy in going over the scene of past triumphs.

From this very place I had introduced to the western world three notable rhododendrons—*R. vellereum*, *R. hirtipes*, and *R. kongboense*. It was here that I had first seen growing in Tibet such plants as *Primula pulchelloides*, *P. atrodentata*, Cassiope, *Adonis brevistyla*, Cimicifuga, and *Iris decora*. The slope above the village, covered with thorn scrub, suggests that the climate here is still very unfavourable to the growth of trees. It is only on the sheltered side of the hill, and in the deep gullies, that there is any real forest. I walked along the path to the big gully on July 24th, and met the Jongpen dressed in white, with his followers, returning from a visit to the monastery high up on the cliff. He had been to pray. I went primarily to see if any Adonis seed was ripe, but failed to find the plant at all. There were *Podophyllum Emodi*, Astilbe, Rodgersia, Polygonum, Codonopsis, Aquilegia, two species of Impatiens, *Primula Florindae*, Cimicifuga, and other plants growing under the trees beside the stream. The vegetation was lush. On the open hillside *Androsace strigillosa* grew with *Iris decora*; both were over.

During the three days spent here (July 24th-26th) I went through my botanical collection to see that the specimens were in good condition; brought all catalogues and note-books up to date; permanently packed all dry specimens; and continued to collect plants. I also developed photographs, and had a good laundry day. Tashi and Pemba worked hard; and as they reported no opposition on the part of the Jongpen to my going to Tongkyuk, I was in tolerably good spirits marred only by continual bouts of insomnia. I was not in fact feeling very well. The weather improved greatly, and we had only a few light showers; but the great mountains to the north-east remained hidden behind a wild flocculence, although the fact that the clouds were broken up in this way was not a bad sign.

I visited the Jongpen, who had been here three years, without ever venturing more than a day's march away. He had only the vaguest ideas of the surrounding country; nor, without maps, was it possible for him to have any but vague ideas. To him, the mountains and valleys of Tibet must spread outwards from the familiar village in zones of ever decreasing precision.

On the evening of July 24th Namcha Barwa again emerged from the clouds, a tapering silver-white cone, tall as a steeple. The day following turned out so warm and sunny that I seized the opportunity to go out and catch a few butterflies and other insects. The wind had changed direction, and was blowing down the Tsangpo valley, off the plateau. The clouds lifted and for the first time the Himalayan peaks were all exposed. At 4 p.m. the air was only 45 per cent saturated, which was remarkable enough for July; or would be anywhere within sight of the eastern Himalayas, except in Tibet.

Small butterflies are abundant round Tsela, about a dozen species being common, including such familiar ones as cabbage white, clouded yellow, tortoiseshell, and a weak but extremely prolific creature, *Neope agrestis*. Small 'blues' were also common and there was a rather striking orange and black species which turned sluggish towards sunset and clung motionless to a twig, while the others were still tiresomely active. I was surprised at the variety of insect life here, at over 9000 feet, amongst an unappetizing collection of thorny shrubs. There was a plentiful supply of grasshoppers, beetles, bugs, hover flies, bees, anonymous Diptera and Tipulidae (daddy-long-legs), to mention a few. As for species, they were legion, including besides at least a dozen lepidoptera, six or eight grasshoppers, some of which were as large as locusts, but all, except the tiniest, lethargic. I even saw a small stick insect, but it was definitely deficient in legs. In two hours I caught fifty-four insects with no better apparatus than a big killing bottle; to wit, butterflies fifteen, grasshoppers nineteen, beetles thirteen, lacewing flies one, other flies six..

The Jongpen had promised me aquatic transport for the 26th, though I decided not to start until I felt better.

July 26th was quite hot; there is nothing like a fine summer day – except a cold winter one – to remind one of the fact that Tsela Dzong is on the edge of the dry plateau. It owes its local forest entirely to the proximity of the Tsangpo gorge, which lets in the rain as through a valve, and to the narrowness and lowness of the Himalayan passes opposite. This advantage is soon lost to north and west of Tsela Dzong, where the country becomes rapidly drier.

I had slept better, and felt fit to start. The Gyamda river was a delicious bottle-green colour, quite clear, whereas the Tsangpo was pea soup; one can trace the limpid water far out into the main river, and where the two waters mingle great numbers of enormous black fish, clearly visible from the bank, congregate. They are probably mahseer, but nobody catches them; not because they are sacred, but because nobody knows how to set about it. But although the Gyamda river is wonderfully clear, it is swift enough to roll quantities of sand and gravel along the bottom. When the current is suddenly checked by the Tsangpo which brushes it contemptuously aside, this burden is piled up to form an archipelago. In summer these isles are verdant, but in winter they are little more than sandbars. Many of them were now half submerged and the thickets of Hippophäe, Myricaria and willow looked like temperate mangrove swamps.

Five coracles had been assembled under the bank at Tsela

Dzong, and in these we embarked, one of us in each, besides the navigator, the luggage in the other two. We had to squat and not fidget. They are queer craft, not calculated to inspire great confidence. Each consists of a dried yak skin suspended from a rectangular wooden frame, to which it is bound by withes. A light inner framework serves to strengthen the hull and to keep the skin stretched.

At 9.15 we pushed off and presently the whole regatta was spinning down the river. The coracle floated high out of the water, the gunwale having at least a foot of freeboard. It was like squatting in a bath tub; I could just see the heads of Tashi, Pemba and the others. Each craft was propelled by its crew, who sat on a crossbar in the stern, facing forward and pushing backward with a pair of sculls. The rowlocks were rawhide, and very swivel, and the sculls were poles.

But if the design of the craft was not modern, at least it floated, and performed evolutions unknown to most pleasure craft. Sometimes it described circles, and whether it moved bow first, stern first, or broadside on, made little difference. My crew sang as he rowed, a plaintive wail of a song with no trace of a nautical rollick; the crew of Tashi's boat merely grunted. There was not a great deal of difference.

At first the boats kept close together, moving very fast down the broad centre channel of the Gyamda river. I felt as excited as though the gun had just gone for the start of a bumping race at Cambridge. Gradually as the speed increased the boats became separated. The bushes on the bank flew past; the water was popply, and we danced over the sparkling waves. Presently we reached the river mouth and got into the slower Tsangpo current, skirting the delta of the Gyamda river. Finally we reached the north bank opposite Tsela Dzong, and in a sandy cove lined by willow trees we disembarked. One by one the coracles drew in to the shore. All of them leaked, and the crew lifted each out of the river, carried it upside down on his head, and up-ended it in the sun to dry. This is part of the care of the ship; it must be dried after each voyage, or the skin rots, to say nothing of the basket work.

It seemed to me we might have voyaged down the Tsangpo for another two or three miles, hugging the north bank, and disembarked much closer to Temo; but it is not the custom.

Immediately below the Gyamda river confluence the Tsangpo expands into a wide tranquil lake, the current flowing under the Himalayan bank. The water is very deep on the north bank, where a rocky spur from Kongbo Peri plunges steeply into the river. Below the spur the Tsangpo comes cranking in. There are sand dunes and backwaters which are filling up to become wide pastures, a warren of dunes, lagoons, marshes, barley fields and grazing. The river has at some time cut a wide arc into the left bank at the mouth of the Temo valley, and has then abandoned it and turned due east. Gradually this warm, sunny bay has become dry land. It reminds me of Turner's 'Bay of Baiae', with willow trees in place of pines.

We disembarked at ten o'clock, the voyage having taken less than an hour. Ponies were to meet us here, but they had not arrived and it was 11.15 before we started overland, following a rough track along the mountain side. It was from this cliff path overlooking the river that I saw many big fish, motionless in the warm clear Gyamda water which clings to the north bank as the heavy sand laden water of the Tsangpo sweeps past in mid channel. I also saw on the rocks a large black lizard, like the ones we had seen farther west, at Chayul Dzong. Tsela is probably its eastern limit, as even the Tsangpo valley becomes wet beyond Temo.

After crossing the high spur which blocks the view of Temo from Tsela, we dropped down to the big sandy bay. The vegetation was much more advanced here than at Tsela Dzong, five miles away. The barley was ripe; and *Iris decora* was in ripe fruit. It grows in masses in the sandy soil. In the hedges *Codonopsis convolvulacea* ramped freely, its big mauve eyes full of appeal. On the dunes I found *Saussurea Kingii*, a curious plant, with silvery narrow leaves and purple flower heads — its flat radiating arms suggested a silver starfish. There was another Codonopsis with pendent bell-shaped, greenish flowers, scrambling in the bushes. I had not time to go across and examine a lagoon which the river had left amongst the sand hills. We changed transport again at 12.30, after travelling for only three-quarters of an hour; this involved another delay. Within sight of Temo Gompa we changed for the third time, finally reaching our destination at 4.30, the last mile or two marching almost knee deep through meads filled with moonlight-yellow primulas, *P. alpicola* in the drier meadow, *P. Florindae* by streams. When I was here in May 1924, the pasture was still short, and patched crimson with *P. tibetica*, another bog plant, but tiny, flowering very early before the summer plants have time to grow up and smother it.

Temo Gompa crowns a sugar-loaf hill at the apex of the wide valley which opens into the bay. It is a large spreading building, in red and white blocks, and looks, as do most Tibetan monasteries from a distance, rather like a pile of children's bricks. It contains about two hundred monks. The inhabitants received me kindly and I was installed in a guest house in the village. In the evening I botanized in the meadows, which were rich in Compositae and other large herbs.

From Temo Gompa to Tumbatse, crossing the Temo La, 15,000 feet, is a long day's march. In 1924 we had taken two days over it. But having rested for three days at Tsela I could not loiter. Daylight lasted for twelve hours now and I was determined to make the most of it. Starting at 7.45 a.m. we reached Tumbatse at 5.30.

We had botanized extensively on the Temo La, and all round Tumbatse in 1924; I saw little now that I had missed then, and concentrated my attention on the geographical problem.

As we toiled up to the pass my excitement increased. Looking west from the top we had a fine view of the Tsangpo valley; in the other direction the snow peaks were completely hidden. As we got down into the valley, 2000 or 3000 feet below, the sky cleared but near mountains blocked the view.

By the time we reached the valley of the Rong Chu below the Temo La, I was feeling the effects of the long march. I had caught a bad cold some days before, and now felt fever coming on. The march northwards down the valley seemed interminable — I had forgotten how many miles it was to Tumbatse. I got separated from the transport, and when at last a house came in sight I crossed the swollen stream and went to it. However, there appeared to be nobody about, and it was a relief when one of my men turned up and said we were not yet arrived. Still greater was my relief when at last after travelling another mile we did reach the village of Tumbatse, and I recognized our house of eleven years ago. It had certainly not been renovated during my absence; but it was something that it had not fallen down. The owner, Lobsang, a typical Kongbo herd, recognized me almost before I recognized him and greeted me warmly. He brought out food and drink, and I felt as though I were the prodigal son returning to my native village after having been away in the great city. Lobsang's daughter, who was a little child playing in the mud when I last went away, had grown into a comely lass about eighteen years old, and taken her place in the economic scheme of her yak world. In her short dark woollen skirt, undyed long-sleeved woollen jacket, and round wide-brimmed white woollen hat, she looked very pretty. All the girls of Kongbo have rosy cheeks and sparkling black eyes, and if their straight, glossy, raven-black hair does smell of stale butter, is it really more unpleasant than the smell of para-di-methyl-benzine? Little 'Rosycheeks' came coyly into my room to say how-do-you-do while I was having my tea, purring like a kitten. She showed me a deep scar on her arm caused by upsetting a pot of boiling water when she was still quite a child. Her father said she remembered me perfectly. I suppose it was an event to have two white men living in her house at the impressionable age of seven; anyhow, she had not seen another one since.

Looking north towards Tongkyuk in the evening, I saw for the first time the snow peaks I sought; and if I had been eager to find them before, I was all on fire now. It seemed to me one of the most thrilling sights I had ever seen.

This is what I wrote in my diary that evening:

'. . . from Tumbatse in the evening a snow range to the north showed up, not more than forty miles distant. Alignment more or less east-west . . . highest visible peak at west end bears 4½°, three summits on a long ridge visible and several glaciers, highest visible peak at east end bears 7½°. Very rocky peaks in between. This is undoubtedly the range Cawdor and I saw from above Tsela Dzong in 1924 – and the view from here places it unquestionably north of Tongkyuk . . . and at or near the sources of the Yigrong Chu. . . . The range seems to run parallel to the Namcha Barwa – Sangling end of the Himalayas, enters Pome, and perhaps curves round to the east or south-east, joining on to the peaks seen from Shugden Gompa in 1933 . . . the range, however, seems to be far south of the Salween.'

Much of this analysis, or reconstruction, proved to be in the main correct; at least I had now got the general location of the range fixed. I was firmly determined to go on and achieve victory – I must *cross* the range. Once I did that its reality could no longer be doubted.

I should have liked to stay a day at Tumbatse with my old friends, but the urge to get on was overpowering, and after a good night's sleep, the fever attack remaining latent, I was ready for the road. Taking a warm farewell of old Lobsang and pretty 'Rosycheeks', we pushed on northwards down the Rong, through meadows blazoned with flowers. A brilliant orange-coloured Pedicularis shone like a flame in the bogs, and the drifts of *Primula alpicola* gleamed like scattered moonlight.

Other flowers were Aster (or Erigeron), Adenophora, mauve Thalictrum, and everywhere primulas, *P. Florindae*, *P. alpicola*, and even *P. tibetica*. In two and a half hours we reached Lunang, built on a large terminal moraine. Beautiful metal work is done here.

There are some shallow ponds at Lunang full of aquatic plants which have an almost worldwide distribution. I collected water buttercup (*Ranunculus aquaticus*), Juncus, Spartium, *Hydrocharis morsus-ranae*, Hippuris (mare's tail), and a grass.

The Rong was not nearly so boggy as I had expected, and to have got even this far, north of the Temo La, without a ducking seemed remarkable after the deluge of 1924.

Below Lunang, the valley narrows and steepens, the meadows disappear, and forest fills the gorge. The torrent, already swift, becomes turbulent, and the path hitherto spongy becomes rocky. The forest consists chiefly of juniper, Picea, *Larix Griffithii*, *Abies Webbiana* and oak, with smaller shrubs, especially *Rhododendron niphargum*, and Lonicera.

At 2.30, we reached Chunyima, and halted for the night. I heard the familiar screech of parakeets here, although Chunyima is 10,000 feet. But it is on the edge of the pine forest country, where one may always be sure of finding these birds in the summer. The pine is *P. sinensis*, which covers large areas of similar high broken country in Yunnan and North Burma. Except that the dominant tree is the same the two forests are of quite different type.

In North Burma this pine forest formation occurs between 4000 and 8000 feet, and is a sub-tropical type of forest. Where pine does not grow, for instance on north slopes, and in deep gullies, it is replaced by sub-tropical evergreen forest, with a great variety of broad-leafed trees, shrubs and woody climbers. This pine forest unquestionably owes its presence to man's interference.

But here in southern Tibet the pine forest occurs only between about 7000 and 10,000 feet, and the climate is by no means sub-tropical; neither is the vegetation.

Outwardly the two forest types look very much alike; in composition and in origin – for there is nothing to show that in Tibet the pine forest owes anything to man – they are utterly different. Yet it is instructive to note how the same general conditions produce the same general results. Pine forest and bracken seem always to go together. They are closely associated in North Burma, and there is much bracken undergrowth here also. Moreover, in North Burma, certain plants with underground stems such as bulbs and rhizomes, which resist fire, are commonly associated with the bracken; notably two lilies, *Lilium ochraceum* var. *burmanicum*, and *L. Bakerianum*. These plants thrive and spread at the expense of others which lack this advantage and so are killed out by the annual fires.

Here, too, in the cool temperate pine forest of southern Tibet a lily is associated with the bracken undergrowth, namely *Lilium Wardii*. Yet I do not think that this pine forest is ever burnt, nor did I see any open grass-bracken covered slopes, devoid of trees, such as are common in the pine forest region of North Burma. It must be remembered, too, that this deeply trenched country we were now entering upon is far more sparsely populated than is the corresponding country in North Burma.

Unfortunately there are no meteorological records for either type of pine forest; but I have travelled extensively in both regions and can speak from experience as to general climatic conditions.

In the first place, pine forest seems to require a fairly heavy annual rainfall, probably not less than forty inches, most of which may fall in the summer, since a degree of winter drought is also common to all the pine forests. The rainfall in the North Burma region, however, is nearly twice that of southern Tibet, and is accompanied by a much higher temperature. Perhaps it will bring out the contrast better if we tabulate the two regions thus:

Factor	North Burma Pine Forest (Htawgaw Hills) *Pinus sinensis*	South Tibetan Pine Forest (Kongpo-Tsangpo region) *Pinus sinensis* and *P. excelsa*
Altitude	4000-8000 feet	6000-10,000 feet
Latitude	25°-27° N.	29°-31° N.
Rainfall	60-80 in. (?)	30-40 in. (?)
Summer Temp.	Hot moist	Warm to cool moist
Winter Temp.	Cool to cold; frost in open at higher levels for three months	Cold to very cold. Severe frost
Snow	None or rare, at highest level only, at night	Little or none, except at highest levels
Wind	Fresh valley winds in winter	Steady gales up valley in winter

Different as the climates are, are the *essential minimum conditions* for the development of pine forest, rather than any other type of forest, the same? And the answer I think is, they must be, since the dominant tree is the same in both, although most of the other plants are quite different.

I was to discover later under what conditions pine forest grows when it is certain that fire has played no part.

We left Chunyima on July 29th. It was a fine sunny day. Almost immediately we entered the pine forest, first pure stands of *Pinus excelsa*, then a mixture of *P. excelsa* and *P. sinensis*. On steep slopes there was a certain amount of open ground covered with bracken, scrubby bushes of *Rhododendron oleifolium*, *Hypericum Hookerianum* and *Gaultheria Wardii*, and plants of *Lilium Wardii*, which although not yet in full bloom were magnificent. The ground was broken and rocky, the path steep and rough, and the high river bank precipitous. The river, in fact, flowed in a deep trench. We halted in the pine forest for half an hour and had lunch. The ground was striped with shadows, the air fragrant and mild. Life in Tibet can be very pleasant. Two strangers joined us; I noticed that they carried coils of rope, and I wondered why. Then, of course, I began to wonder who they were, and what they were doing. In another hour we reached the precipitous descent to the Tongkyuk river, and I peered between the tree trunks for the wooden bridge.

There was no bridge. For fifty feet on either side of the mud-coloured river which rushed sullenly between enormous chunks of stone, there was no forest either. It was as though an earthquake had violently shaken the whole valley, and sent a tidal wave to complete the work. The devastation was immense. As far as I could see, up and down the valley, splintered and crippled trees lay inextricably mixed up with rocks, which glistened white in the sunshine. Some lay as they had fallen; others were reduced to matchwood. For miles, both banks were composed of bare rock and gravel, fifteen or twenty feet high without a blade of green anywhere.

A crowd of men were gathered on the opposite bank. At first I thought that the disaster had only lately taken place and that the local inhabitants of Tongkyuk were surveying the damage and bewailing the loss of their bridge. Then I saw that they were working on a temporary and very hazardous-looking rope bridge, the rope being passed over timber tripods to keep it out of the water. The tripods stood on rocks. Meanwhile we had descended into the river bed, and the Chunyima people were unsaddling my boxes preparatory to taking their ponies back. They seemed in a hurry to get away. There was quite a stir amongst the crowd on the far bank when I appeared, and now the reason for the two men carrying coils of rope became clear. They began tying up my loads to haul them across the rope bridge, the sight of which filled me with misgiving; for the bank did not lend itself to this type of bridge.

I decided to be hauled across myself first. One or two of the men had come over and gone back, so the apparatus appeared to be working smoothly. Luckily the formidable

Tongkyuk river is not very wide. I was soon trussed up into a helpless cocoon, suspended from the rope by a flat wooden triangle to which a life line was attached, and the word shouted across to haul. I bumped slowly across, the line sagging badly; but the men hauled with a will, and presently my feet touched solid earth again. I was standing on a ledge of rock, my bonds being loosed; then I clambered down to the group hauling on the line. 'Good evening!' said a suave voice behind me. 'I am Colonel Yuri. Who are you?' I turned round to find myself face to face with a military looking man who saluted smartly, as he drew his heels together with a click.

CHAPTER XIV

EXPLORING

COLONEL YURI, a well set up, sturdy man of fifty-two, with good features and a pleasing expression, was in uniform. He wore riding breeches, army boots and puttees, and a thick khaki jacket, not well cut. He had brought his pony down to the bridge to meet me, and now he insisted on my riding it back to the dzong. This was a mile distant by the ruined river bank, ending with a steep climb to the top of the cliff.

The Colonel himself had only arrived in Tongkyuk from Lhasa two days ago. One of the first things he learnt was that I was at Tsela Dzong and might be arriving at Tongkyuk any day. Thus he was ready to receive me. Through Tashi I learnt that Yuri was Chief of the Lhasa Police; that he had come to Pome on special duty; and that he was looking for a mysterious and sinister person, Urush Marpo, though who Urush Marpo might be I could not at first discover. It was confidential.

The dread shadow of Bolshevism was believed to have fallen across eastern Tibet, and it was thought that agents inoculated with that fearful virus had secretly arrived. It was only too patent, however, that the Colonel believed he was at the end of his sleuthing. He had found his man. In short – *I* was Urush Marpo!

Tashi had some difficulty in convincing the Chief of Police that he was in error; and I helped to allay suspicion myself.

The Colonel possessed two rifles, a long Lee-Enfield, and a heavy Manlicher, both the worse for neglect. He wasted no time but as soon as I had finished my meal, produced them for my inspection; and I got through the examination with honours.

Like many simple souls, Yuri believed himself to be full of guile, and he asked me a number of questions designed to test the truth of my denials. It was a transparent device, and by the end of the evening, when he had drunk a gin or two, we were very good friends. Colonel Yuri had lived in Gyantse, and had known MacDonald[1] there; no doubt he had enjoyed himself with the polo-playing young officers of the Trade Agent's guard, and he had a soft spot in his heart for the mad English.

Having cleared myself of suspicion, I was allowed to proceed. Then came the question of what route I was to follow. Showa was still on the agenda; but when I suggested it, the Colonel received it with disfavour. Pome in the rainy season was intolerable, he said, and strongly advised me not to go there. Since it was not, so far as I knew, essential to my plan of discovering the great snowy range, I withdrew the motion, and Yuri then said I might either go to the Po-Yigrong, or to the Pasum Lake, via the Nambu La, as we had done in 1924. The Po-Yigrong was my goal; but I was sorry to give up Showa.

Before leaving London in January I had jokingly made a date with my young friend, Ronnie Kaulback, the Tibetan traveller, for July 1935. We were to meet at Showa, he from the east, I from the west. Kaulback, in the course of a brilliant journey did actually reach Showa, though not till the end of September. His companion, Hanbury Tracy, preceded him there by a different route, awaiting his arrival, according to plan; but even Hanbury Tracy did not get there till the end of August. Even had I gone to Showa I should not have met either of them, as they were both more than a month late for the appointment. Yet it was a good effort to keep a difficult tryst.

It is interesting to record that on his arrival at Showa, Kaulback heard I was in the vicinity. He writes:

> On the way down the valley I heard that an Englishman with two servants was somewhere near the Yigrong Tso. It could

[1] J. MacDonald, British Trade Agent at Gyantse and author of *Twenty Years in Tibet*.

only have been Kingdon Ward, and I was very sorry that I had not the time to pay him a visit.[1]

Actually, by the end of September I was a long way from the Yigrong Tso, but there is a time-lag in the publication of news in Tibet.

Yuri himself was going to the Po-Yigrong in a few days to recruit Pobas for the army. This was lucky; he probably felt at ease recommending a place to which he himself was accredited by his Government. I suppressed a desire to say that I was in a hurry and must start at once. I felt instinctively that to appear anxious to remove oneself quickly from police observation would be in the worst possible taste. Anyhow, Yuri would not hear of my starting the next day, so I stole another day's rest, and botanized discreetly. I found starved plants of *Campanula glomerata* in the turf which covered the gneiss rocks – a rather local British species; Thalictrum, saxifrage, *Polygonum capitatum*, Allium, Strobilanthes, Polygala and various shrubs, including Deutzia, Berberis, Rosa, yellow jasmine, Daphne, *Leycesteria formosa*, and Lindera. On the pine trees a species of Loranthus was common; the conifers do not often support mistletoe!

I learnt now that the catastrophic flood was not due to an earthquake; and far from having just happened, it took place four years ago. Either there had been a cloud burst higher up the valley, or a temporary lake, formed perhaps by a landslide, had burst its dam and emptied itself quickly. Whatever the cause, there was no doubt about the result. A wall of water fifty feet high had swept down the valley, overwhelming everything in its path. For fifty feet above normal high-water level it had smashed, pounded and pulverized the landscape and carried away the remains; and for fifty feet above that, the undermined banks had broken and crumbled, throwing trees and rocks and sand into the flood in the utmost confusion.

[1] *Salween*, by Ronald Kaulback. Hodder & Stoughton, 1938.

The sections of the bank revealed on what foundation the forest grows. The pine forests of Tibet begin where the glaciers left off. In other words, they cover the old moraines and the vast accumulation of coarse gravel rock and sand, derived from moraines, which the rivers have laid down since the retreat of the ice. It is a poor, hungry, well drained acid soil, deficient in humus in spite of considerable rainfall, and probably highly deficient in nitrogen. Pine forest is the climax formation for this soil and climate. But the sub-tropical pine forests of North Burma, and the low-lying pine forests of Rima on the Assam-Tibet frontier must also be regarded as climax formations, since they too grow on glacier gravels of exactly the same type. But here fire has played an important role, to the advantage of the pine. It is doubtful whether there would be any pine forest but for fire, which kills off seedling broad-leafed trees, but leaves the young pines scatheless. Rivers easily plough deep valleys through this loose material, which is perpetually being carried down to lower levels. Immense accumulations of moraine gravel may be seen in the Tsangpo valley at the head of the great gorges, where the river is passing below the glaciers of Namcha Barwa.

I should have liked to follow the river down below the junction of the Lunang and Tongkyuk streams to see what damage had been done, but I had not the time. The gorge becomes deeper and steeper, and the river more shut in until the great Po-Tsangpo itself is reached near Lubong. This section is almost uninhabited. Cawdor and I had marched up the Po-Tsangpo from its confluence with the Kongbo-Tsangpo at Gompo Ne in 1924, in pine forest all the way. Gompo Ne, where the pine forest ends, is 5247 feet, and below that the gorge is filled with sub-tropical evergreen forest. One would have to climb a couple of thousand feet up the sides of the gorge before meeting with pines again.

It would be interesting to know whether the Tongkyuk flood, pouring at high speed into the Po-Tsangpo, which it hits at right angles, piled up the waters of that river, and raised the level at Showa. The Po-Tsangpo itself is so large, particularly in the summer, and its gorge so ample, that I suspect even the Tongkyuk flood could make little impression. But I make the suggestion in case future explorers in these valleys should find traces of action which they find hard to explain.

So the full force of the flood was gradually spread out: and although the few bridges were carried away — and below Tongkyuk they are only rope bridges — the villages, which in the Po-Tsangpo gorge are far above any possible flood, could not have suffered. Tongkyuk itself must have felt the full pressure of the wave: luckily the dzong stands on solid rock 150 feet or more above the river and well out of reach of any flood.

On the evening of our arrival, when the sky was an exquisite turquoise blue, I saw down the valley, to the south-east, three snow peaks. The first bore 113° from Tongkyuk, and was north of Gyala Peri; the second, bearing 132°, that is almost due south-east, was Gyala Peri itself. The third was south of Gyala Peri. All three peaks stand on the great Makandro ridge which runs due north from Namcha Barwa, the Tsangpo having sliced through it between Namcha Barwa and Gyala Peri. What happens to this ridge further north I was presently to discover.

July 30th was fine but without much sun; clouds hid the snow peaks. There was a howling wind up the gorge in the middle of the day, which always means no rain; it is a stiff price to pay for fine weather. Yuri promised me transport for the following day. That night the temperature fell to 57° F.

Next day, the last of July, after saying good-bye to Colonel Yuri, we started up the valley at 8.30. Signs of the flood were visible everywhere, more or less, according to the breadth of the valley and the height of the wave. I hardly recognized the scene, so greatly was it altered. At one point where the bank had been stripped bare to the living rock, a timber gallery had been built round the cliff. But the main lines of communication had been kept open; although everywhere was improvisation.

Terraces of gravel and sand had been left in some bays: they were almost naked, but occasionally one saw a shrub which had withstood the onslaught. Grasses, and a species of mullein were amongst the earliest colonists.

At Paka, the first big village above Tongkyuk, the river splits into two, the main branch coming from the Nambu La, while a large stream flows in at an acute angle from the mountains to the north. In 1924 from both sides of the Nambu La, Cawdor and I when we could see anything at all had seen glaciers and snow peaks up every north valley. At the time we had little reason to think that this was our great snowy range: but it was at least a snowy range. When drawing our route map, however, I began to suspect it was the real thing, and further believed that the north-west valley at Paka would lead us directly to it. Here then we were at Paka; and here too were my coolies calmly trudging on up the main valley towards the Nambu La. Had I been toiling a lifetime towards the golden gates only to be refused admittance because my passport was not in order when at last I reached them, I could not have been more furious. I halted the party and calling Tashi and Pemba, questioned them closely as to what Yuri had said; and they talked long and earnestly with the coolies. I had no fear of double dealing: Colonel Yuri was not the man for that. As for Tashi and Pemba, they shared my enthusiasm and were almost as anxious to see the snow range as I was. Nobody seemed to know where we were bound for; but of course the coolies would be likely to stick to the main path, until forcibly diverted. What I really wanted to know was, were we or were we not going to cross the Nambu La?

'No,' said the leader.

'Right,' said I: and we went on.

After half an hour it became certain that we were continuing up the main valley, and that the Paka stream, at first close to us, was diverging farther to the right. This was more than flesh and blood could endure. I again halted the coolies.

'Are we or are we not going to cross the Nambu La?' I asked.

'Yes,' said the leader.

'Back to Tongkyuk,' said I, in bitter mood.

Reluctantly we turned and trudged down the rough track. It had begun to rain. Tashi had told me of a pass we were to cross, and of a hair-raising trail, which was certainly not on the Nambu La route. He said we were bound for the Po-Yigrong. Yet here were the coolies saying they had been told to take me to the Pasum Tso, a lake which lay far down the other side of the Nambu La! I could make neither head nor tail of it. I had chosen the Nambu La as an arbitrary boundary; by hook or by crook, I must cross the northern range *east* of the Nambu La. I felt that the key to the mystery of the great snowy range was within my grasp. The obvious route seemed to be up the Paka valley. But the coolies said there was no route, although in my book, *The Riddle of the Tsangpo Gorges*, I had categorically stated that there was a route.

In December 1924, Cawdor and I had walked two miles up the valley beyond Paka to a village called Lumo, from where we had seen a snow peak and glaciers. It appeared however that the glaciers completely filled the valley, and the coolies were emphatic that beyond Lumo there was no road. To travel where there is no path in the gorge country of eastern Tibet, a country which in spite of the most appalling obstacles is criss-crossed with paths, is simply asking for trouble; at least without the most careful preparations beforehand. People who have never travelled in this country would hardly believe some of the paths; I was destined to have a taste of the incredible myself before long. If the Tibetans could not follow a route, it was certainly a difficult one.

With a heavy heart, then, I went slowly down the valley towards Tongkyuk. Sheafs of *Lilium Wardii*, growing on a huge rock, above our heads, scented the air. There were a score of plants in a single clump, each with a dozen blooms open, giving a bouquet of some two hundred and fifty sweet scented pink lily blossoms. In that wild setting their beauty was indescribably overpowering, and did something to restore me.

Hardly had we re-crossed the Paka torrent near its confluence with the Tongkyuk river and another torrent which was like any small mountain torrent, than I came up with the coolies who had halted to argue. Presently one of them, hard pressed by Tashi, volunteered the surprising information that the direct route to the Po-Yigrong lay up this small torrent! I might well be astonished. The mountain was as steep as the roof of a house, and the torrent itself came leaping out of a chasm which offered no possible ingress. True, it came from the right direction, that is to say due north; but the wide Paka valley, up which one walked with comparative ease for a mile or two, seemed to offer an infinitely simpler approach to the northern range. However things are not always what they seem in the high mountains of Tibet. Anyhow here was a trail, because at least one man had been on it; he had not merely heard of it.

I told Tashi to make an immediate bargain with the coolies to go to the Po-Yigrong, no matter what the previous arrangement might have been. Nobody seemed to know, anyhow. I offered them a good reward, and after some hesitation they agreed to the new plan, if I would camp for the night at this spot, and let them return to their homes for extra supplies and more coolies. I willingly agreed, whereupon Tashi and Pemba set about putting up the tents. The moist cool glen out of which the torrent poured was filled with a lush growth of temperate herbaceous plants, mixed with shrubs; an association which contrasted strangely with the pine forested outer slopes. I collected three species of impatiens, geranium, salvia, hydrangea, and Piptanthus. There were a number of rampant twining and scrambling plants also, notably *Leptocodon gracile*, which has tubular bells of pale violet, very delicate. That evening I had wild raspberries and milk for supper; I also bought a few green peas which had come from Paka, where I saw peach and quince trees. There are several fruits and crops

cultivated in the deep valleys of Tibet which it would be hopeless to try and grow in the much milder climate of Britain. And yet the Tibetan winters, even at the comparatively low altitude of 7000 or 8000 feet, are far more severe than an ordinary English winter. Why then are these plants not hardy in Britain? The answer I believe is that they *are* hardy, but that while the English winters are not cold enough to harm them, neither are the English summers hot enough to ripen them. They would simply exist, unable to produce flowers, fruits or seed; a useless sort of existence. The climate of Atlantic North America, with its hot summers and cold winters is far more suited to such plants. There is a close correspondence between the climate of many parts of eastern Tibet, and parts of eastern North America. Most plants from this region would grow more successfully round New York than round London.

About dusk who should join us but a solitary traveller who had come from the Po-Yigrong. He sought warmth and lodging, and perhaps company for the night, before continuing his journey. After he had chattered with the men for some time, Tashi came in to tell me his news. It would take us, he said, three or four days to reach the Po-Yigrong, and two more to reach a village called Talu. He was not very sure what happened after that; but by following up the Po-Yigrong, which as shown on present maps – admittedly speculative – came from the north-west, I expected to reach some known point on the Gyalam, or China Post Road, in about a fortnight. This forecast turned out to be reasonably accurate.

The path went straight up the hillside, through high meadow, but after crossing a shoulder, we dropped gradually back to the torrent, and found ourselves in conifer forest and on a comparatively good trail. Whenever the forest thinned out a little, and I could get a bearing, I found we were marching almost due north. When we had gone only a few miles – but that took three hours – I could see the tails of one or two small hanging glaciers higher up the valley; an hour later we reached open meadow.

After leaving the forest we went on for three-quarters of an hour, covering another mile, then camped in the bush; it was two o'clock, so we might easily have gone on some distance, but I had collected so many specimens, and there was such a wealth of plants round me, that I was glad to halt. Moreover, I wanted to get a view of the peaks.

There had been bursts of sunshine, and we could see big patches of blue sky to the south, but the snow peaks themselves were hidden. Looking back over the top of the forest, I noticed a high rocky peak across the Tongkyuk river, almost due south of us. There were no glaciers in that direction. I was surprised at the small extent of forest and the dominance of alpine meadow here, though there were still islands of silver fir and a few other trees on the sheltered slopes above us. We were in an alpine meadow valley, pasture alternating with scrub, and the stream spilling over to form wide meads where bushes grew thickly in the sand. But looking back down the valley, it was evident that we had climbed higher than I thought. The Tongkyuk river, about five miles away and of course invisible, was probably 3000 feet below us. Tongkyuk itself is 8441 feet, and our camp by the river was over 9000 feet. We were now at least 12,000 feet above sea-level, or much the same height as Tumbatse, and with much the same type of vegetation.

And now I must describe in some detail the day's botanical work, since nothing was previously known of the flora of this region.

The main valley between Tongkyuk and Paka is within the pine forest belt, although there are fewer pines and more broad-leafed trees than below Tongkyuk. But no sooner had we entered this narrow gash in the hills, between 9000 and 10,000 feet altitude, than the forest changed completely. The dominant conifer was no longer *Pinus insularis* but Picea with scattered hemlocks (Tsuga) and junipers; *Pinus excelsa* was rarer. Broad-leafed trees were those commonly found in the temperate forests of eastern Tibet, namely birch, maple, holly and oak. The canopy was open; but a second tier of shrubs and smaller trees included a few rhododendrons, honeysuckles, *Quercus Ilex*, and others. The path hugged the steep mountain side above the torrent, and there was a dense undergrowth of ferns and herbaceous flowering plants. I noticed small colonies of *Primula latisecta*, a plant I had discovered in 1924 by the Pasum Tso, on the other side of the Nambu La, about fifty miles to the west. It belongs to the 'Geranioides' or geranium-leafed section, all shade plants found in temperate forests. Farther on grew *P. chungensis*, and beyond that colonies of *P. Whiteii*. But all these forest species were over, and it was not till we came out into the open meadow that I found primulas in flower – *P. alpicola luna*, the moonlight meadow primula, with lambent yellow bells, softened with silver meal, and deliciously scented; and in boggier places *P. Florindae*, the giant cowslip primula, not so giant here as at Tumbatse.

Other flowers of the forest were *Oxalis acetosella*, impatiens, yellow salvia very abundant, thalictrum and presently a small colony of a new species of Ligularia (*L. tongkyukensis* Hand. Mazz.). The ligularias (Senecio) are typical of Tibet; they are mostly big, sometimes coarse, meadow plants, and are often found in astronomical numbers, as the dominant herbs over large tracts of open country. A few are shade plants, growing under rhododendron bushes at fairly high altitudes.

An even more interesting shade plant here was Plectranthus. It has ternate leaves, yet is one of the Labiatae, a family which normally has simple leaves. Unfortunately the flowers were over; but it is not a rare plant.

When we reached the meadow at about 12,000 feet altitude, a wealth of flowers greeted me, and I was kept busy, collecting first those that I did not know at all, and later those that I thought I did. Amongst the first were two fine species of Allium with large pompom heads of purple flowers, and a stout Ligularia with large mace-shaped leaves. *Notholirion campanulatum* was in flower, and there were masses of smaller plants, polygonums, anemones, Pedicularis, Phlomis, Corydalis, geranium, ranunculus, aster, and a deliciously scented ground orchid. The proximity of the great snow peaks to the hot damp gorges in Pome seems to compress the forest zones. The transition from one type to the other is more abrupt, and some types disappear completely. We were now in the topmost zone, silver fir forest (*Abies Webbiana*), and that patchy. Shrubs were scattered about the open valley and in places formed dense almost impenetrable thickets. There was not the variety here that there is in Tsari; willow, honeysuckles (*Lonicera tomentilla, L. Webbiana*), and *Quercus Ilex*, with several species of rhododendron, including the dwarf *R. lepidotum* on rocks and the purple *R. nivale* on the wet sandy chutes, formed the bulk. Here and there between shrubs I noticed *Salvia Wardii*, a robust plant with large leaves and deep violet flowers, in long branching spikes. There were more flowers preparing to scatter their seeds than to open their buds, for winter in Tibet comes with a violent suddenness. However on August 1st there were still a lot of plants in bloom, with all the gentians and cyananthus to follow. In the high places of the earth plants flower when they can, as I was to learn next day.

Meadow plants whose seeds were almost ripe included Trollius and *Primula bellidifolia*; and there were several others. But although most of the June flowering plants, including those great patrician genera, rhododendron and primula, were over, there were still many alpine plants in flower. This was in a south valley, in which the snow melts early.

It was about three o'clock when we camped, and I wandered about for an hour or two collecting plants, then retired to my tent to write up field notes and have some tea. We had passed a bothy a mile back, but it had not been recently occupied, and there was no sign of herds here. But the bottom of the valley was mostly water and thick bush, and the flanks were mostly forest, cliffs and screes. In fact the pasture was really limited to intermittent patches consisting of tall moist meadow of a type ill suited for grazing.

After blue sky at dawn, it had clouded up rather fast, as it so often does in this land of high and deep, even in the finest season. From time to time the sun had broken through, and shone for half an hour, and it was warm and pleasant in the green valley. At five o'clock, the sky was completely overcast, yet it hardly looked like rain.

It was about six when Tashi came running across to my tent, which I had closed against a rather chilly wind.

'Sahib! Sahib! Come outside quickly! Look! Look!' I heard him shout.

CHAPTER XV

TRIUMPH AT LAST

At Tashi's shout I jumped up and ran outside. Ever since we emerged from the forest, only the dribbling snouts of glaciers to the north, and the dark heavily timbered ranges to the south had been visible below the cloud ceiling. Now the ceiling was breaking up in swirling eddies. Rents and holes of turquoise blue appeared in the soft marble whiteness, and vanished, to reappear elsewhere as new eddies formed. It was as though some giant were pouring rivers of milk into a limpid sea, clouding it for an instant until the currents swept it away. The opaque fluid still hung in streaks and clots. The struggle between mist and dry air continued, but the final result was never in doubt. Quicker and quicker the air drank up the mist until as the last shreds of curd dissolved depths of infinite blue stood revealed. Now the whole valley was sunning itself like a gorgeous butterfly which has just cast off its chrysalis shell.

'Look Sahib! It is like the view of Kinchinjunga from Darjeeling!' Even the stolid, unemotional Tashi was moved.

I gasped. The valley, which had looked big before, had suddenly become dwarfed. A mile above our camp the slope began to rise more sharply; terrace succeeded terrace, each steeper than the last. At the head was a high jagged wall, joining two snow peaks, and one could see where the Soḅhé La crossed it, if not the actual pass; it was four or five miles off. This was the only gap in a glittering semi-circle of snow, the highest peak lying to the west of the pass. I counted five hanging glaciers — none of them reached the main valley. We were clasped within the icy claws of gigantic pincers. Snow peaks rose directly over our camp, like the spires of a cathedral above the cottages which cluster round its base. It was impossible even to estimate their height; I can only say that they were more than 20,000 feet high.

If any lingering doubt remained, it was now finally set at rest. We were in the heart of the mysterious snowy range of Pome. The lost range was found! The enormous flight of bergs which Cawdor and I had seen far off, eleven years earlier, arching across the world for over a hundred miles, a glittering skyway joining east and west, was here in front of me. No wonder I felt uplifted!

For some minutes Tashi and Pemba, who had now joined us, and I stood there looking up the valley. The sun had dropped behind the ridge on our left; but his last rays still shone on the peaks at the head of the valley, and on those to the east of us. Violet shadows crept swiftly over the glaciers. The valley, roofed with its ribbon of darkening sky, now looked like some wonderful fjord with the sky for deep sea, and fantastic white rocks plunging down into its depths; it was all upside down, but it was easy to believe oneself gazing into a mirror. Everything in that light was ethereal, almost spiritualized; and presently when I heard the sound of distant song I was not very surprised. There was a solemn hush about the mountains with their changing lights, the ghostly peaks shining through the oncoming darkness, the red shafts from the setting sun which still sprayed through the western wall and caught the tops of the spires opposite, and the abyss of the Tongkyuk river far below. I was in that fanciful mood, when one might hear voices singing. Perhaps I was half asleep; certainly it was all like a dream, if a dream come true. It gave me rather a shock therefore to see a group of black specks moving down the meadow beyond the next belt of trees. Not men surely! Spirits? The singing drew nearer; men's voices! They *were* men, and presently they came into camp, a happy band of pilgrims; they had been singing to scare away evil spirits as night came on. They had seen the smoke of our camp fire and approached joyfully.

I ate my simple supper with relish. Then Tashi came into my

tent to tell me all the news. The visitors were Kampa pilgrims on their way to Lhasa. They had been working in the corn fields of the Yigrong during the harvest, to earn enough money to enable them to continue their journey. They had intended to go down the Yigrong valley and round to Tongkyuk by the ordinary winter route. But in summer it is impossible to get down the lower Yigrong, and so they had made the arduous traverse of the snow range via the Sobhé La and would reach Tongkyuk the next day. Of course, their quickest route to Lhasa was up the Yigrong valley, or at any rate up the Tongkyuk river and over the Nambu La. But there is no rhyme or reason in the routes chosen by pilgrims. It seemed they wished to visit certain monasteries, especially Temo Gompa, which is a very holy place, and other shrines in the Tsangpo valley.

As may be imagined I was up early on August 2nd. I had waited eleven years for this day, the day I would cross the last mountains; and I wanted it to last a long time. The temperature in my tent went down to 40° F. but the air was keener outside, and a heavy dew drenched the meadow.

It was scarcely light when I got up and dressed, but the dawn came swiftly. The sky was incomparably blue, and the arc of snow peaks looked as sharp as crystal quartz. But no sooner had the sun heaved itself above the embattled ranges to the east, than the atmosphere began to smoke and a thin mist went curling up, to dissolve and reform, gathering round the snow peaks as though to warm their cold hearts. Up to ten o'clock there was sunshine, and the views were intermittent.

I had an early breakfast, and started off for the pass with one man carrying my camera. Had I been on the pass when I started from camp, I should have had wonderful views, but unfortunately, long before I got there, the cold range had drawn up all the moisture from the warm valleys, and the peaks had sunk in a cloudy sea. This was only to be expected in August; I was lucky not to have had to cross the pass in teeming rain.

As I was leaving I remembered that the previous day the

tea in my thermos flask had not been very hot. I called out to Tashi to fill the flask with strong boiling tea, and added – rather gratuitously – '*not* cold water'; Tashi is a little deaf.

The Sobhé La was not more than four miles away in a direct line, perhaps five as we went; but it was hard going and the ascent of 4000 feet made it a grind. It took us four hours to get there, partly owing to the fact that I and my companion took a 'short cut' – which added an hour.

For a mile or two we had to make our way through thick willow scrub and over hassocks and tussocks of *Rhododendron nivale* still covered with a froth of purple flowers. The only path was the bed of the stream, where a foot of icy water rattled over the stones; and we had to paddle across numerous streams which burst in over wide alluvial fans. As we forced our way through the bushes, water showered on us, so we got soaked anyhow. Gradually we left the scrub and the last scattered silver firs behind. Then there opened out before us a limitless wilderness of boulders and gravel, in a series of immense overlapping moraines. The ascent became steeper and steeper. I saw the fretted ridge far above us, and made straight for it, ignoring a valley to the left, which happened to be the way to the pass. We had long since lost sight of any track, and were clambering up the sliding mounds of gravel as one might clamber up the side of a lunar crater, having landed unexpectedly on the moon. My coolie did not know the way any more than I did. It was not till we found ourselves on some awkward crags, which we could not climb, that we began seriously to take stock of the position; we were still hundreds of feet from the crest of the ridge, and I had to confess that this route simply did not 'go'. Looking back, we caught sight of the last coolie disappearing up the valley to the left.

Meanwhile I had noticed many scattered high alpine plants; the sky-blue poppy *Meconopsis speciosa* and the sulphur *M. integrifolia*, *Primula sikkimensis*, or *P. alpicola luna*, or both; and young plants of the giant rhubarb, *Rheum nobile*, pale yellow cones destined to elongate into pagodas encased in bracts. The only other rhododendron besides *R. nivale* was the aromatic leafed *R. anthopogon*.

There were only two possible routes to the pass, and we had certainly chosen the wrong one. I looked at my coolie and he looked at me. He said, '*Dro-sa min-duk*' ('There is no going place', i.e. no road); and I felt that he was entirely right. A cracked and broken ridge separated us from the other valley. The choice lay between retracing our steps, and descending a thousand (or more) feet, before striking the path; or trying to cross the ridge and descending to the path higher up. I disliked the idea of going back and decided to risk the ridge. It was no easy walk to the top; we scrambled up a gully. From the crest of the dividing ridge we looked down into the other valley, and saw the coolies far below; the pass itself was out of sight round the corner. We must have been almost on a level with it, but there was not the slightest hope of getting along the top of our ridge to the pass; spiky rock towers and sheer cliffs on both sides made that out of the question. As it was, we had reached the highest point it was possible to reach, nor was I yet certain that we could get down the precipitous slope in front of us. Luckily for us, we got into snow in some of the worst places, and descending on a long slant, reached the path at last. It was not, I felt, an ideal short cut.

The coolies were ahead of us; but the last 500 feet of the ascent was so precipitous, that we reached the top as soon as they did. Meanwhile, the sky had grown completely overcast, and all the snow peaks we had seen from camp were hidden, only the tails of the glaciers being visible. This was unfortunate; yet so close under the high peaks were we, that we would have had a poor view of the great range, even on the clearest day.

If the view southwards to the Tongkyuk river was disappointing, the view northwards was worse. There was no view. As soon as I reached the pass I dodged behind a rock to get out of the howling wind; and now I found myself looking straight into a blank wall of grey mist. There was nothing for it but to sit down and wait.

The height of the Sobhé La is a matter of guesswork, but no Tibetan traveller will accuse me of gross exaggeration if I call it 16,000 feet. The Nambu La, which is covered with vegetation including dwarf rhododendron, is about 15,000 feet: and the Temo La is the same. But there were no plants on the Sobhé La, and on the north slope there was a lot of snow, even in August. The Drichung La, a like pass which I had crossed in June, is about 17,000 feet, and the Sobhé La is not much less. Passes 17,000 to 18,000 feet high are usual in Tibet.

Our general direction up the valley had been almost due north. But now we had swung round, so that we crossed the range on a line roughly WSW-ENE., then gradually worked back north again during the descent.

At last there came a temporary break in the clouds, and I saw the gleam of water far below, and then snow peaks. I was looking down a narrow gorge, and had a glimpse of the Po-Yigrong framed between cliffs; across the river I saw cultivated slopes, and beyond that again two lofty snow peaks. Then the clouds closed again like a shutter.

The south side was as I have said steep; but the north side was precipitous. Almost immediately we got off the broken rocks on to a hard snow slope tilted at about 70°. A climber would have roped his party here, and cut steps. Not so my coolies. We had no rope, nor did that fact dismay them. The party of the previous night had stamped – not cut – a track, and we followed. It was a wonderful sight to watch these men calmly traverse that snow face in single file. A false step meant certain death; and they sang songs. I was scared; but I was the only one who was. We met another party of pilgrims shortly after we left the top. There were two women, one of whom carried her baby in a basket on her back.

Presently we left the snow and found ourselves going

cautiously down an almost precipitous rock ridge placing our feet in rough steps. For a thousand or fifteen hundred feet the descent was more arduous than the ascent had been.

At length we came to the rim of a green bowl, and the slope eased off. It had taken us an hour and ten minutes to come the half mile from the pass, and the Sobhé La may fairly be described as difficult. Besides it is only open for three months in the year. No doubt in exceptional seasons one might cross it before July, or after September, but I should not care to be caught on it in a snowstorm, or in thick weather at any time of year.

This snow range is not a rain screen, at least not at this end where the monsoon current has free access to the gorges. The north side was no drier than the south: but because the snow was deeper on the north side, and lay much longer, the ground was better watered, and we soon came to alpine vegetation.

The green bowl seemed a good place to halt for lunch. It was chilly, but we were out of the wind. The climbing of the last two hours had exhausted me. It would be pleasant to rest for half an hour, and warm one's inside with hot tea. I sat down on the grass, and Tashi brought my thermos flask. I unscrewed the top and took out the cork, and poured out a cupful of — ice-cold water!

On our right was a deep gully, partly filled by a glacier from a peak north-east of the pass. The glacier had shrunk far down into its bed leaving a high earth cliff. Pushing through a fringe of rhododendron bushes which lined the edge of the cliff, we scrambled down to the glacier; after that the going to the bottom of the bowl, over the crisp snow, was better.

We were now in a marsh, fringed with rhododendron bushes, and buzzing with innumerable flies. On a rocky mound which poked through the bog stood a herd's bothy, but I saw no cattle, nor did there appear to be any grazing, only bog, rock, and glacier. We halted here for half an hour. The sun peeped out; and but for the myriads of flies it was pleasant. By this time I felt I could eat a biscuit, which previously with nothing but cold water in my flask, I had been unable to swallow.

We were, as I have said, at the bottom of a gigantic bowl, formed by the semi-circle of peaks. To the north-west, that is on our left front, a fine snow mountain flung a large glacier almost across the bowl, half blocking the exit and giving origin to the bog. A second glacier overhung the bog. Thus at least three glaciers were pouring their waters into the green bowl, from the lower end of which the stream was trying to escape. It had to squeeze between the foot of the glacier and the opposite cliff, through the narrowest of passages, before leaping over the lip of the bowl into the forested valley below.

The sky was heavily overcast, but now one could get a rough idea of the landscape. Peaks more than 20,000 feet high rose on three sides of us, so close that even had the sky been clear they would not have looked impressive. Their flanks were festooned with glaciers, converging on the bowl, at the bottom of which we stood like ants in a bath tub.

Meanwhile I had not neglected to note and collect plants, and I may begin with three species of dwarf rhododendrons in full bloom on the rocks which fringed the bog. These were *R. pumilum*, *R. riparium*, and *R. trichocladum* – and they grew mixed with dwarf willow. *Rhododendron pumilum* is a dwarf undershrub with pink flowers borne singly on long pedicils; *R. riparium* another dwarf, forming tussocks, has purple flowers borne in compact heads so close together that the whole plant is smothered with bloom. *R. trichocladum* is larger, with greenish-yellow butterfly-shaped flowers and deciduous leaves.

To return to the pass: coming down the precipitous gravel slope I found two new species of gentian with delicate cobalt-blue flowers. They were not large enough to be conspicuous, nor numerous enough to paint the hillside; in fact, to tell the truth, I only just spied them, and they impressed me more as botanical than as horticultural discoveries. However, *Gentiana Sherriffii* (named in honour of the Tibetan plant explorer, Captain G. Sherriff, who also found, and I believe introduced it a year or two later) would make an excellent rock garden plant. The other, *G. pseudophyllocalyx*, is smaller and perhaps less cult-worthy, although it is not to be despised.

Other plants seen were the small purple flowered *Allium Forrestii*, quite a pretty thing; a yellow flowered primula which might have been either a pale *P. sikkimensis* or a broad-leafed *P. alpicola luna*; *Nomocharis nana*, an anemone, its leaves covered with a mat of silver hairs, soft and glistening as floss silk, a potentilla also with brightly silvered leaves due to protecting hairs — this formed small carpeting colonies studded with large yellow button flowers; and the bent red pokers of *Polygonum Griffithii*. The highest alpines met with, hardly lower than the pass itself, were Diapensia, *Primula dryadifolia* var. *Jonarduni*, *P. purpurea*, and a composite. The south side of the pass, where very little snow remained except in a few sheltered places, was indeed impoverished; and what plants I saw were half starved, as they might well be in such a bitter hungry soil. No yak grazed here, and the soil was short of nitrogen.

I am convinced that this great snowy range will offer a rich harvest of novelties to the next botanical explorer.

After resting half an hour at the log hut, which was occupied by a man who had come to meet Yuri, we started down the valley, splashing ankle deep, in places knee deep, through the chilly glacier water. The stream, already quite large, was swift and deep; but it had not cut a channel deep enough to carry off all the water which poured into the bowl, consequently it overflowed. It was difficult in places to see where the channel was — until I suddenly stepped into it, almost waist deep. However, the bowl must have been a lake quite recently, and when more silt has been washed into it from the glaciers it will become dry land.

There were no rhododendrons in the marsh: they ceased abruptly as soon as we left the rocks. But there were other plants, including a second species of willow, horsetails, sedges, grasses, and Luzula, with an abundance of soft sphagnum moss.

At last we came to the end of the bog, where the stream suddenly plunged with a roar over a precipice and seemed to be tumbling down an endless flight of stone steps. It was a remarkable sight, this abrupt change from placid marsh to dynamic action. The track followed the crest of a high moraine on the left bank. We descended very steeply, past the snout of the glacier which had recently blocked all exit from the basin, the torrent tumbling through the natural sluice with a crash and a roar, on our right. One side of the moraine was covered with shrubs, but we soon reached the forests of silver fir and tree rhododendrons which filled the glen below the waterfall.

So far it would have been almost impossible for anyone unacquainted with the route to have followed it, but after leaving the moraine we got on to a path. At the foot of the fall, with the torrent, now vastly swollen, plunging headlong down the valley, we had to cross to the right bank by a flimsy log bridge. There was nothing to hold on to, and having lagged behind to collect plants, I found myself alone. I am no braver than my fellow men, probably less so, and am not ashamed to confess that the sight of this bridge almost unnerved me. Half-deafened by the noise, my head reeling at the savage rush of water, cold and hungry, I crept slowly across the wretched bridge to safety, thinking every moment would be my last.

I was surprised to find that Colonel Yuri really was coming by this heroic route, for men had very recently been along to clear the way, slashing the branches off the bushes on either side of the path. It was more than they could do to make the rough way smooth, but they had done what they could. Logs had been thrown across streams, tree trunks laying across the track had been cut up. The Colonel was expected any day now. I wondered whether he would ride and if so what — Tibetan officers hate walking. We ourselves had brought ponies as far as the first meadows, close to our camp on the other side, but had sent them back to Tongkyuk from there. On this side, they could have come up to the bridge. I do not think either ponies or yak could cross the Sobhé La, certainly not the north side of it. They might be dragged and pushed over unladen; but it would be simpler to have meeting convoys, using human transport for actually crossing the pass.

By this time I was feeling extremely hungry and dead beat, having had scarcely anything to eat since early morning. My companions were some distance ahead, or I would have told them to halt anywhere, although there did not appear to be a possible halting place hereabouts. Suddenly to my great joy I heard the sound of somebody chopping wood, and knew that camp was being made. Turning a corner, I caught sight of my tent pitched in the forest, and a curl of smoke going up from a fire. It was five o'clock, and we had been going for nine hours.

That night I tried to discover where I was, from my own observations. It seemed that we were twelve or fourteen miles north of the Tongkyuk river, and must very soon reach the Po-Yigrong — the river we had glimpsed from the pass. I estimated that from our previous camp to the Sobhé La was about four miles, and another three from the pass to our camp. Thus we had taken eight hours to do six or seven miles. Such is travel in the mighty gorges of Tibet.

August 3rd dawned no less crystal clear than the previous day, the only difference being that the clouds formed more rapidly. I had an hour's writing to do before we started, because the night before I had done no work except put my plants in the press. This I always did as soon as we reached camp, no matter how long the day; otherwise they were wasted.

We were camped in a little meadow where a glacier stream rushed through the forest, which I found to be full of the purple lily-flowered *Notholirion campanulatum* and Rodgersia, a tall herb with dense bunches of small white flowers borne on the end of a bare stem, surrounded by large independent leaves shaped like those of a horse chestnut. The forest consisted principally of silver fir and rhododendrons of several species, but as we descended more and more temperate deciduous trees appeared, also hemlock.

We continued down the right bank of the big glacier torrent, keeping close to it, on a bearing a little east of north.. On occasions we had a clear view up stream, and caught a glimpse of glaciers and snow peaks with the clouds frothing amongst them. The streams we crossed were all born amongst glaciers. It was the most awesome and tremendous scenery I had passed through since we left the plains more than three months ago. The forest was full of amazing trees and shrubs. One tree had leaves very like a chestnut (Castanea) but I could not identify it for certain without flowers or fruit. There were oaks, maples, hollies, and many other kinds. After descending the valley for four hours, we stopped for half an hour and lunched. Gigantic hemlocks and pines (*P. excelsa*) appeared. These last few miles were through some of the finest and most beautiful forest I have ever seen in Tibet. We must have come down a long way, because I noticed a climbing fig, and the charming yellow flowered *Briggsia longifolia*, which is a sub-tropical epiphyte, grew on the mossy tree trunks. I reckoned we were down to 9000 or even 8000 feet by this time: and still we went down.

Without warning, the narrow ravine widened, the forest ceased; we were on the edge of a level plain, as it seemed. To our left was a stout bridge over the glacier torrent. We crossed it and surprised a crowd of Pobas, seated round a fire. At sight of me they all sprang up, took off their hats, put out their tongues, and spread out their hands – the Tibetan greeting to an official.

'Welcome, great Chief, welcome.' They bowed low.

I felt slightly embarrassed.

CHAPTER XVI

MYSTERY RIVER

THEY gave me a royal reception by the Po-Yigrong! Carpets, woven in Lhasa, were spread; buttered tea was quickly prepared and poured into silver-lined bowls, both for me and for my personal following. We were invited to seat ourselves on the ground, and a low wooden table was set before us, with tsamba, fruit, and tea.

Tashi, in a rapid aside, told me that the Pobas were awaiting the arrival of Colonel Yuri whom they expected every day. When we turned up they had naturally mistaken me for him. I seemed fated to be mistaken for anybody except myself on this fantastic journey!

How easy it would be, I reflected, to impose on these simple people, and give out that I was the new dzongpön, sent from Lhasa! Or adopting a religious bearing, proclaim myself a Holy Man, a Reformer, even a new Messiah! But could I keep up the deception?

As a boy I had read of 'Dr. Nikola', that arch-impostor in the cause of science who, disguised as a great Lama, had lifted the veil of the most sacred and secret monastery in Tibet long before anyone had ever heard of Changri La. In fact, it was 'Dr. Nikola' who had fired my youthful ambition and in later years set my feet on the road to Tibet.

I had little trouble explaining to the Pobas that I was not Colonel Yuri, but I think they were disappointed when they realized the truth.

The Pobas now led us to their village, called Temo Chamna, close to the river. On reaching the plain, which was well cultivated, we had turned sharp left, that is to the west, and presently we reached a village of small scattered wooden houses.

The fields were strongly fenced, and contained cattle, but no yak.

It was a deliciously warm sunny afternoon, with spacious views all round. The plain was about eight miles long and a mile wide, clearly a silted-up lake basin. After tea I strolled across some fallow sandy fields to the river. Its size and speed surprised me, it seemed greater than the Po-Tsangpo, of which it forms no more than half; the other half being the Showa river called Po-Chu. But I saw the Po-Tsangpo in December, and I was looking at the Po-Yigrong in August. Tibetan rivers, especially in the eastern part of the country, completely change their appearance winter and summer, and the larger the river the greater the transformation.

The Po-Yigrong flows from west-north-west almost due east, then turns gradually southwards at the other end of the plain which was hidden from view by a spur. To the west a large tributary joins in, rushing through a gorge from a group of snow peaks to the north-west. In fact the plain is ringed by ranges of snow mountains, the glaciers on the northern range being visible, as those round the Sobhé La would be from the north side. I regretted I had no time to go round the lake, and view the Sobhé La from the other side of the river. Northwards I could see bare granite peaks, as well as clusters of snow peaks. Towards the south-west was another group of stark peaks, continuing the range into Pemako. All these rock peaks are on outliers of the main range, not on the main range itself.

The fact that there are snow mountains on both sides of the Po-Yigrong is interesting.

The river, grey with glacier mud, was strewn with dead timber, whole trees sticking out of the sand. A number of short dugouts, more like coracles than boats, were drawn up on the bank, and fishing nets were spread out to dry. I did not get any fish here, but rather to my surprise I did get fresh milk, and some potatoes.

The corn was ripe in the fields, for Temo Chamna is only 7300 feet above sea level; even in winter it is not very cold here. At 4 p.m. the temperature inside my tent was still 77° F.

The valley is thickly populated for Tibet and I saw a number of villages on the left bank of the river. The whole district is called Po-Yigrong or simply Yigrong and is really part of the tribal province called Pome, although under the Jongpen of Tongkyuk. The people are Pobas. At the west end of the plain, perched on a mound where the two rivers unite, is a small monastery, Samling Gompa. Not far from Samling Gompa, on the left bank of the river, is Tongbe Dzong.

F. M. Bailey, who with the late Major H. T. Morshead, R.E., discovered the Po-Yigrong in 1913, records that a lake was formed here about the end of last century owing to a landslide blocking the lower end of the valley. There is ample evidence of a great flood in the Dihang river at that time, and its effects were felt throughout the hills as far as the plains of Assam. Such floods are not very rare although perhaps seldom on the scale of the Yigrong flood. The fact that the wide plateau valleys are pinched into bottle necks lower down would encourage the formation of dams, and lead to floods.

The Po-Yigrong lake is about the same length as the plain — eight or ten miles long perhaps and half a mile wide. At its western end the water is flowing swiftly for its full breadth, so that it looks like a river. But at its south-eastern end the current is slacker and it has more the appearance of a lake. All this was hidden from my view owing to the bend. It is probable that during the Pleistocene glaciation, glaciers from the west ploughed out this valley, and that when the ice retreated a big lake was left behind. Later the Po-Yigrong cut its gorge to join the Po-Tsangpo and the lake emptied itself. That happened many thousands of years ago.

The journey down the Po-Yigrong to the confluence appears to be very difficult if not impossible during the rainy season. It takes four days to reach Showa and the same to Tongkyuk; but even the pilgrims go by the Sobhé La, and do not attempt the lower road.

The plain is rather dry, as the snow peaks on either side take the bulk of the rain. There are a few trees, chiefly willows in the villages, and shrubs are scattered about. The only noteworthy herbaceous plants I noticed in the fields were an aster, Verbascum, Phytolacca, and a crimson-flowered ground orchid, *Spiranthes sinensis*.

After a warm night, minimum temperature 60° F. with heavy dew, the fine weather of the last few days came to an end. August 4th was cloudy, showers alternating with bursts of sunshine. I decided to follow up the Po-Yigrong, if possible to its source. The Tongkyuk coolies went back, and a fresh relay from Temo Chamna took over; they were to take me to a village called Ragoonka, several days' march up the gorge.

Starting at 8.20 on a bearing two points north of west we reached the end of the plain and of cultivation in an hour. Immediately beyond a large glacier stream men were ploughing the light sandy soil, using cattle for draught animals. Presently we were clambering up an old moraine, covered with pine trees. As we got deeper into the gorge the forest rapidly grew richer in species. Under the big trees there was a second tier of large shrubs and smaller trees, such as *Rhododendron niphargum*, hydrangea, Lonicera, and laurels; here and there were colonies of a tall coarse-leafed labiate (Notochaete) with purple flowers, and of impatiens, and I noticed such plants as Chirita, Sarcococca, and another more curious undershrub allied to the barberries *Caulophyllum robustum*, Podophyllum, Arisaema, Elatostemma, polygonum and *Pyrola uniflora*. There were many big lianas – vines, Lonicera, clematis, and others, and the trees were festooned with moss and smothered with epiphytic ferns.

Before noon we halted half an hour for lunch – not our first halt either – having come three or four miles from Temo Chamna; ahead of us was a high buttress. We had been ascending gradually ever since we entered the gorge and were now several hundred feet above the river which we heard but could not see. Progress through the gorge of the Yigrong was going to be almost as laborious as it had been through the gorge of the Tsangpo eleven years previously. But not quite. There is no trail through the Tsangpo gorge below Pemakochung; it was go as you like, or rather as you could. Here we were on a path, albeit a rough one. Of the difficulties and dangers which lay ahead I had as yet no inkling.

After the lunch halt we toiled up to the top of a ridge, a mile long climb through grand forest. The veteran trees were of great girth, but I could not distinguish what they were except a species of oak, and another beautiful tree with large compound leaves which may have been either Cedrela or Ailanthus. The canopy was close, and the tangle of big vines, the wealth of moss and epiphytes, and the luxuriant undergrowth made identification, and even collecting, difficult. I think, however, that this mixed semi-evergreen moist temperate forest was confined to a narrow belt lining the bottom of the gorge and that a few hundreds of feet up the cliff, one would come to more stereotyped forest with some dominant conifer, either hemlock or pine. We were at least 8000 feet above sea-level, and completely hemmed in by gigantic ranges of snow mountains. Moisture was assured, but only at the bottom of the gorge could there be enough warmth, shelter, and perpetual damp to nourish such forest as this.

From the top of the ridge we could see nothing, but a short steep descent brought us to a powerful torrent which came from the south. There being very little traffic through the gorge, it is nobody's business to attend to bridges and that sort of thing, at least across minor torrents. This bridge consisted of a tree trunk, and was rather sketchy. Ascending the far bank, which comprised a series of boulder-strewn terraces arranged in echelon, we camped on one of the higher terraces amidst lush herbaceous undergrowth – evidently an old clearing. It was about two o'clock; but our actual marching time, excluding short halts, was not much over four hours, and we had penetrated about two miles into the gorge.

I went for a scramble round camp. We were some little distance from the river, and high above it. I tried to reach it via the torrent but soon came to impassable cliffs; in fact between the exit from the gorge and Talu, we rarely saw the Po-Yigrong itself. The walls were sheer and naked; I could see the north wall rising from the invisible river for many hundreds of feet, shutting out the ribbon of sky from my view. The forest was filled with the thunder of waters, and rather baffled by the noise and darkness, I not only lost my way, but for a time my bearings. For half an hour I searched in vain for our camp, nor was it till I had descended again to the torrent, and worked both up and down stream that I picked up the trail and ascended to the terrace where the men had lit a big smoky fire and pitched my tent.

They were fine fellows, these Pobas from Yigrong, beautifully made, like a sculptor's model. The Greek athlete has been held up as the classic example of human physical perfection, but many of the eastern Tibetan mountaineers are equally well-built. Some of the Pobas, like so many of the Eastern Tibetans, are tall and lithe, yet one would not say they were of athletic build; they are more of the 'strong man' type. Another curious thing is the number of Pobas who have naturally curly hair, instead of the lank straight locks one expects a Tibetan to have.

Nothing in the Yigrong gorge surprised me more than the abundant and varied bird life. It is clear that birds are not persecuted here with the same ruthless determination that they are in other parts of Asia, in spite of the fact that there is no moral law against taking life in Pome. Had I the means, and the time, I might have made a most valuable collection of birds and small mammals here. This day I shot an Indian red-billed liothrix (*Liothrix lutea calipyga*) and collected a few beetles, including an extremely active tiger beetle.

August 5th turned out fine, although it was cloudy at the start after a night of rain. We made little progress up the gorge in five and a half hours' marching, but the way was hard, and I was fully occupied with my botanical work. I was torn between two incompatible urges: a desire to press on quickly, since we were plunging ever deeper into the unknown, and I wanted to be back in India by the end of October; and a desire to march slowly, so that I could make as good a botanical collection as possible.

Although we had only just crossed a big glacier torrent, the day's march began with a steep up and down climb round a re-entrant. We were on the more sheltered side of the gorge, and the cliffs were covered with forest: but we had to keep on climbing in order to cross even the smallest stream which had eaten through to the living rock, high up; there was no other way. Having crossed a small stream slithering down the cliff, we climbed once more. Looking back I caught sight of the head of Yigrong plain, bearing a point south of east and, as I estimated, about six miles away. The path now plunged down the flank of a spur for several hundred feet, until I thought we really should reach the river. We did not; we were still considerably above it, and now we worked away from it once more, climbing again. But I caught more than one glimpse of roaring waters. The river raced along, a furious welter of foam.

There was a terrifying fascination in watching this huge force at work, which was able to destroy utterly whatever tried to thwart it, yet for the moment was held like a tiger in chains. Here in the gorge you feel that the defence has beaten the attack. Nothing could dint that granite armour, towering a thousand feet sheer above the water line, and reinforced below it with blocks of stone as big as the dome of St. Paul's.

There appear to be vertical falls, though of no great height, between Talu and the plain. Such falls or rapids on a main river generally occur at the confluence of tributaries, and it is probable that there was one near our first, and another near our second camp – both camps were situated on big glacier torrents. But I am doubtful whether it is possible to get down to the river, even at low water. The few glimpses I had suggested that, like the Tsangpo, it filled the gorge from wall to wall. At no point between the plain and Talu were we less than two hundred feet above the river, and more often than not we were a thousand feet above it, buried in the forest.

The gorge of the Yigrong impressed me more even than that of the Tsangpo had done, perhaps because I had not expected such violent scenery. But more terrific sights were to come.

Our general direction was still slightly north of west, but I reckoned that as our pace up the gorge could not average more than half a mile an hour, we were not making much northing. After halting three-quarters of an hour for lunch, we made better progress for a time, but at 2.45 we had to camp by a big stream from 218° (i.e. practically south-west).

It was a pleasant sunny afternoon, comfortably warm without being hot; such fine weather in August is unusual. It was curious to see the coolies covered with flies; I don't know where they came from.

The blue weeping pine (*P. excelsa*) was abundant now, and this is a tree which will not stand excessive rain, certainly not a combination of rain and heat, such as the moist heat of Sikkim; I suspected that the gorge was becoming drier as we went west. *Rhododendron niphargum* reached a huge size; I have never seen larger rhododendrons. Many trees were six to eight feet in girth, and must have been two or three centuries old. What a wonderful sight the gorge would be in the spring! But when I examined the trees closely, I could see no sign of their having flowered the previous year, or the year before that. Nor were they going to flower next year, since they did not bear any flower-buds. Were the trees so old that they were past flowering at all? It looked like it.

Hemlock had become common again, and I noticed at least three species of oak, some of them enormous trees. Cedrela was tall, graceful and slim, not bulky like many other trees, and there were small laurels (Litsaea), and yew. I was surprised to see so few species of rhododendrons, but these though very conspicuous in flower are easily passed over at other times; and although *R. pankimense* was the only other species I noticed, there may well have been several I missed. Of small plants on the ground there were plenty, notably saprophytes (species of Monotropa) and ground orchids. Climbing plants such as clematis, Zanthoxylum, *Cyanchum auriculatum*, and *Lonicera Henryi* were also abundant. Here and there one came upon colonies of salvia or Strobilanthes, big coarse herbs with brightly coloured flowers: and scattered undershrubs such as *Desmodium repandum*, with purple flowers in long racemes, like wistaria.

In the afternoon sunshine I heard a bird singing just like an English blackbird; also parokeets screeching. The latter (*Psittacula Darbyanus*), are large brilliantly coloured birds, the male having a rosy red bill. After dark sand flies were troublesome, a sure sign that we were approaching conifer forest, in which they thrive. My tent also became a refuge for many Tipulidae (daddy-long-legs), stupid insects which seem quite incapable of managing so many legs.

Rain began in the night, and fell steadily. It ceased shortly after we started the next morning, but the clouds remained low. Crossing the torrent, we climbed to the top of a ridge and saw the Po-Yigrong below us. The gorge opened out into another plain, and there were thirty or forty huts in view, with intermittent cultivation on the left bank for a mile; fewer on the right bank. We were looking down on to fields and villages again.

The mountain had slipped here, taking the path with it, and we had to descend a dreadful mud slide, clambering over fallen trees. Arrived at the bottom, we came to a rope bridge, and preparations were made for our first crossing of the Po-Yigrong. It did not look a pleasant business, and in fact had the water been a foot higher it would have been impossible. As it was the rope sagged so much that passengers struck the water near the far bank. A few hundred yards below the bridge, the river swept magnificently into the gorge.

The Pobas pulled themselves across, and it was a good long haul; but the baggage was pulled across with a rope, and so was I. The river was wide and turbulent, with a current of eight or ten knots. It looked a typical grey glacier river, thick with impalpable mud. The rope, a quarter of an inch in diameter, was made of roughly plaited bamboo, fastened to stout wooden posts on each bank, and on it travelled a triangle of hard flat wood, with a notch cut in either arm to secure a rope of twisted yak hair, forming the base. To this rope the passenger tied himself with leather thongs, in such manner that his arms were free and he could pull himself over. Neither the bamboo rope, nor the yak hair rope, nor the leather rope, looked very strong; and the slider was awkward. You felt that the friction, and the jerking motion inseparable from the method of hauling would put too great a strain on it. Once in the river, the strongest swimmer would have been helpless. Yet accidents are, I believe, rare. It was not a nice bridge, but I have no particular fear of Tibetan rope bridges, and the crossing did not worry me.

The day was still young when we reached the village of Talu, less than half a mile from the bridge. We had started at 9 that morning, and by 10.30 had reached the top of the cliff, and were looking down into the comparatively broad cultivated and inhabited valley, not unlike the Yigrong basin we had lately left, but smaller. The descent to the river had taken an hour; and although crossing the river took a long time, it was now only two o'clock. We had advanced about three miles from our last camp, and the total length of the gorge between the two plains was eight or ten miles. It was a wet afternoon, and the view was poor. I could not see a single snow peak in any direction, and began to wonder what could have become of my great range. However, the sight of a glacier across the river to the south-west restored my confidence in its existence.

The houses of Talu are of timber on stone foundations. The inhabitants were friendly but a little shy. They were grubby, under-sized, and ugly. I found to my joy that I could get milk here, also fowls, eggs, and flour; I could even buy a sheep if I wanted one; but no vegetables were obtainable.

The whole open valley – it is hardly a plain – with its three villages is called Tagé, just as the lower one is called Yigrong. I had to stay here on August 7th while the coolies prepared food for the next stage of the journey. It rained all day, and I worked in my tent. The most beautiful plant I saw here was *Lilium Wardii* which became ever more abundant as we marched westwards into the pine country. But it does not extend far north of the 30th parallel or west of the 93rd meridian.

CHAPTER XVII

MOUNTAINS UNKNOWN

I HAD gone to bed the previous night when the clouds hung low over the sodden fields and a fitful drizzle charged the air with mist. I awoke to clear skies, a soft breeze, and a strong healthy vegetation sparkling with dew, minimum temperature 60° F. I hardly recognized Tagé, and saw for the first time a valley to the north-north-west. I was told it led only to cattle pastures.

It seems strange that one should speak of heat, even in August, at an altitude of 8000 feet. Most people, sweltering on the plains of India in August, would give two months' pay for a fortnight in the hills at half that altitude. But it must be remembered that we were in a low latitude, only about 30° north of the equator. The very narrowness of the gorge made it warm up quickly. Yet the same cause which helped to make it hot in summer, made it colder in winter, in spite of the fact that, with so thick a garment of vegetation, there could be little radiation.

Our Tagé coolies were the sweepings of the village, the serfs, the hags, the crones, the deformed and the half-wits — 'pitiful rascals'. I felt as ashamed of them as Sir John Falstaff did of his ragged conscripts; but like him I could say:

> Faith for their poverty I know not where they had that, and for their bareness I am sure they never learn'd that of me.

But if they were the worse citizens for it, they were none the worse workers; they marched from 8.15 a.m. till 4.15 p.m. with halts.

It may be imagined how much I enjoyed the day's march

through such glorious country, never before seen by a European. The mountains and glaciers, the cliffs, the rushing river, the trees and flowers and birds, all helped to make up a scene of ever varying beauty and unfailing interest.

We walked across cultivated fields — the barley was reaped — and green pastures to the end of Tagé, and then a mile beyond Talu the cliffs drew together again. Just before entering the gorge, we crossed a stony valley which suddenly gaped to the north-west. I could see the tip of a snow peak, called Tamchokpa, at the head of the valley, and I was told of a village about a day's journey distant. My informants, however, denied that there was a thoroughfare, although the valley had such a used look that I doubted the truth of this statement. I would wager that there is a route northwards over the snow range from Talu, although this particular valley might of course be blocked by a glacier. We crossed the torrent, swift, grey and turbulent, by a plank bridge, above which the bed widened till it was a hundred yards across. A small monastery stood on the right bank; beyond it we entered the forest again. A stone wall had been built across the path at the entrance to the gorge to keep the village cattle within bounds. As I climbed over it, I saw a small brown bushy-tailed creature dart amongst the rocks. It might have been either a squirrel or a tree shrew (Tupaia). Though I watched for ten minutes, it did not reappear.

Back in the forest after our brief sojourn amidst cultivation, I strolled along happily botanizing — which means something more than collecting plants! The commonest trees on the north bank, exposed to the full weight of the sunshine, were *Pinus excelsa* and *P. sinensis*, with *Rhododendron niphargum* between; on the other more sheltered side of the gorge, hemlock spruce was dominant, and broad-leafed trees also were common. It was difficult to distinguish them, in spite of the narrowness of the gorge. Oaks seemed to be rare; but there were poplars, also several trees with compound leaves, one of which was certainly a Cedrela, as I had picked up cedrela fruits in the gorge below Tagé; others may have been walnut, Ailanthus, or even ash. Many midsummer herbaceous plants were flowering wherever there was an open space, especially round a small village called Ba, about four miles from Talu; we stopped here half an hour for a snack. Two species of geranium were common wayside weeds, their small flowers dimmed by the harvest moon flowers of *Hypericum Hookerianum.* Wherever pine and bracken grew together on the rocky slope, festoons of *Lilium Wardii* scented the air. Climbing plants flourished luxuriantly – woody climbers like Schizandra, and big vines, and slender herbaceous twiners like the yellow pea-flowered *Dumasia Forrestii.*

Rhododendron niphargum suffered appallingly from 'blister blight', which causes unsightly disfigurement of the sick leaves. They bulge up in leprous white pustular inflations, and the disease is undoubtedly spread fast and far by contagion, although it seems to be confined here to a few species of ericaceous plants, including *Pieris ovalifolia.* Generally speaking this foul fungus – another species of which attacks the tea bush in Assam – indicates a moist climate. From the prevalence of the pine-bracken association, I had already come to the conclusion that the rainfall here was not very heavy. But when next morning, I found bushes of *Rhododendron megacalyx* in the forest, I was nonplussed, for this shrub too indicates a fairly damp climate. No doubt I was partly misled by the exceptional August weather; probably the rainfall of the gorge is nowhere less than 40-50 inches, most of which falls in six months. The winters are fine and dry, but long droughts are probably unknown. It was evident that owing to the enormous height of the mountains, which, within a few miles of the river reach over 20,000 feet on both sides, the bottom of the gorge gets little sunshine. Even now it was noticeable how early the sun sank behind the southern range and at how late an hour it reached the water in the morning. These conditions would keep the gorge damp even in the brightest weather.

Throughout August 8th and 9th we were marching almost due west, while the glaciers on the southern range were coming closer and closer to the river. We were groping between two great ranges in a lost world of ice peaks.

Beyond Ba we crossed a rugged spur, but presently returned to the river, where there was a rope bridge; so I suppose there was a path, and probably a village, on the other bank, although I could see nothing but solid forest, with an occasional glimpse of spiked peaks pricking the turquoise dome of heaven.

Late in the afternoon we came to a big torrent flowing from the north-west, and turned up stream. We had to scramble some little distance along the cliffs before we reached a plank bridge and got across. Far up the valley I saw a constellation of snow peaks to the north.

Just here the Yigrong makes an S-bend to the south-west, and for a time passes out of sight (but not out of earshot) round a high buttress. We halted for the night inside the loop of the S, my tent being pitched at the foot of a smooth wall like a sea-worn cliff, against which the river had dashed in an earlier age. Now it had retired some little distance, baffled, while forest had grown up in the old river bed, lapping along the base of the cliff. Enormous spongy cushions of *Campanula cashmeriana*, silken-leafed and purple-flowered, and long, loose streamers of Silene hung down. The base of the cliff, for twenty or thirty feet, was almost bare owing to the darkness; but above that I saw a wealth of plants; unluckily they were well out of reach.

It was a pleasant spot for a camp, and after supper I sat outside my tent listening to the soft hoot of an owl. The moon shone brilliantly in a sky phosphorescent with stars, and through the flickering leaves of the trees I watched it whiten the snows before it slid behind mighty peaks. Sand flies were bad here.

At Talu I had been puzzled by a flock of birds in the fallow fields which appeared to be singularly tame. It was a dark coloured bird, about the size of a dove relieved only by white feathers on back and rump, and white lateral tail feathers. In fact, as usual, the forest was full of birds and I had seen enough in the course of the day to delight the heart of the most blasé ornithologist. But with the exception of woodpeckers, of which there were several species, I could not recognize any of them, from the glimpses obtained while attending to my own work.

We were eight hours on the road next day (August 9th), although we marched only five and a half during which time we covered about seven miles to the village of Tongdu. The weather was perfect, blue skies with fleecy white clouds and brilliant sunshine; again it was almost too hot in the afternoon. One expects that in forested Pome, but it does not fit in with the popular idea of Tibet. By August, after absorbing an immense amount of heat, Tibet has definitely warmed up, except of course in the immediate neighbourhood of the snow peaks and on the open plateau. But the summer is all too brief, and the stored heat is quickly lost as winter approaches.

At first we were in mixed forest, but as the gorge narrowed and deepened only pines seemed able to maintain their hold, with scattered oaks (*Quercus Ilex*) and shrubs. *Rhododendron triflorum* was common. It is not a handsome plant but it is interesting owing to the ingenious method by which it ensures cross-pollination of its flowers. The corolla is flattened, and the short tube pinched so as to leave a narrow groove, leading to the nectar secreted round the base of the ovary; the entrance to the groove is fur lined. Any large insect such as a bee in search of honey must thrust itself well into the groove. Meanwhile its legs and body are picking up pollen threads which form a web across the path; a tangle of these is carried away and brushed off by the fur-lined groove of the next flower visited. The second step is to transfer this pollen to the stigma. That is easily done, not by the insect but by the flower itself, a more subtle arrangement. The long style sticks out well beyond the stamens, and the stigma is not receptive till some time after the pollen is ripe. The style slants downwards to start with, but towards the end is bent more sharply upwards; it is capped by a large blob – the stigma. When the corolla becomes detached, it does not immediately fall to the ground. It slides down the style, until stopped by the bend; caught up by this, and by the large stigma, it remains suspended for some time. Gradually the style becomes flaccid, droops; the fur-lined groove drags over the stigma, the sticky surface picks up the tangled pollen threads, and the corolla drops to the ground. It is unlikely that self pollen will be transferred in this way, because stamens and style occupy different relative positions at different stages of the flower's life, as well as ripening at different times.

This method of cross-pollination is found in several species of rhododendron.

We started off on a bearing just south of west, marching at the bottom of the gorge. The river was awe-inspiring. The bed is sharply tilted here, and choked with enormous blocks, fallen from the granite cliffs. The speed and force of the water are irresistible, the roar of the leaping waves as the river batters its way over the boulders deafening. It was difficult to find a point from which I could photograph the scene and do justice to the river's might.

At eleven o'clock we halted for an hour, having reached, of all unlikely places, a sandy cove. From the line of driftwood washed ashore, it was evident that the river had lately fallen several feet. We had not covered more than four miles, but it was pleasant to lie on the hot dry sand in the sunshine, close one's eyes, and imagine that one was listening to the roar of the sea in some rock-bound Cornish cove! In the strip of forest between the cliffs and the river bank I had found fruiting bushes of *Rhododendron megacalyx* and several small ground orchids, some in flower – a Goodyera, *Neottianthe cucullata*, *Neottia listeroides*. Small saprophytes, such as two species of Monotropa, are common, but there are few herbaceous flowering plants in the forest, the undergrowth consisting mostly of ferns, especially Lomaria.

In the afternoon the path took us across cliffs where *Iris decora*, steeped in sunshine, was shedding its coffee brown seeds amongst dwarf Cotoneaster and other shrubs. The slender *Codonopsis convolvulacea*, whose big lavender-blue flowers stare like unwinking eyes at the traveller, twined up every solid stem which offered support; and from crevices of the rock the dwarf *Allium Mairii* shot up in fountains of green threads at the ends of which the flowers congealed like pink pearls.

Crossing several pine-clad terraces we made excellent progress, and before evening reached the small log hut village of Tongdu; it had all the appearance of a new settlement. Right opposite to us on the other side of the river was a glacier bearing due south-west.

That night I wrote in my diary these words: 'I cannot imagine whence all this water comes unless there are some large glaciers farther west. This river (the Yigrong) drains the northern flank of the range, as the Tongkyuk river and Pasum river do the southern.'

It was raining when we were ready to start at eight o'clock on August 10th after a wet night – minimum temperature 58°. It looked as though it might clear up, so we waited till 8.40, by which time the rain had stopped although the clouds did not lift for some time. Later the sun came out.

We covered another five miles in a general westerly direction, a short day, and an easy march. At the village of Boyu, reached in an hour and a half, we halted twenty minutes to change coolies. Two hours later we were astride a spur, looking down on to the village of Shonggyi, on the banks of an enormous torrent. At first sight I thought that the Yigrong had divided into two equal streams; but presently I saw that this was not so. The main stream flowed from the west, as hitherto; the big torrent had its source in a group of snow peaks and glaciers visible to the north. The valley was strewn with large erratic blocks of granite. It would have been an easy matter to ascend this valley to the nearest glacier, which ended at some little height above the village; and from there one would have had a magnificent view of the southern range. I felt half inclined to stop the night at Shonggyi; but in the end we went on for another half hour, camping by the river.

Right opposite Shonggyi, to the south, rose a conical snow peak from which a glacier flowed to within a thousand feet of the river. It formed a dramatic background for the confluence of the two furious streams.

So easy had the march been that I began to think all our difficulties lay behind us: soon the valley must merge on to the plateau. But where? and how? If we continued to march westwards we must presently cross explored country; in fact, we must reach the very region Cawdor and I had explored in 1924, when searching for the range. I had a queer sensation of being lost, knowing that there was no map in existence which would show me whither we were going. I was making the first map of the Yigrong river as I went along, a crude plan to scale of the relative positions of rivers, mountains, passes, villages, glaciers, routes – everything: and crude it was, yet better than the blank, or the guess-work which was all that existed. Every night I went through my table of bearings and distances and added something to the sketch-map I was roughly drawing in my note-book; all I knew for certain was that we were somewhere north of the Nambu La and Pasum Tso (or at any rate north of the Tongkyuk river); and I guessed we were probably west of Tsela Dzong, and north of the Gyamda river.[1] We might eventually reach either the Gyamda valley, below Gyamda, or the Gyalam – that is the Peking-Lhasa highway. This surmise proved roughly correct; the mistake I made in our location was due not so much to underestimating the distance to known ground, as in overestimating our speed.

[1] I was wrong. At Boyu we were practically due north of Tsela Dzong, and still east of the Gyamda Chu.

In spite of a fine evening, it began to rain during the night, and August 11th was a wet day. We got soaked to the skin, pushing through the tall undergrowth, and cold too, the minimum having dropped back to 55° F.

At first the path was fairly level, the river twisting and turning like a snake; we were still marching through pine forest, gloomy in such weather.

Soon after starting we crossed a torrent of crystal clear water which certainly did not rise in any glacier. But on the right bank a small glacier almost overhung the river. Here the Yigrong gorge seemed to be entirely waterworn, and we found ourselves marching along the base of conglomerate cliffs which had been left high and dry by the ceaseless erosion of the river bed.

After we had crossed another torrent a complete change came over the appearance of the gorge. The landscape now became violently stereoscopic, where formerly it had looked as dramatic but as unreal as a scene in a theatre. Climbing away from the river which slewed towards us from the south-west, we approached a distant skyline by a rough track. An immense ridge swept in steep folds from the northern range, and flattened out in a saddle before plunging vertically down to the river. On this shoulder I could see fields, and silhouetted against the V of sky behind, houses. Hitherto, villages, few and far between as they were, had stood on the river bank, or on terraces just above, wherever a large enough torrent debouched into the main valley. Here was something entirely and extraordinarily different – a village on a skyway. Had it been a great monastery, or a castle, I should have been less surprised; since fifteen hundred feet above the river one might reach a new world inhabited perhaps by creatures either not quite human, or superhuman.

As we ascended the cliff diagonally, the gorge began to take on yet stranger forms. From a black slit in the south-west wall, the violent river came galloping out towards us like Aphrodite's foaming seahorses; and, behind a maze of mountains, seemed to divide into two, three or even four streams. Was this the end? Were there just glaciers and torrents pouring their contents into a vast sump in the bowels of the earth? When at last we had toiled up the mountain face, and come to the gently sloping saddle, where we found ourselves in fields golden with ripe corn, there in front of us was the gorge, stark in the west, as before. The sudden reappearance of the river, as big as ever, and 1500 feet below, which I had thought broken into a thousand cascades, was quite startling.

On the edge of the barley fields we halted. The sun had come out; it was midday, and pleasantly warm, so I sat down and had lunch. A hundred harvesters, men and women, were at work on the terrace. Some were reaping the golden ears, others putting the corn into stooks; processions of men were carrying huge bundles up to the village. They looked at us curiously. Who was this stranger? A man like themselves, and yet different. Presently several men approached. The leader was dressed in a red robe, and wore boots; clearly he was a man of means — the village headman, Tashi said. He bowed to me, and holding out his hands over which he draped a coarse scarf, he invited us to his village.

Tashi and Pemba were soon in friendly conversation with the deputation; I could always rely on Tashi to tell a simple honest story, and to make friends with the people, who after all only wanted to be friendly. His ugly cheerful smiling face, and his complete lack of self-importance at being *sirdar* to a great *sahib* from India were enormously to his credit. I never knew Tashi use his position to put the screw on the people amongst whom we travelled.

But first we must drink with the headman, and he poured some spirit from a stone jar into a cup and handed it to me. So we sat down again, and I sipped the colourless spirit, which was vile. After that we walked up the slope above the broad saddle, through more terraced fields to the village of Ragoonka.

It was a big village. There were at least eighty houses, stoutly built of timber on a foundation of stones, scattered up the slope: and though the houses were not large, I reckoned the population of Ragoonka must be over three hundred persons. On the way up the street, which happened to be the bed of a stream now brimful of water, I noticed large colonies of *Primula Florindae*, a plant I had not seen for some days. On dry ground *Cyananthus insignis* was in flower, and little tuffets of *Rhododendron lepidotum*. The forest below still consisted mainly of Pinus and *Quercus Ilex*; and an assortment of gaily coloured herbaceous plants such as crimson-flowered geranium lined the path, with a big Senecio or Ligularia hiding under the bushes.

Although the houses looked substantial, this could not be said of the little monastery in which I stayed. It was a most decrepit place, and highly insanitary, since the courtyard round which the sagging shacks formed a lopsided parallelogram, was the public latrine. Nor were we the only inmates; several monks and five or six soldiers shared it with me. It was like a concentration camp; and when it began to rain and water poured through the rotten roof, I felt aggrieved. However, I did have a room to myself, albeit a tiny one, which with its single exit on to the common veranda (and the public latrine) did not allow of much privacy.

But these were small matters; the warriors and monks were friendly souls, and it wasn't their fault if the peasants held both religion and war in such contempt that they would not house the praying and fighting services decently.

It turned out that the soldiers were on their way to Tagé to meet Yuri. I held a rifle inspection, and am unable to report favourably on the care of the rifle in Tibet. There were several British Lee-Enfields, and one Manlicher, none of them less than thirty years old. However, they would have been quite serviceable weapons had they been even moderately clean. Unfortunately, gun oil is not a government issue.

The soldiers were fine looking fellows, well set up, and

muscular; they looked more like Kampas than Pobas. Properly trained and led, what tireless stubborn hill fighters they would make.

I was neither surprised nor sorry to hear that I would have to stay here a day while coolies were collected and food prepared; but I was surprised to hear that it would take us four days to reach the next village. Evidently I was still a long way from the source of the Yigrong. But the rate of progress can be judged from the fact that it had taken us four days to do the twenty-eight miles from Talu; and the most difficult section of the gorge lay ahead.

Ragoonka is about 2000 feet above the river and perhaps 11,000 feet above sea-level. On a fine day it commands a superb view of the southern range; but unfortunately it was not fine. Yet I could see a long way eastwards down the gorge towards Talu, and southwards up a smaller gorge which cleaves the immense barrier. There is a path up this gorge to the south which crosses the main range by the Ba La, and drops down to the Pasum Lake on the route we had followed in 1924.

To the east, south and north I could see snow peaks looming through the mist, and glaciers; while from this height with more and more peaks poking up their heads, and crowding into the picture, the gorge itself became a minor operation, and looked quite impassable. We were too close under the northern range to get a good view of it, but I could see a small hanging glacier above the village.

After dark it began to rain, and it continued all night and most of the following day — August 12th. The minimum temperature was down to 53° F. I was not feeling very well, and spent most of our day of rest in my room, classifying my plant collection; the water dripped dismally through the wooden tiled roof, and the courtyard turned to liquid manure and stank to heaven.

Ragoonka stands on the ice shelf — all that remains of the

old glacier valley bottom; the rest has been worn away by the river. To south and west snow peaks have their very roots in the gorge. The highest peaks and largest glaciers lay to the south; it is here that I should look for a mountain exceeding 25,000 feet in height – for the high peaks on the southern range stand in close groups, as I judged from the torrents which flow from them.

The river coils itself round the great spur on which Ragoonka stands and is then joined by the southern stream. The confluence is invisible from the village. It was now obvious why there was no sign of ice action down by the river – since there never had been a glacier there.

I began to picture the Yigrong gorge in course of construction. At one time the main glacier reached the lake at Temo Chamna, for there is a moraine at the head of the lake. The chain of lakes, Temo Chamna, Tagé, and perhaps Boyu, may mark temporary halts in the retreat of the glacier. At the height of the Himalayan ice age, the Po-Yigrong glacier was a majestic river of ice almost a hundred miles long, fed by innumerable glaciers from north and south; or perhaps a vast ice field stretching between the two ranges, fifteen or twenty miles wide towards the west, narrowing towards a snout at its eastern end, and covering about twelve hundred square miles.

August 13th broke fine, but the mountains had hidden their heads behind banks of cloud. The coolies were ready; so we packed and resumed our march.

CHAPTER XVIII

SHOUTING WATERS

I NOTICED we had enlisted three extra coolies, making a total of fifteen. The Ragoonka men carried axes and long coils of thin but new yak hair rope, black and white strands being twisted together. This looked like serious business.

Viewed from the saddle, the river appeared to fill the gorge completely; nevertheless we plunged headlong down till we stood under high cliffs. Once inside the gorge, we made slow progress and for the next three hours the coolies were compelled to halt continually, while they moved one at a time cautiously across some dizzy gulch. We crossed a torrent from the north and passed a rope bridge, which did not look as though it was often used. Probably it led nowhere. The river was very powerful; what it had lost in quantity it made up in velocity. Glaciers from the southern range ended only a few hundred feet above the river, and a snow bed jammed in a gully dipped into the water. Under the glaciers, the rapids were fiercer than elsewhere, the ice having pushed enormous blocks of stone into the river bed.

It was a warm sunny day, and the march along the river, often in forest, was pleasant. We had come only four miles from Ragoonka, when we halted for lunch. While we were resting a party of about thirty Pobas, passed, and stopped for a chat. They were on their way to Ragoonka to join the army—it sounded strangely familiar. That the lust to kill and kill should have penetrated to so fair a part of the world was a bad augury. For thousands of years while men were striving and struggling all round the southern fringes and peninsulas of the Eurasian continent, Tibet must have been a peaceful land. But now the echo of the gathering storm had become so loud and insistent, that the repercussions reached to the remotest corners of the earth.

These men carried no arms, except the short Tibetan sword. They wore their hair long and were finely built, well set up fellows: some of them were Kampas. They told us we could get along the river the whole way to Nye, the water being comparatively low; thus we would avoid having to cross a range of mountains.

After lunch we climbed a spur, from the top of which we had a good view back to Ragoonka; I noted a conspicuous snow peak bearing 129°, that is about south-east, and therefore south of the river. For the last mile or two through the forest the path was good, and we found an unexpectedly pleasant camping ground at the base of a towering cliff. A change had come over the forest, larch and spruce trees appearing by the river. I also found a lilac – *Syringa villosa*, with softly pubescent leaves, though the plant is never so hairy as the name suggests. This species was first known from the neighbourhood of Peking; it is a far cry from Peking to the Yigrong gorge. Unfortunately the seeds of my plant were not ripe, and I saw only a single specimen. It had been a mass of blossom earlier in the year. There are at least two other lilacs in eastern Tibet; *S. microphylla*, on the cold dry plateau farther north-east, and *S. Potaninii* in the wet valleys along the Burma frontier to the south-east. Another common shrub in the pine forest was *Rhododendron triflorum*. Species of clematis, *C. connata*, and another in flower, helped to brighten the villages; and *Lilium Wardii* was still common on the granite cliffs, with huge pleasantly scented cushions of *Primula Dubernardiana*. This last is a slow growing plant, the woody stems lengthening only a fraction of an inch each year, and retaining their dead leaves for several years so that the plant gradually comes to resemble a bath sponge. It is possible to calculate the age of the plant by its whorls of dead leaves and leaf scars, as one counts the annual rings in a tree trunk; some of the specimens were nearly half a century old. The leaves are white with meal beneath, and covered with sticky gland hairs, to which they owe their fragrance.

Next day the rock climbing began; the path by the river ended, and we started up the cliff. Higher and higher we climbed hand and foot, till we were a thousand or fifteen hundred feet above the river. The cliffs were often bare for hundreds of feet. Pine forest (*P. excelsa*) was still dominant, with occasional spruce, and big poplars, willows, and *Quercus Ilex*. Soon we had a wonderful bird's-eye view of the river far below. But we did not leave the gorge, and presently we began to go down again, descending some awkward, rickety notched logs, which leaned drunkenly against cliffs, and wobbled, threatening to tip us into space. Then came a difficult bit.

'Be careful, sahib', Tashi warned me as I went ahead; 'wait for us to help you over.'

In front of me was a very nasty traverse across a smooth granite face, which immediately below dropped sheer to the river; where the path crossed it was not quite vertical, but sloped at about 75°, and was eight or ten feet wide. How four shallow cup holes had been ground in that hard rock I could not imagine; they would take one's toes, the rest was a matter of balance.

Hitherto the path up and down the cliffs, though not easy, had offered no insuperable difficulty to an active man. Here was a nerve tonic; and I had taken the first step before I fully realized the nature of the traverse. Then I looked down the slab, and saw that it ended a few feet below, and beyond that – emptiness, till you came to the river, so far below that I could not hear the thunder of the water. It made me giddy, and I shrank back with that awful stab in the pit of the stomach which sudden fear can induce – as though one had been violently kicked in the solar plexus. Then the coolies came up to the end of the path and halted; one by one they crossed. I watched the first man, fascinated; it gave me a sinking feeling akin to what I

myself had felt when attempting to cross. The coolie, with a forty pound load on his back, one hand against the cliff, and his body slightly inclined inwards, took the few necessary steps, slowly, methodically, and with cool assurance. Step by step, by sheer balance, with his toes thrust into the shallow steps, he swung himself across to safety; and the next man followed. My heart was in my mouth; the sight gave me physical pain. One slip, a momentary loss of balance, and he would crash to his death on the rocks six hundred feet below. It was the most nerve-racking cliff traverse I had ever watched. I told Tashi I wanted to cross and get the suspense over; no use standing there with my courage fast ebbing away like blood out of an artery!

Tashi, seeing my hesitation, at once crossed the gap, to show me how to do it.

'It's easy, sahib! Look!'

'I can't balance like that, Tashi! I shall certainly slip.'

'But see, sahib!' Tashi went half way across, stopped, turned round, and came back, while my heart stood still. It was almost unbearable. So again I tried, with Tashi just in front to give me a lead; but it was no use, I could not go on.

Then I remembered the rope. All I needed was moral support; there was no technical difficulty in the traverse. In a few minutes two ropes had been tied round my waist, and Tashi crossed first, holding the end of one rope. Then he planted himself on the path. I followed, another man on my side paying out the second rope gradually, while Tashi held the first one just taut. I did exactly what he told me to do without a hitch, never felt a moment's giddiness, and kept my balance perfectly. It was easy!

Gradually we scrambled down the cliffs to the river bed again, and found a cove, piled with gigantic boulders. Here we halted for lunch, having come two miles in four hours. Shut in by granite cliffs so sheer and smooth as to be totally devoid of vegetation for hundreds of feet, I was not certain that we could get any farther. Could we pass through the gorge, or must we get out of it? The mighty Po-Yigrong had at last become no more than a brawling mountain torrent, on a big scale. The water poured and cascaded intermittently in violent pulsations over rocks too big to be submerged; fountains of spray shot up, as waves hit the cliffs. The thunder of the rapids filled the gorge; looking up stream I found myself looking up a visible slope.

We continued to climb and scramble till four o'clock, then halted for a consultation; we had reached the most terrific part of the gorge. The cliffs towered up for thousands of feet, till only a ragged ribbon of sky was visible; and they were bare. There seemed no way either through or over. I wondered what was going to happen next. I had not long to wait. There was a joint in the cliff here filled with a dense growth of dwarf bamboo (arundinaria). The leader parted the bushes, and revealed a hidden path which zig-zagged up the cliff, behind the thick screen; it brought us to a rickety wooden gallery built round the face of a vertical buttress, hundreds of feet above the river. I marvelled at the courage and resource of the people who had built this remarkable road. It was like a scenic railway, curving round the cliffs of an imaginary world at a fun fair — without the fun. It was thrilling, but very serious. We seemed to be suspended between the sky and the river, amidst Cyclopean scenery.

The gallery continued for more than a hundred yards, pinned to a bare wall as it seemed. The logs we trod on moved underfoot, and sometimes were not there at all, leaving a yawning abyss across which we stepped. You could have dived off the edge into the river far below. It was exhilarating, but I was thankful the logs sloped inwards, so that I could hug the cliff. Presently we reached firm rock again.

Two alternatives were open to us. We could descend to the river once more, and if the water was low enough, clamber round the scalloped cliffs by means of a 'bridge', or gallery;

or we could leave the Yigrong gorge altogether by climbing out of it. The latter route would take a day longer; but as the 'bridge' would probably need repairing, if not rebuilding – if it existed at all – there could be little in it. We decided to examine the river route. But first we cut out a nest for the night in the bamboo thicket.

Then, while one pioneer party started up towards the crest of the range another went down the green crack in the cliff at the top of which we had embedded ourselves, to examine the river. I followed this party and found them standing in a tiny cove by the hurtling water. Out in the river bed was an enormous whaleback rock, and round it the vast volume of water poured in two streams, forming a vortex below. Immediately above rose the overhanging cliff, which beat back the roaring tide. A gallery sloped up the face of this cliff and was lost to view in a bay round the corner. The lower end of it hung 12 feet above water level, and was reached by a notched log, lashed to some staging; but there was a gap 30 feet wide between where we stood on a safe rock and the foot of the ladder, with heaving deep water between. The rest of the bridge had been washed away. Clearly the soldiers we met had not come this route, but in winter it would offer no difficulty. Could we build the missing part of the bridge? The experts, after studying the problem for some time, decided that we could. We returned to our camp – my tent had been pitched amongst the bamboos as though camouflaged from air raids; and that night the coolies, like tireless spiders, spun a 100-foot rope of split bamboo strands.

Early next morning (August 15th) we descended to the river taking the rope with us. First the coolies spent an hour studying the water under the cliff, which appeared to be about 4 feet deep; it was not its average depth which interested them, but the rhythm of the 2-foot waves from the main rush of water which surged in, causing eddies and rebounding waves. Then the bridge building began.

A grove of alder saplings grew at the base of the cliff, and several trees were felled. Gradually a fence was built out from the rock on which we stood, till it reached the ladder; the stoutest poles, 20 feet long, were plunged in the river and cross pieces tied to them with rope and strands of bamboo, one or two muscular men working waist deep in the pulsing swell. Then the ladder itself was secured, and finally the loads were carried along the fence one by one, and dumped on the gallery. The gallery ended in mid air, 20 feet above the river, and a shallow gulf yawned between the cliff and the beach. The resourceful bridge builders, with some difficulty, waded the gulf, almost up to the armpits, Tashi giving them a lead. Then an upright pole was fixed amongst stones, and finally the bamboo rope linked the gallery with the shore; loads and men slid down it, and we were over the last obstacle.

The bridge building had taken us eight hours: we did not leave the cliff till nearly four o'clock. The morning had been radiant, the deep blue sky setting off the fantastic outlines of the mountains which towered thousands of feet above the river; but rain was coming.

During the late afternoon we made better progress, still hemmed in by cliffs, but able to keep close to the river. We turned north-west, and looking back, saw snow peaks again. Although we had no more bridge building to do, the path climbed high up a cliff above violent rapids, and so reached another flimsy gallery. There were some nasty places here owing to broken logs. Finally we descended to a broad arid valley, almost a plain by contrast. The stream, now eighty yards wide, flowed tranquilly but swiftly; we were out of the gorge.

Ahead, the high bare granite ranges and the wide flat valley, with sand banks dividing the river, proclaimed that we were in a corner of dry Tibet; the wind was warm and almost caressing. Behind us the Po-Yigrong plunged into the bowels of the earth, through sixty miles of fairyland. I had thought we would reach a village, but there was no sign of one; and having marched till dark, we had perforce to camp in the best place we could find. At least the ground was level.

About eight o'clock next morning the men we had met near Ragoonka arrived in camp on their way back, and took over my loads. Had they been rejected for the army, I wondered?

When travelling by themselves, Tibetans will often start before daylight, after drinking buttered tea which is quickly and easily made; then halt for a meal when the sun is up. They halted now, and ate just as we were getting ready to start, delaying us. In less than half an hour we reached a cliff, and a rope bridge.

On the cliff the white-flowered *Allium Gageanum* was scattered amongst thickets of *Cotoneaster bacillaris* and other cramped shrubs. There was even a species of rhododendron, unidentifiable, with rust-coloured leaves. The type of forest changed very suddenly from open woods of *Pinus excelsa* in the gorge to open woods of birch, poplar and Picea on the slopes above the arid valley. Nearer the river grew stunted bushes of *Quercus Ilex*, and a thorny scrub of *Rosa Moyesii*, *R. sericea*, and Caragana. Common also was a dwarf paeony, scattered on the stony scrub clad slopes. It looked something like a starved form of *P. Delavayi*, but there were no flowers, and the seeds were mostly lost, though I collected a few.

Exploring the granite cliff ledges, while the loads were being taken across, I found a striped toad (*Bufo viridis*) lurking under the bushes.

It was now high noon and very hot. A strong wind blew through the valley, parching the vegetation. The cliff from which we were launched out on to the rope bridge stood about 30 feet above the river, and as the far end of the rope was fastened to a pole only about 10 feet high, stuck in a sandbank, one slipped down it at a cracking pace. When it came to my turn, the Tibetans trussed me up as though I were Houdini. I kicked off from the cliff and shot into space. A gust of wind caught my topee and tipped it over my eyes; next minute it fell off, the chin strap carrying my spectacles with it. I was powerless to save them as I dared not leave go of the slider; had my hands touched the rope it would have cut the flesh to ribands. Topee and glasses plopped into deep water. My topee was caught up in an eddy, and was eventually fished out, not much the worse for its ducking; but my spectacles of course I never saw again. This resulted in violent headaches.

Just above the rope bridge from a deep slit in the mountains, the Alado Chu flows peacefully into the Po-Yigrong from the north-east; had we crossed the mountain the previous day instead of pushing through the gorge, we should have descended to the Alado Chu. There is a road up this stream, which, after crossing a pass, the Alado La, joins the Gyalam at Lharigo Dzong.

Across the river we came to barley fields, so we sat down under some bushes and had lunch. Presently men arrived from Nye with ponies, to conduct me to their village. They said it was quite close, but it proved to be a good three hours' walk along the river bank. At last we came in sight of houses and strips of cultivation on each side of the river, and a wooden bridge; for the river is here only thirty yards wide, though swift and deep. Behind the fields the mountains rise abruptly, exposing a great deal of flashy white limestone rock, dotted with juniper bushes, as on many parts of the outer plateau. I felt confident that we had now reached the Gyalam, somewhere between Gyamda and Lharigo.

We did not stop at the first group of houses, nor at the second; nor when we reached the wooden bridge, did we cross over to a group of houses on the left bank. It began to rain; we continued to plod across wet barley fields by slippery winding paths; and we got wetter and wetter. The sudden change of weather, from brilliant sunshine and deep blue sky to a blanket of dark cloud, pelting rain, and a raw wind is typical of Tibet in summer. But I could not help feeling that the arid appearance of the valley in the morning was a complete fraud, or at least an optical illusion. Anyhow the drought conditions were confined to the bottom half of the valley, and were the result of the raging winds which tear through these gorges; a thousand feet above the river the mountains were covered with fir forest. It is a question of degree. The Po-Yigrong at Nye, the altitude of which is about 11,000 feet, is not so dry as the country to the north twenty-five miles distant, where the Gyalam runs; but it is a great deal drier than the Tongkyuk valley about the same distance to the south. We were between the wet river gorge region and the dry outer plateau.

At last we reached a collection of stone houses built round the courtyard of a small gompa. The courtyard was crowded with almost pygmy people, dressed in filthy rags; slaves, I imagine, from Pome. I was conducted to a room in the dark gompa and changed my wet clothes. Presently Tashi brought me hot tea. He told me we were still seven marches from Gyamda, and that we had not yet reached the Gyalam. This gave me a shock. I was beginning to feel the effects of altitude and the long tiring marches.

I spent the night in the monastery, above the paved courtyard which, slimy with black mud, and surrounded by noisome rooms, or rather kennels, in which the workers lived like dogs, looked and smelt unsanitary.

CHAPTER XIX

WORLD OF ICE

It poured all night, and next morning (August 17th) showed no improvement. Under the grey dripping sky, Nye looked repulsive. It is a considerable village, scattered in a trough nearly two miles long and about a quarter of a mile wide. The fact that the crops are irrigated shows that it must enjoy—or suffer from—periods of drought; but this was not one of them.

At this point it will be as well to put on record a few facts I had discovered about the Yigrong gorge.

Between Temo Chamna and the top of the gorge at Nye, the river receives eleven large tributaries on the right, or south bank, and only eight on the left or north bank, in a distance of about sixty miles. The southern tributaries are larger than the northern, proving that most of the water comes from the southern range. It may, therefore, be assumed that the main range lies south of the river; the highest peaks certainly do. Either the river is cutting its way diagonally across a single range, or there are really two parallel ranges, about twenty-five miles apart. The difficulty of accepting the latter explanation is that it leaves them with very little width; a range of mountains with peaks over 20,000 feet high must have considerable width, as well as length and height.

On the other hand, the mountain ranges of Tibet rise from the plateau, which here averages 12,000-14,000 feet, leaving a height of only 11,000-13,000 feet for the fold ranges from base to summit, supposing the peaks to attain 25,000 feet. In that case the width at the base would not be so great. We do not yet know what is the real relationship of these ranges north of the Tsangpo to the Himalayas and to one another.

The gorge is 8000-12,000 feet deep and is mostly water worn.

Above Nye (or Nyomé) the Po Yigrong, henceforth called Nye Chu, becomes a boisterous torrent, rushing steeply down between forested mountains.

We started in the rain, and did a long stage of about fifteen miles up the valley, to a village called Kongma. Just above Nye the river divides into three big streams. We kept to the main stream, and at once entered the forest. The pine country had been left below; here the dominant conifer was Picea. Mixed with it were a few larches, also oak, birch, poplar, Sorbus and other trees. In the open grassy glades, the herbaceous flora was at the zenith, and many plants were in flower, notably the big mauve-flowered *Thalictrum diffusiflorum*. Here and there I came upon colonies of milk-white *Primula alpicola*, deliciously scented, and in one place, *P. latisecta* in fruit. *Morina Coulteriana*, a stiff aggressive plant with prickly leaves like a thistle – though it is a member of the scabious family (Dipsaceae) – had ripe seeds; and many shrubs such as Ribes, Lonicera, Rosa and cherry were in ripe fruit. Long ropes of *Clematis montana* bearing little lovers' knots of pink flowers trailed over the bushes, and there was a second species in flower at Nye. Yet it seemed that autumn threatened us. Above 12,000 feet the Tibetan summer is distressingly short.

In four hours we reached a forest village called Tor, and halted for a meal. We had not come far, but the path was very rough and we made slow progress. It was early to halt for the night; but had I known how far it was to the next village I would gladly have stayed here.

Just above Tor we crossed to the left bank of the torrent. Then came a long up-hill march, through pine forest. As we approached Kongma the valley began to open out a little, and give a hint of the alpine region. Grassy glades grew wider and more numerous. Birds had been scarce all day, but I saw several small squirrels in the fir trees, and tried unsuccessfully to shoot a couple with my .410. About a mile from Kongma we crossed a large glacier torrent, and from time to time I caught glimpses of glaciers on both sides of the river.

Kongma is in the forest, but we were now close to the alpine pastures, and there were plenty of cattle here, besides some cultivation.

We had been marching south of west all day, and I was again getting a little confused as to where we should finish up.

August 18th was another long day, and the weather was still wet. In fact it was becoming apparent that, although on the edge of the dry country, we were now so high up that we might expect continuous rain in August. The thick coating of forest, though predominantly conifer, required abundant moisture; and it was obvious that the surrounding glaciers were amply nourished. Much of the precipitation on the snow range falls in winter, as I had learnt in January 1925, when crossing the Nambu La from Tongkyuk to Shoga Dzong. But above 20,000 feet there is a heavy summer snowfall too. The wonderful weather we had enjoyed coming up the gorge was probably local, although it may have coincided with a break in the rains.

Four hours' marching through forest, up a very rough track, brought us to the last village, Nyoto Sama. The name covers three or four clusters of stone houses in a wide flat valley, about two miles long. The upper end of this green pasture is blocked by a large glacier, which completely fills it, and at the foot of the glacier is a small fjord-like lake.

Two streams, one from the north, the other from the south, cascade over cliffs into the main valley, probably from small hanging glaciers; and up the valleys to the south an ascending series of snow peaks can be seen.

We stopped at the first cluster of houses and had lunch. A Lama showed me an ecclesiastical flute, on which, he said, the monks played ceremonial music. I could not play a note on it, but that may have been due to reflex inhibitions set up by the knowledge that what I was putting to my lips was a human thigh bone. It was a rather gruesome object, but not very new.

The sun shone brightly for an hour in the middle of the day, and after lunch I decided to push on, in the hopes of seeing some of the great peaks I suspected to exist here. Had it rained I would have stayed where we were for the night.

Continuing along the northern edge of the pasture, I noticed a large torrent pouring out of a chasm to the south and less than half a mile up it a glacier. The mouth of the chasm was blocked by a moraine covered with trees. A village nestled at its foot. Opposite it, on the left bank, was a third hamlet, overshadowed by a ramshackle gompa. Our road took us past the gompa. Finally, near the lake at the foot of the ice wall, was a fourth hamlet, poorer than any of the others. In spite of all these houses — and there were between forty and fifty altogether — I noticed very few inhabitants, nor did I see any animals grazing.

Nyoto Sama is literally ringed round with ice, and must be bitterly cold in winter; for though not very high as places go in Tibet — the fact that barley ripens here would mean that it is not much over 12,000 feet — it lies in a bowl, in the very heart of the great snowy range, overhung by peaks which probably reach 25,000 feet. But what a base camp for a botanist! I can imagine nothing more ideal!

When we reached the foot of the main glacier, I naturally supposed we had at last reached the source of the Po-Yigrong. Leaving the lake below we started climbing steeply up an execrable track, through a belt of silver fir fringed with bushes of *Rhododendron Wardii* and *R. vellereum.* From time to time we could look over the cliff on to the glacier which fell over two high steps, and was split into tall séracs.

Meanwhile the sky had rapidly clouded over, and now it began to rain, gently at first, then harder. After we had climbed some hundreds of feet we reached the top of the cliff and found the valley wider. We were in a meadow overlooking the great honeycombed glacier, and here the men decided to camp. It was a far from ideal spot, a wet sloping hillside above a glacier;

but in the deluge which was now coming down, anything was preferable to marching. The sooner we camped the better, I thought, especially as night was coming on. Now the mystery of the glacier which filled the main valley, yet was not the source of the Po-Yigrong, was solved. Right opposite us, across the glacier, that is to say due south, was a constellation of enormous snow peaks, far higher than anything I had seen yet. They were half smothered in clouds; but the dawn might reveal them, and to this rather slender hope I clung. It was in this cluster of incomparable peaks that the great glacier had its source. It swept down upon the valley in a majestic curve, and the cliff on which we were camped held it up, and turned it eastwards towards Nyoto Sama, where after tumbling over two cliffs it reached the meadow and stopped.

This great ice river quite lately reached the end of the pasture; for the terminal moraine where the wide valley narrowed to the wooded ravine below Nyoto Sama was intact.

Thus the Po-Yigrong consists, as it were, of a chain of lake basins threaded on a gorge. The topmost basin, that of Nyoto Sama, still contains a glacier, above which is a typical ice-worn alpine valley, fed by glaciers. Twenty miles below is the lake basin of Nye. Below Nye the real gorge begins, and fifty miles farther on is the lake basin of Tagé. The largest basin of all, Temo Chamna, is fifteen miles beyond Tagé.

At no remote date, each of these basins contained a lake.

Was the entire Po-Yigrong valley once occupied by a glacier? The length of the river from its source near the Lochen La to Temo Chamna is almost exactly a hundred miles; and the total length to its confluence with the Po-Tsangpo one hundred and twenty miles. The gorge is, of course, water worn, and as I have said, shows no trace of glaciation. But it is clear, both at Ragoonka and at Shonggyi, that the upper plateau valley was scooped out by a glacier. The terminal moraine at Temo Chamna is a further proof. Ten or twenty thousand years would suffice to cut the gorge in the floor of the glacier valley. It is obvious that the gorge, apart from its depth, must quickly take on a water-worn look, since the sections between the lakes are the steepest pitches, and would be rapidly corroded.

It was dusk before we had the tents up, and could begin to dry ourselves, and dark before we had a fire burning, all the wood being soaked. Altogether it was an unhappy evening; I regretted we had not halted at Nyoto Sama.

It rained all night and was still pouring when day broke. I was feeling ill. The clouds ebbed and flowed over the great peaks opposite, affording tantalizing glimpses, which promised much but performed little. A great ice stairway unrolled itself, leading up from the tumbled frozen sea below us to vast, smooth snow fields. We were actually behind the glacier, and could see where the river passed beneath it. Even now a gorge was being cut out under the ice! In the upper valley, herds tended their flocks in wide, wet pastures. It was useless to wait for a view; we might have waited a week. So we packed up, and from the cliff on which we had camped, descended gradually to the upper valley. This was fairly level.

We had left the last trees behind; they were junipers, with stringy bark, gnarled and aged but not tall. But there were clumps of small bushes and shrubs and thousands of bright alpine flowers, forming vivid patches of colour. Brightest of all were the species of Pedicularis, such as *P. bella* and *P. globifera.*

We camped above the last herds' tent. Now the Po-Yigrong (Nye Chu) was so shallow we could ford it. We were at the foot of the Lochen La, which we could see about a thousand or fifteen hundred feet above us, on the opposite side of the stream. Our camp was at 15,000 feet.

And now I must say something of the late summer alpine flora in this high-level glacier valley. It was a very considerable flora, in spite of the lack of woody plants. Dwarf rhododendrons numbered only two species, *R. anthopogon*, and *R. nivale.*

Primulas included, besides *P. alpicola* already mentioned, *P. sikkimensis*, *P. Florindae*, the tiny tot *P. tibetica*, and the magnificent *P. macrophylla*, colonies of which grow in the cold trickling alpine streams. It has large rather flabby leaves and sends up stout stems to end in a hemisphere of mauve flowers, and is the highest primula in Tibet. Other interesting plants included the violet-flowered *Ajuga ovalifolia*, growing under dwarf shrubs, and the lily-like Notholirion. Then, scattered here and there were species of aconite, one with toilet-paper coloured flowers, another with violet flowers; three species of larkspur, one a dwarf plant; the magnificent *Cyananthus lobatus*, var. *insignis*, *Gentiana sino-ornata*, its rich blue flowers just opening, and *G. detonsa*, besides various Compositae, species of Polygonum, geranium, impatiens, a blue-flowered Allium and many more. All these I saw, and collected, as we walked along. Had I spent a couple of days with the herds in this valley, I would have seen many other plants.

August 20th was our last day in the Po-Yigrong valley. Starting at eight o'clock we forded the river with ease, the secret of its mighty strength like that of Sampson, exposed. It rose from a large glacier not far above our camp. Now we began to climb the forbidding wall opposite, ascending by a precipitous zigzag path towards a bare notch on the sky line. It was hard work, the scree oozing water at every step. There were millions of flowers; a dwarf pale form of *Primula sikkimensis*, the water-loving *Allium calcophengos*, with dull purple flowers, two yellow-flowered cremanthodiums, *Trachydium napiforme*, Pleurospermum, several saxifrages, *Meconopsis integrifolia* and *M. horridula*, Oxytropis, anemone, ranunculus, *Polygonum Griffithii*, and *Saussurea laniceps* are a few I collected. Leaving the scree, we got on to bare rock, where boulders lay in confusion at the foot of the cliffs. Alongside, a miniature glacier was fast being reduced to the status of a snow bed. There were no plants here because there was no soil; nothing but hard crystalline rock.

We had started in mist, the mountains hidden behind a veil of cloud. Just as we reached the top of the scree and were entering amongst the rocks, I glanced back to the Po-Yigrong for the last time. At that moment, as though it had been preordained from the beginning of time, a miraculous transformation took place. Suddenly the amorphous cloud thickened and curdled; the veil was rent, and there was revealed the most wonderful view of the actual source of the Po-Yigrong my wildest fancy could ever have painted. If I had waited and dreamed for ten years for that brief glimpse only, I had not lived in vain. It epitomized a life's ambition; a worth-while discovery in Asia, truly finished.

The head of the valley was gripped in a ring of ice. One large lop-sided glacier flowed right down to the floor of the main valley, at its head a broad snowfield beneath an astonishing spike of rock. Other large glaciers occupied high valleys, or were plastered to the cliff face; the cluster of rock spires and steeples suggested a Gothic cathedral, and was almost as unexpected as the cathedral would have been.

The atmosphere remained clear for several minutes, leaving blue ice, grey rock and white snow violently outlined on a turquoise curtain of sky. Then the cloud materialized again as suddenly as it had been absorbed, and the vision disappeared. It was our final glimpse of the lost range. As we reached the pass, which was perhaps 17,000 feet high, without further warning a blizzard swooped up from the other side. A low sangar, or stone wall, had been built across the gap; the men immediately crouched down behind it, and I did the same. The air was full of sharp ice crystals, whirled along at gale speed, and they stung like bees. The wind screamed amongst the towers. I had often wondered what these walls, found on many of the Tibetan passes, were for; when I saw not only the hardy Tibetans but the caravan ponies, mules, and dogs seek shelter, I realized it was not a trench behind which men fought for command of the pass, but a shelter against storm.

For twenty minutes we lay low while the wind, supercharged with snow, roared and shrieked over the bare slabs and tombstones which strewed the mountain. We could see nothing through the flickering veil, but the noise was terrific. Then came a lull. The caravan at once started down the opposite slope; I climbed up a steep boulder scree above the pass to get an all round view. I had barely reached the top of the ridge with much effort, a few hundred feet above the pass, when a second barrage was unleashed. There was no sangar here; so I crept behind a rock on the lee side of the ridge and waited in discomfort. After a time the blizzard went off to wherever blizzards go to, and I surveyed the scene.

I had a marvellous close-up view of the sharp tower which is the highest peak at the actual source of the Po-Yigrong; and an incredible view far down the Po-Yigrong valley to the big glacier, six or eight miles away. Far away in the east, half buried in yeasty clouds, I could see the tops of snow-covered mountains, probably the Markandro group above Tongkyuk. But of the great snow peaks to the south-east I could see nothing; a near ridge blocked the view.

I returned to the pass, then descended by a series of abrupt steps into larger and larger glaciated valleys, going first south, then west, then south again, and finally west; at the head of each valley were snow peaks and glaciers, and the valleys were stepped up, one above the other, the larger valley being always overdeepened. At four o'clock we reached a herds' camp and halted. We were still fairly high, probably 13,000 feet, but there were scattered juniper trees, not forming forest, and thickets of shrubs. Twining species of Codonopsis, especially the stinking *C. sylvestris*, were plentiful, and *Primula sikkimensis*, with most of the alpine plants already mentioned.

Nothing interested me so much as finding *Primula vittata* with claret-coloured bell flowers, here; it is a Chinese plant. But more and more of the alpine plants of western China are now being found on the Tibet plateau, on the northern slopes of the Great Himalayan range, and even on its southern slopes. Yunnan and Szechwan indeed have no endemic alpine flora; they can boast, in the alpine region at least, fewer endemics than was formerly supposed, and their claims, even to those which have not yet been discovered in Tibet, are likely to be falsified in the future. *Primula vittata* adds one more to the list of alpines which is neither Chinese, nor Tibetan, nor Himalayan, but Sino-Himalayan.

While descending from the Lochen La, I saw several marmots, and watched one swim across a torrent; I had always supposed that marmots resembled cats in their horror of water.

Thus for the second time we crossed the great snow range. The flora of the Lochen La was interesting, but, so far as I could see, predictable. Only the rocks looked peculiar. The slabs at the top were crowded with small oblong porphyritic crystals, larger than the matrix crystals. There were other kinds of porphory with big crystals, also gneiss.

With the passage of the Lochen La we finally turned our backs on the Po-Yigrong, which we had been exploring since we crossed the Sobké La on August 2nd. We had now entered the basin of the Gyamda river, but were still within the drainage field of the Tsangpo, which indeed practically fills southern Tibet. The great snowy range we had just crossed forms part of the watershed between the Po-Yigrong and the Gyamda Chu.

During the eighteen days I was in the valley I collected over a hundred species of plants and noted many others, but there must be several hundred more species I did not see, and I know of few areas of Tibet that would better repay exploration for hardy plants than the great Po-Yigrong snow range.

CHAPTER XX

POST ROAD TO CHINA

AUGUST 21st was wet and cold. The day began with what is usually called a 'scene' and ended in the most cheerless and uncomfortable camp I had known for years. Nevertheless, it was memorable also for things by no means unpleasant, including an unparalleled display of *Meconopsis integrifolia* in its dwarf alpine form; not for the world would I wish to forget it!

There was some delay, and before long a violent altercation arose between two Tibetans, one belonging to the party who had brought me over the Lochin La, the other the gipsy king of the camp where we had spent the night. The two men bawled each other out and gesticulated like madmen; called each other unpleasant names, and in fact almost came to blows. What it was all about I could not discover; me, I suspect.

About 9.30 the transport was ready and we started. For the first time since leaving the Tsangpo I had a pony to ride. Heavy demands for transport are difficult to meet in country of vast distances so thinly populated as Tibet is. It often means sending messengers in several directions, a day's journey to another encampment, preparing food, and similar delays. But my needs were modest as we had only twelve loads, and the smallest capitalist had no real difficulty in finding enough transport. Still, he didn't always want to do so.

We continued south-westwards down the valley for an hour, and came to a larger valley. The brimming stream was too swift and deep to ford, at any rate just here. We crossed it by a very unsafe wooden bridge, and turned north-west again, up stream. I had a vague sensation of having seen something like this valley somewhere; the vision was distorted and half forgotten as in a fleeting dream. It was an intuition, not an intellectual effort, yet the sight of this valley had conjured up a memory, even if I could not remember what it was that I was trying to remember. It was an unconscious recognition; and the sensation was recurrent. A man riding a pony who had accompanied us so far, turned down stream as we turned up stream; he said he was bound for Shoga Dzong, which could be reached in a day or two. That remark too set a chord of memory vibrating. That night enlightenment came and I wrote in my diary: 'I believe this is the valley we came up in 1924 from Drukla Gompa to the Pasum Kye La. Otherwise how could we have got from Shoga Dzong to Atsa without crossing the Po-Yigrong *somewhere*?' (The significance of this will be apparent from a glance at the map.)

Presently we recrossed the stream by a second bridge, then jogged along through flooded pastures for a couple of hours. There were bushes and large shrubs by the stream, and even scattered juniper trees; but no forest. Above us was a small almost invisible hanging valley in the western range. The steep slope below was covered with thick bush, which hid the path. We now set about fording the swollen stream. It proved a difficult business. The pony carrying the tents lost its footing, capsized, and nearly became a total loss; it took three men to get it on to its feet again. Pemba too was washed off his feet, and ducked; I dashed in to give him a hand and got ducked also. We were all wringing wet by the time we got over, and I was glad to halt for lunch.

It was two o'clock. The coolies said we could cross the next pass and reach a yak camp on the other side before dark; a piece of fatuous optimism as it turned out. I was half in favour of camping on the spot, but succumbed to the allurements of the promised yak camp.

So we started up the steep slope, and again got drenched to the skin forcing our way through wet bushes. My bedding also got soaked, which always puts me in a bad humour. Arrived at the top of the wall, a wide valley opened out before us, and we marched for a couple of hours. Crossing a stream my saddle girths broke, the saddle twisted under me like a live thing, and I fell headlong into the stream for a third ducking. I decided to walk the rest of the way.

The rocky peaks at the head of the valley were still far away, and I saw no prospect of crossing any pass before nightfall, and said so. The coolies agreed they had been misinformed; and we made up our minds to camp before we reached the end of the scrub — and faggots. So about 4.30 we camped in a sulphur sea of poppies. A very dilapidated old hag was sent out to collect firewood, and she gleaned a little from the inhospitable waste. It was still raining. We were wet to the skin, tired, cold, and hungry. In such circumstances it is distinctly difficult to feel cheerful; but when, about seven o'clock, Pemba brought me some hot tea, I felt better. So passed August 21st, a day memorable for the fact that I had crossed my route of 1924 just above Pungkar, thus closing another traverse through south-eastern Tibet.

It was a party subdued in spirit who ate a tepid breakfast in the pouring rain next morning, after a night of discomfort. But spirits rise with the rising sun even when the latter is quite invisible; and by the time we had packed up with numb fingers and chilled feet, I cheered up, despite a racking headache.

Continuing up the stony valley towards a great buttress from which hung a horseshoe-shaped glacier, we presently turned aside, and made for a notch in the chipped ridge. After a sharp climb up the grey screes, gold flecked with nuggets of saxifrages, we reached the Tse La, a pass about the same height as the Lochen La. From the top I spied glaciers and snow peaks to the east, and also to the west and north-west, quite close to us. Immediately to the west was a pyramidal peak from which four glaciers rolled towards the valley at our feet. Due east, two more glaciers fed the same valley. We could see some distance down this valley towards Laru and the China road. Right below us was a black tent. It did not take us long to descend 1500 or 2000 feet to this sheltered nook in a deliciously green pasture, and here we halted for two hours.

On the cliffs, I found the dainty little *Primula Baileyana* in half-ripe fruit. The short stems each ending in an umbel of violet flowers spring from amidst a tuft of rounded buttercup-like leaves, snowy-white underneath, the whole drawn closely down to the rock crevice, which is the plant's normal habitat. *P. Baileyana* is a typical plateau plant. Unfortunately after a brief though brilliant career in Britain it has been lost to cultivation.

We marched down the stony valley for three hours, dropping abruptly from level to level, till we reached a herds' camp at about 13,000 feet, and bedded down for the night. During the last hour the weather cleared, and our clothes dried on us; but just before reaching camp we had to wade the stream waist deep. There was no forest, only scattered trees here and there; we were back on the edge of the plateau, after spending fifty days in the river gorge region.

We were not yet clear of the glaciers. Glancing up a valley to the east, I caught a glimpse of shrinking white snouts. But as nearly all the side valleys are 'hanging' valleys, it was generally impossible to see anything at all from below. In fact so deeply scored is the country, and so narrow even the largest valley, that high peaks may be close at hand, yet quite invisible.

We now began to meet the typical plateau flora again. A fine form of *Salvia Wardii*, with flowers of pastel-violet, grew under the bushes. Clumps of the coral-budded *Stellera Chamaejasme* — though the fragrant flowers open chalky-white sometimes with a blue-violet tinge — grew amongst the boulders. The lavender-blue bells of *Codonopsis Bulleyana*, so carefully suffused with crimson as to suggest an intravenous injection of aniline dye, mingled with the pale yellow bells of *Primula alpicola*. Contrasted with these elegant plants were clumps of aconite, with white, yellow, and violet flowers, delphinium, violet Cyananthus, and purple Allium, and under bushes the white starry-flowered *A. Gageanum* again. Amongst the shrubs which partly covered rocky slopes *Lonicera bracteata* was ripening its orange berries.

No sooner was my tent pitched than the rain came down in torrents. Even in this part of Tibet it can rain heavily, though the rainy season is short compared with what it is in the deep river gorges close to the mighty peaks of the Assam Himalayas; and to judge from the lateness of the flora the rain does not begin till high summer.

It was still raining on August 23rd. In two hours we reached a scattered village called Nyemna, and the valley broadened again. Also it grew drier. There were bushy growths of *Dracocephalum Hemsleyanum* here, smothered in bright violet-blue flowers, but with ripe seed also. We were now hardly a mile from the main valley and the China road. Another long delay over transport occurred, because every able-bodied villager was out at work, but in spite of it we reached the Gyalam about one o'clock, and halted at Laru for lunch. Laru is a long stage from Gyamda; we could arrive there the following afternoon if we slept the night at Laru; but we could not possibly get there by nightfall, leaving Laru at two o'clock. As there were several good hours of daylight left, I decided to make a start after lunch and camp on the road.

In three hours we reached a village of hovels where we spent an unblissful night fighting the fleas. On the road we passed a large Kampa caravan carrying tea from Batang to Lhasa. The leaders were resting under blue and white cotton tents, or rather awnings, and the great bales of tea bricks were piled up into walls all round them. They had more than a hundred animals, mules, ponies and donkeys.

The valley for some miles above Gyamda is shut in by high cliffs, which are well wooded though with shrubs rather than trees, especially *Quercus Ilex* and a species of juniper. Amongst large shrubs were several species of Lonicera, and Salix, Rowan, cherry, birch, and buckthorn; smaller shrubs are rose, spiraea,

Berberis, Caragana, Cotoneaster, Ribes, and Wikstroemia. Thus there is considerable variety. On the more exposed cliffs grow perennial herbs, of which the most impressive are the fine deep blue *Gentiana Waltonii*, an abundant 'Kabschia' saxifrage, its white flowers dotted yellow, Pedicularis with large bicoloured flowers orange and pale yellow, Adenophora, and a splendid orange-flowered Corydalis.

So we came to Gyamda on a bright sunny day, which could not gild the squalid town; in eleven years it showed no sign of improvement, architectural or sanitary, and the solitary shop it boasted in 1924 had closed its shutters. But a new bridge had been built over the Gyamda river.

I put up in a large house. Pemba and Tashi went out to see what they could buy, and thanks to the tea traffic passing through, returned with some brick tea bought at wholesale rates. There was nothing else; neither matches, sugar, nor oil were on the market. But the post office was functioning, with the same old Chinese postmaster who had been in charge eleven years previously; I bought up all the Tibetan stamps I could lay my hands on. There had been a second edition, and the new ones, in four colours, were a slight improvement on the old, though hardly fine examples of the stamp engravers' art.

I spent four days of rest here, and the weather was fine, sunny, and warm. I was thankful for this — Gyamda can be awful when the winter wind is blowing — but regretted it had not been fine while we were crossing the Lochen La. The situation of Gyamda at the junction of three valleys ensures a wind.

It was now clear why the Gyalam turns to the north after passing through Gyamda, namely to avoid the difficult Po-Yigrong country. The chord across this arc of main road described by the Laru-Nye-Alado route to which reference has been made, is not exactly a short cut, but is certainly used by the inhabitants of the upper Po-Yigrong, as is the route through the Yigrong gorge itself.

Two Jongpens share the duties of administration for the Gyamda district. One of them, the 'people's Jongpen', who might be compared with the 'people's consul' in Imperial Rome, was away on pilgrimage, but the other, the military Jongpen, was in residence. The fact that he took not the slightest notice of me – other than to send a man round to borrow my field glass – augured no good.

Having borrowed my field glass, he soon returned it, saying he could see nothing through it. Neither could I; in his hands it had developed something like a squint.

I made short excursions from Gyamda up the slope behind the town, along the river bank, and down the valley. There is a rather scanty growth of thorn scrub on the hills, becoming more luxuriant and richer in species when protection from the wind is guaranteed. Between the shrubs grow herbaceous plants such as *Milula spicata* which looks and smells like an onion but differs from the ordinary Allium in having the purple flowers arranged in a club-shaped spike instead of in a spherical head. Sometimes this spike reaches a length of two inches. *Incarvillea lutea* – the flowers were over – is abundant round Gyamda. I saw plants with a main stem six feet tall bearing twenty to thirty flowers, and six or eight branch stems with fewer flowers, rising from the same rootstock. In flower on the stony slopes were two species of delphinium, crimson Pedicularis, *Dracocephalum tanguticum*, Cynoglossum and other plants, many with blue or violet flowers. Another common plant is *Codonopsis convovulacea* which falls short of being first class only because so few blooms open simultaneously. If it could only let itself go, ramping and tumbling over the bushes like a clematis, it would be a great success.

My quarters, overlooking an insanitary yard, were not pleasant, and the roosters, crowing from three a.m. onwards, made the night hideous. I would have left Gyamda immediately, but I could not hire any transport till the missing Jongpen returned, which he did on August 26th. A pair of swallows had a nest just over my window, and used to visit it daily, as though taking a fond farewell of the old home before flying south.

The Jongpen's return was an event. There was a great tintinnabulation as the calvacade swept up the narrow street, two mounted men forming the advance guard. One of them had an umbrella slung on his back, the other a rifle. Which was the more lethal I cannot say; it is improbable that either of them had any ammunition. Followed a file of three ponies, each bearing a small male child built into a saddle. They at least wore sparkling raiment bright, for they were beautifully dressed in vivid scarlet and green silks, the colour scheme only vitiated by the fact that they wore magenta Homburg hats. That wrecked it. Finally came the Jongpen himself, jingling along on a gaily caparisoned pony, and looking as though he had just slipped round from Captain Bertram Mills's Circus; for he was completely disguised from head to foot as a Chinese mandarin of the first class, even to his conical white hat with long vermilion tassel. It is curious how the Tibetan ruling classes, who profess to loathe the Chinese, nevertheless ape them. Their contempt for the drab dress of their own lower orders is only equalled by their admiration for the scintillating magnificence of that worn by the former Chinese Amban in Lhasa. In short, the Tibetans do not like the Chinese, but they admire and envy them.

I went round to the post office and talked with Mr. Ma — Hsiao Ma, 'little horse', he called himself. There was not much business, and the tiny cubicle at the top of the rickety stair with its paper-covered Chinese window frame, where Mr. Ma slept, ate, smoked opium and transacted postal business, was always empty. A wooden box, about the size of a small dispatch case, with a large Chinese brass lock, contained all the stamps, cash and accounts that Mr. Ma ever kept. You could send a letter to Lhasa, or to Chamdo, or even to India, with reasonable assurance of its ultimate arrival at destination; but you could not telegraph, or buy a postal order, or a post office savings certificate, or a dog licence.

Mr. Ma was a little man, the tightly drawn skin of his yellow face like cracked ivory, his bright almond eyes screwed down to slits against the glare and wind of this harsh climate. His teeth were yellow with age, and a straggling moustache and beard proclaimed his years. He wore a long blue gown, much patched, and a short sleeveless sheepskin jacket over it, short velvet boots, and a hard round black silk skull-cap with a scarlet button. His eyes and cheeks were sunken, the cheekbones almost protruding through the tight sallow skin – he seemed to be wasting away from within owing to his opium-smoking excesses.

'When does the mail leave for Lhasa, Ma Hsien-Seng?' I asked.

'The day after it arrives here from Lhasa, Hwa Hsien-Seng.'

'And when is that?'

Mr. Ma shook his head; he did not know. Perhaps to-morrow, perhaps the day after. The post arrived from Lhasa when there were letters to come, and as the courier had to go back, he took letters to the capital – if any. It was a sliding service. Mr. Ma was not overworked. Lately there had been a good deal of correspondence passing to and fro between Lhasa and Chamdo, and between Lhasa and Shoga Dzong, he told me.

Just then I heard a jingle of bells below. Another Jongpen arriving? Mr. Ma said suavely: 'There's the Lhasa post.'

I went to the window, and looked through a hole in the paper. All I saw in the cobbled street was a mangy dog scavenging, and a woman in rags, shooing some pigs away from a tray of grain which was drying in the sun. Mr. Ma lay down and began preparing his 'gun' – the Yunnan colloquial for opium pipe. There was a light footfall on the rickety stairs – a visitor to the post office was a rare event. However, it was only a small boy who put his head rather shyly round the corner; seeing only the two of us, he stepped into the room. Although little more than four feet tall, he was dressed in a long *chupa* and cloth boots, and carried a sword stuck horizontally across his stomach like a full-sized man. He had a round, almost cherubic face, and red cheeks, and he looked hot – which was not surprising as it was now midday and the sun beat down fiercely on the mud town. I wondered what he wanted – had he come to buy a stamp?

For a few seconds he stared at me, then at the Chinese postmaster. He said, 'Yong-song: lam yakpo mare' (I have come: the road is bad). Then he put a grubby hand inside the ample bosom of his *chupa*, and pulling out a grubby letter, handed it to the little postmaster with an air. It was the Lhasa mail!

Letters travel from Lhasa to Gyamda in four days, by relays of couriers, who go at the double – or are supposed to do so. The courier carries a stick with bells loosely attached, which jingle as he jogs along over the mountains, warning all whom it may concern that he is carrying Government mails – very few private letters are sent in Tibet. Approaching Gyamda the regular courier had apparently flagged, and sublet the contract to the cherub, who had sauntered and dallied along the road like any boy on his way to school; but he had undoubtedly run the last half mile in the orthodox manner. Hence his arrival all hot and bothered.

I could get little information as to what was going on in Lhasa or anywhere else. However, the cherub assured me that a British Mission had arrived there – and a whole crowd of Englishmen! This I knew to be untrue; but to a country Tibetan, anyone dressed in European clothes, from an Indian officer to a doctor babu, would be an Englishman! In fact, the Political Officer, Mr. Williamson, had recently arrived in Lhasa.

Had I on receipt of this intelligence gone straight to Lhasa and seen Mr. Williamson and the high Tibetan officials, it is quite possible – that is, supposing I had not been stopped on the way – that everyone would have calmed down. Probably my travelling in Tibet without a passport would have been overlooked, and the matter settled out of court with an apology from me, a promise not to err again, and – who knows? – an invitation from the Tibetan officials, who are nothing if not polite, to come again! Mr. Williamson, indeed, whom I knew personally, hearing what had happened, did his best to smooth things over with the Tibetan officials. He was popular in Lhasa, and highly respected, and if anyone could have moved the Tibetan Government, he would have; indeed it is probable that his endeavours were not without effect. Most unfortunately about this time he fell seriously ill, and before the end of the year 1935, to the deep regret of his many friends, died in Lhasa. His death was a real loss to the Government of India.

My purpose was to continue my botanical reconnaissance, and to this end I now decided to return to Takpo and Tsari by the most direct road. There are two direct roads from Gyamda, followed by traders and pilgrims, one via the Sho La, the other via the Ashang Kang La, a little farther west. Both leave the Gyalam west of Gyamda, and turn due south.

On August 28th we set out along the famous highway which leads to Lhasa. It is a rather long stage up the main valley of the Gyamda Chu to Chinda, and it took us eight hours. The morning, however, was gloriously fine, although towards evening a strong wind rose, bringing a threat of rain. The slopes and stony terraces were bright with flowers, and some plants, notably Onosma, Dracocephalum and Morina, were in ripe fruit, and I collected seed of them all. I enjoyed the march, and revelled in the colourful scenery – the clouded bottle-green of the river, the deeper green of the thickets, the delphinium-blue sky, and the grey rocks overspread with a film of many coloured flowers.

Gyamda marks the extreme western limit of the gorge country. There the houses are still roofed with wooden boards, as they are throughout Kongbo. Farther west, at Chinda, we returned to the flat mud roofs of dry Tibet. The rocks also change. The granite, so conspicuous round Gyamda is, at

Chinda, replaced by metamorphics, perhaps due to contact between the igneous rocks of the Po-Yigrong range and the sedimentary rocks of the Lhasa region. I first noticed the change after crossing a big torrent from the north.

Numbers of pilgrims, both men and women, were on the road, some going to Lhasa, others returning to their homes after visiting the holy shrines. They carried large blue cotton umbrellas, made in China, and spears which they used as staffs. Their garb was picturesque, and added a touch of wildness to man in harmony with the wildness of the country. The conventional attire for a pilgrim of either sex was apparently a white — or off-white — *chupa*, tied round the waist with a scarlet sash; scarlet boots; and white felt hat with low crown and wide brim, rather like a clergyman's hat. Everyone carried on his or her back a bamboo hoop-shaped frame, into which was strapped his worldly all, clothing, food, and cooking pots. These people, some of whom came from the far frontiers of Kam and had been walking all the summer, had certainly solved the problem of travelling light.

A few miles out from Gyamda, I noticed a snow peak on the range to the south; but the northern range was hidden from us, although the fact that we crossed two large torrents indicates that there are some high peaks in that direction also. Probably the Po-Yigrong range continues west of the Laru-Gyamda road, and both the Tro La and the Pasum Kye La cross it.

Swallows were numerous at Chinda.

The fine weather continued, at least in the valley, and on August 29th we marched for seven hours, only stopping half an hour for lunch at the mouth of a valley which leads to the Sho La.

There were milestones along the road, some of them approximately a mile apart. Each consisted of a huge pile of stones, enclosing an inscribed tablet, something like the foundation stone of a public urinal laid by the borough engineer. Inscribed on each were Chinese numerals in black paint. One would expect this to be the mileage to Lhasa, but since that could hardly run to three figures, perhaps, with the perversity of the Oriental mind, it recorded the mileage from Chamdo.

Traffic increased; pilgrims, tea caravans, and Lamas passed us. A noble Lama, belonging to one of the great Lhasa families, was concealed from the vulgar gaze in a magnificent tent close to where we halted for the night. It recalled those colourful pavilions depicted in the history books in which the knights of the Middle Ages lived, during the campaigns in Picardy. We met also a wealthy merchant, dressed in purple and fine silk.

The road was still blazoned with brilliantly coloured flowers, and every cliff clothed with rock plants, or with trees and shrubs. I noticed twenty-four species of woody plants, not counting undershrubs, some of the more important being *Spiraea laevigata*, rhododendron, poplar, and two species of clematis. At higher altitudes juniper was the last tree. There was plenty of red birch, the translucent bark of which is made into paper.

On the cliffs were clumps of gold-buttoned saxifrages, the blue *Gentiana Waltonii*, Adenophora, Androsace, geranium, and numerous charming little ferns. *Primula Florindae* I had seen the previous day, perhaps for the last time; but *P. sikkimensis* was still abundant, scattered amongst the bushes on sheltered slopes. Only the hard gravel river terraces were rather barren; here I found Thermopsis in half-ripe fruit, Allium, Dipsacus, and the two dracocephalums, not uncommon where there was a suggestion of turf.

I also caught a curious vole here, a species of Microtus.

August 30th, our last day on the Gyalam – bright in the morning, but clouding over ominously after noon.

We reached a large valley. Since leaving Chinda we had been marching south-west, and so we continued to a village called De, the Gyalam here turning due west. De is not more than a mile off the main road, but hidden from it. We halted only to get fresh transport, then continued up the valley.

Shortly we reached a yak camp in a broad open pasture where juniper trees were widely scattered, and halted for the night.

I watched a girl milking one of the cows, and saw her put her lips several times to the animal's vulva, and blow hard; when the creature had emptied its bladder with a convulsive movement, the milk began to flow.

Tashi told me that most of the Lhasa officials were at the monastery of Chögorche, on the far side of the range ahead of us and not far from where we were camped. Cawdor and I had passed through Chögorche in 1924, and I had intended to do so now in order to visit a mysterious sacred lake I had heard of, in which the devout see visions wrapped in rainbows. But learning of the church convention I decided to alter my route; I am neither very sociable nor very devout.

CHAPTER XXI

SOUTH

IT was the last day of August, and not fine in the mountains. Heavy storm clouds circled round, threatened us, then spilled part of their contents, and passed on to water a hilltop a mile away. We caught one severe irrigation in the middle of the afternoon; and as by this time we were fairly high up, it was an unpleasantly cold douche.

The march was a long fourteen miles, in a general south-easterly direction, and though we kept as close to the stream as possible, we had some arduous climbing over cliffs.

Generally the valley was broad, and it had been heavily glaciated, although the peaks we saw both to north and south did not look more than 20,000 feet high. Such glaciers as we saw were small. This range, which I had already crossed in 1924 farther west, forms the watershed between the Gyamda and Tsangpo rivers. If it continues beyond the Gyamda Chu, as it may do, parallel to the Great Himalayan range, then the Gyamda Chu must cut through it between Gyamda and Tsele Dzong.

There is a wide blank space on the map here, and until it is filled in, it is impossible to be sure of the directions of the mountain ranges.

A blue-flowered garlic (Allium) was very abundant in the turf, also *Milula spicata* again. *Gentiana sino-ornata* in both dark and light blue was beginning to flower, and on a scree I noticed *G. amoena*, a pinchbeck flower very different from the deep blue trumpets found on the southern slopes of the Himalayas though this too is *G. amoena*. Another common alpine was the dry plateau form of *Meconopsis horridula*, shooting up a sheaf of short 1-flowered scapes. On the scrub covered slopes, where common Tibetan shrubs grew in shivering congestion, the dwarf *Iris goniocarpa* (section Pseudo-regelia) was in fruit; in flower it is a pretty wee plant, with mottled violet falls, recalling *I. kumaonensis*, but darker and more handsome. The spathes are usually 1- sometimes 2-flowered. The large aril on the seed is a warning that germination may be long retarded.

We had yak transport, which though slow, is sure. Yak are queer animals, full of consuming curiosity which makes them poke their noses into everything. My tent always intrigued them. They hung round it sniffing gustily. Then, when I suddenly emerged from it, up went their short bushy tails into the air, stiffly erect, and wheeling round, they galloped a few yards, and halted; curiosity had triumphed over fear.

After a good night's sleep, I felt fresh during the morning's march across broad acres of rolling turf, where few flowers grew. Even when we climbed a steep, wooded cliff, I noticed nothing I had not seen many times before. But during the afternoon, when it rained, and I was getting more tired, more cold, and not unnaturally more disgusted with life at every mile, I found plenty of interesting alpines; saxifrages, and incarvilleas and monkshoods and alliums and sedums, to mention a few. These ought to have cheered my drooping spirits; but I was too deeply awash by this time and almost foundered beyond caring. We reached a cold yak camp at 5.30, the highest in the valley; we had passed hundreds of grazing yak between the lower camp and this one.

We made a late start next morning, but reached the pass by two o'clock, having halted twenty minutes for lunch; it was too cold and gloomy to linger.

As I had expected, the climb to the top, even starting from 15,000 feet, proved arduous. And so on September 1st we crossed the Ashang Kang La, a bare saddle about 17,000 feet high, covered with loose rocks of arkose the colour of dried blood. There were a few widely scattered plants in flower even at the very summit, including a most attractive dwarf saxifrage with large spotted flowers, an ultramarine Corydalis, Saussurea, its wool all fluffed out, Cremanthodium, Aconitum, *Meconopsis horridula*, Polygonum and gentian. From a little distance one would say that these bleak stony mountains were utterly barren; it is with a shock of surprise one finds so many charming flowers close to the sky. In fruit were two species of primula (*P. purpurea* and *P. macrocarpa*), and *Meconopsis integrifolia*. Just below the north side of the pass the valley divides, and the more westerly branch crosses the range by another pass, the Gechi La, which leads into the Chögorche valley. As already stated I had intended to follow this route in order to visit the 'rainbow' lake; but on hearing that the Ministers of Tibet were at Chögorche, I altered course two points to the east.

There was only a limited view from the Ashang Kang La and I found myself looking down a long remarkably straight ice-worn valley, between high sierra-like ridges. There was a small lake at its head, but no glacier. The scenery was grim.

Descending, we reached a yak camp, about three miles distant in one and a half hours, and halted.

This massive range, stretching eastwards from Lhasa, is one of the greatest pastures in Tibet. We saw hundreds of animals grazing; and there are scores of long, level, ice-worn valleys like this, and they contain thousands of yak and zo (half-bred yak), ponies, mules, sheep, and goats. The yak are mostly black with white face, a few almost entirely white, while chocolate-coloured specimens are not rare. The herds decorate favourite animals with coloured ear tassels and pompons, boring holes in their ears for the purpose.

Next morning, September 2nd, before continuing our journey south (the valley here runs south-east) we visited a sacred lake called Gyalam Tso, situated in a hanging valley right above the camp. It is a spot greatly venerated, whither many pilgrims come; and the Ministers had recently honoured it with a visit, and set up a picturesque shrine, flanked by tall poles. The lake, however, is just an ordinary glacier lake, sombre and deep.

Mile after mile we stumbled down the endless valley, until in the afternoon it joined a larger one, with a snow peak visible at its head near the Sho La. At this point we turned south.

As soon as we entered the large valley, I noticed cultivation. 'Good!' I thought, 'we must be near a village.' Yet still we went on mile after mile, and still the valley seemed endless. I felt ill, and was in some pain; it was a pity the marches were so long. As usual I had started off full of enthusiasm, but by four o'clock I was a total loss, unable to take any great interest in anything. I began to think we were going on until we reached the Tsangpo!

The yak plodded on unconcerned as yak do, blowing hard, or uttering the curious grunting noise which is responsible for their unlovely name – *Bos gruinens.* Sometimes they quarrelled amongst themselves, and an incensed elder would pursue a too fresh juvenile for a short distance at astonishing speed.

Towards evening we reached a broken-down bridge, which looked in imminent danger of complete collapse; it was horribly rickety, and the yak seemed to think so too. In the gathering dusk I thought it *had* collapsed, so many important bits of it were missing altogether. The nearside sagged dangerously to starboard, the off side more violently to port; and because it was made of a solid whose resistance to tension is notoriously uncertain, you felt something might happen at any moment. On a boulder beside it was inscribed in letters a foot high: 'O māni padme hum!' which was ominous enough. However, the Tibetans undismayed drove the squeamish yak across one by one, and I followed; the stream was rough and could have been relied on to end one's troubles quickly, but we got across safely if not with dignity.

It began to rain again. Everybody agreed we ought to have reached the village by six o'clock. It was now nearly seven. Obviously nobody really knew where the village was – or cared. Perhaps there wasn't one. Nevertheless, at 7.30 we arrived at Nye in the dark, and a wretched place it proved to be — four cold stone houses! All the good people of Nye had to offer in the way of accommodation consisted of two walls with a leaky roof; the other two walls were missing. It was draughty; it was damp. Luckily the altitude was hardly more than 12,000 feet and it was not cold.

The first thing I learnt was that it would take us another two days to reach the Tsangpo. As we had now been marching for fifty-six days out of the seventy-two since we left Chayul Dzong, I decided to rest a day.

We were now down at tree level once more, but the only forest was in the ravines, though there were thickets of shrubs and bushes.

The alpine bogs were gay with a nodding yellow-flowered Cremanthodium, and with the blue *Lomatogonium deltoideum.* There were not many species of alpine plants, at any rate not in flower, but some, such as gentians and Cyananthus, occurred in countless numbers. At high levels *Primula sikkimensis* was still flowering so thickly you would have said there was not room for another plant. Yet two months earlier the ground had been equally thickly carpeted with *Primula Roylei,* which was now ripening its seed. Such succession is typical of the grazing country, and seems to be a direct result of the yaks' rich manuring of the ground.

Tashi had shot a hill partridge, a common Tibetan bird (*Perdix hodgsoniae*) of which we saw numbers scuttling about in the low scrub, running when disturbed, and rising quickly to settle again not far away.

I skinned the partridge, and curious to know what these birds were picking up so eagerly in the scrub, I extracted the contents of its stomach, and classified the contents. Here is a list of casualties:

six small grasshoppers, damaged about the legs;
six unidentified larvae, more or less intact;
one small spider and one large ditto, apparently unrelated;
four small moths, very worn;

one large ant, and a collection of ants' eggs, easily recognizable;

a promiscuous collection of small beetles (more than fifteen);

several flies, with parts missing;

numerous seeds of grasses, and of polygonum.

A varied and omnivorous diet!

It rained all morning, but the afternoon was fine and I took a country walk. A fat and prosperous-looking Ligularia, a genus split off the vast and rampant race of Senecio, was very conspicuous on the turfy slopes. Though not tall, its big pale ace-of-spades shaped leaves buttressing the short fat yellow spike of typical ragwort flowers suggest prosperity. These ligularias are often invasive weeds which have come as an answer to man's interference with the vegetation. They occur on the open turf slopes round villages, where the forest has been cut and burnt, and once there nothing will eradicate them. They increase rapidly and choke out all rivals by sheer brute strength.

Nye, the highest village in the valley, provided no rest cure. The house where we stayed was the usual farmyard of chickens, cats and dogs, living on the brink of starvation, sad-eyed, desperate and unhappy; except perhaps the fowls. I got little sleep the second night, but felt better for the halt.

Long marches now seemed inevitable, and September 4th was a very long day. We covered about fifteen miles to a village called Shām in ten hours, and it rained nearly all the time. Narrow as the valley was, and wide the swift stream, the path followed it closely, and we were spared climbing; we could hardly have descended five hundred feet.

As might be expected at the end of the summer in a valley used only twice a year when the yak are going up to and returning from the alps, the path was exceedingly rough, and almost completely overgrown. Often we had to force our way through the bushes.

Meanwhile the broad ice-scooped valley above Nye had given

place to a narrow water-worn gorge, between bold bare granite cliffs. A fringe of forest lined the river, but in some places the birch trees had been drowned where they stood owing to flooding caused by some stoppage lower down. Tranquil pools alternated with steep narrow channels where the water raged furiously.

Except that there was more forest, and that oak replaced juniper, there were as yet no revolutionary changes in the vegetation. Though we had left the alpine zone, flowers were plentiful, the old familiar flowers; and the fruiting plants likewise. *Dracocephalum tanguticum* replaced *D. Hemsleyanum*; *Milula spicata* grew by the thousand in open ground; some specimens had white flowers. Three common species of androsace were in unripe fruit and far from rare, with *Primula sikkimensis* and the finest form of *P. pulchelloides*. By evening near the village of Shām, thick colonies of the giant cowslip, *P. Florindae*, had appeared, crowding the bogs and attaining nearly four feet in height. Other well known plants were *Incarvillea lutea*, the delicate lavender bell-flowered codonopsis, little *Iris goniocarpa* again, and *Onosma Hookeri Wardii*.

Far down the wooded glen, patches of forest clung like moulting fur to the cliffs, and thickly filled the slot-like ravines. The river broadened out, and the wide expanse of swift rippling water shone like quicksilver in the evening light. Pine trees appeared on the stark cliffs, black against the leaden sky, and the mountain tops grew barer as we approached the Tsangpo valley.

A sapphire crust of flowers covered the bushes of *Cerotostigma Griffithii*, now at its best, and piptanthus was still sheeted with yellow. Frothing seas of polygonum surged round the clearings, and mingled with it were the violet trumpets of *Cyananthus incanus*. Other meadow plants, such as thalictrum with mauve or lilac drop flowers dangling on the ends of fine wires, grew amongst the bushes. I picked a little wild fruit here and there as we went along — small cherries, rather tart, red and black currants quite tasteless, and a few raspberries.

At half-past six we reached Shām, a poor-looking agricultural village of half a dozen houses scattered on both banks of the river. The inhabitants, mostly old, were friendly souls, but they had no accommodation to offer, so I pitched my tent and was much troubled all night by mosquitoes.

For the last march to the Tsangpo we used coolie transport again, and a few ponies. An attractive rosy-cheeked little woman with a disarming smile and raven black hair carried my camera. A few hours' march, passing through two villages, with much changing of men and ponies, brought us through the jaws of a rocky gorge into the hot sunshine of the Tsangpo valley. A mile down stream was Tromda, a village on the right bank. Abruptly the rock changed from granite to metamorphic, and tree growth except in the villages ceased. All crops are irrigated.

The Tsangpo winds its solitary way between dry hills and is lined with sand dunes and stony terraces on which a characteristic thorn scrub grows, consisting mainly of *Sophora Moorcroftiana*, with a few deeply rooted herbaceous plants.

Shortly after we reached the Tsangpo, a squall came up from the south, and assailed us with lightning and wind of gale force, but not much rain. In an hour the sky was as blue as the Mediterranean. I saw big fish leaping in the swift muddy river. We crossed in a boat like a box, sculled by one man, reaching Tromda on the ninth day out from Gyamda.

I was compelled by sickness to rest two days at Tromda. The corn was being reaped, that is to say pulled up, and the peasants could be heard singing in the fields, long after dark. They were bright moonlight nights, and pleasantly warm.

I had finished my supply of Indian tea some time ago, and was using Chinese brick tea, which is a poor substitute. Tashi shot a hare (*Lepus oiostelus*) and I had hare soup and fried liver one night, and hare brain for breakfast.

On the sand flats in the river bed, which were occasionally inundated, grew plants different from those of the loose sand hills. They included Artemisia, Euphorbia, samphire, and a little ragged grey-mauve aster. Here hares were plentiful.

I enjoyed my rest, and was feeling well enough to continue the journey on September 8th. Marching up a stream from the south, past the picturesque monastery of Ganden Rapden surrounded by a welter of unsavoury hovels, we reached Guru Namgye Dzong about six miles from the Tsangpo. The original dzong was finely placed on a spur which rises like a wall high above the ravine. It is in ruins, and the modern dzong was built tamely by the stream. Though insignificant in size it is important because the magistrate controls Tsari. Paper is made here from the bark of a shrub.

At Ganden Rapden Gompa, where we had lunch, two young men with close-cropped heads welcomed me. They wore long dark red robes. But what impressed me was that one of them spoke a few words of English — he had learnt it in Lhasa, he said. In spite of his youth, he was the head monk of the monastery, which contains a hundred and thirty monks. Many years ago the Chinese soldiers came to the gompa which submitted to them and was well treated, but Guru Namgye Dzong was heavily fined.

Our next march was a longer one. In a couple of hours we reached the confluence of two streams, the western valley well cultivated. Continuing south-east, we came to a quaint monastery called Boomda Semung, built round a large *chorten*. This monastery has some title to fame, because its holy founder had conveniently buried beneath the *chorten* a large army of devils who had been in the habit of interfering with pilgrims on their way to Tsari. We stopped here for lunch, and I was shown an iron chain curtain hanging before the door which led to the holiest place.

Just before we reached the monastery, a holy monk rode by. The man who was leading my pony snatched off his hat and bowed his head, for the Lama to lay his hand on gently, as he passed. It was a friendly act, and the man was highly gratified.

A short distance beyond Boomda Semung cultivation ceases. After going another five miles, and ascending steeply, we reached Trupchuka, the last village, and halted. There was no cultivation here, the altitude being 14,000 feet; a windscreen of brushwood had been piled round two sides of the village.

Had we turned up the other valley to the west, we could have crossed either the Karpo Ra La or the Kamba La, and reached the Char Chu above Sanga Chöling; as it was, we had to cross two passes, although both of them are over the same range. There seems to be no lack of passes over this range, which forms the watershed between the Tsangpo and the Subansiri. We might have taken any of half a dozen which are close together hereabouts. I crossed the Kongmo La because I wanted to revisit Chösam before returning to Sanga Chöling.

The Kongmo La, 17,520 feet, is not a difficult pass, but the approaches on either side are exceedingly steep, and we experienced horrible weather, with snow and heavy rain. It took us altogether nine hours to do the remaining seventeen miles to Chösam. We reached the pass at noon, having done the hard ascent of six miles from Trupchuka in rather good time; it was the terrific deluge we caught on the far side which almost brought us to a standstill. I noticed a small glacier or snow bed in a corrie on the south side, but visibility was poor and I could not see far. A large number of alpine plants were in flower, between 16,000 and 17,000 feet. On the north side the woolly mantles of Saussurea were dotted about like snowballs; but on the south side there were hundreds of dwarf yellow cremanthodiums, gentians, monkshoods, and other flowers, contented with the rough screes.

After descending for about six miles, we reached the junction of three valleys. We had passed this spot after crossing the Cha La on July 1st, so I was again on familiar ground. It would have been easy to cross the Cha La now, but instead we turned down the valley, and reached Chösam at 6.30, just before it got dark. It had stopped raining, and I felt more able to cope with the many plants I saw, amongst them Cyananthus, a Cremanthodium with scented fruits, and masses of white-flowered delphinium. But I was very glad to reach Chösam; the day had been long and the deluge at 17,000 feet was an unpleasant reminder that Tibet is a hard land.

We were now definitely embarked on the return journey, and though there was more exploration still to be done, yet the thrill of a high enterprise, which had buoyed me up on the outward journey, was waning.

CHAPTER XXII

EAST WIND

My object in returning to Chösam was to collect seed of *Adonis brevistyla*, a beautiful perennial with finely cut leaves like sea-weed, amongst which float the gaping pearl cups freighted with golden stamens. The silky petals have a delicate sheen and are sometimes shot with razor blue. The next day, therefore, Tashi and I rode three or four miles down the valley to the cliffs. Although by the second week in September, autumn has breathed heavily over Tibet, in moist Tsari there were still more flowers than ripe seeds. The alpine slopes were coloured with the pale periwinkle-blue *Cyananthus microphyllus*, mingled with the glossy indigo of *C. lobatus*, var. *insignis*, both abundant. Less flamboyant were yellow Corydalis and saxifrages, and there were several plants with duller flowers such as the purplish *Kingdon-Wardia codonopsidoides*. Brilliance was added by the reddening leaves of dwarf Lonicera. Several gentians were in flower.

The seeds of Adonis were barely ripe, those of Notholirion half ripe, but *Nomocharis nana* and the saffron-flowered *Primula Barnardoana* were thoroughly ripe, although it would have been rash to have collected them much earlier. No rhododendron seed was ripe yet.

That night at Chösam the minimum temperature dropped to 42° F., about the same as it was on July 2nd.

September 12th was fine, with a cloudy sky. We crossed the shrunken Tsari Chu, and went straight up the mountain making for the Rip La, a pass of over 16,000 feet which we reached in two and a half hours. Beneath the rhododendron bushes was flowering the beautiful sea blue *Gentiana trichotoma* var. *tsariensis*. The country was very steep and wild here, and I could see snow peaks in a north-easterly direction, heavily engaged with clouds. The slate cliffs on the pass were violently crumpled and twisted, as though the strata had been gripped in a vice. Many alpine flowers coloured the rocks, the gayest being *Lomatogonium oreocharis*, a fairily dainty gentian with inch-wide flowers striped darker and paler pansy-blue. The lomatogoniums, which may be described as high alpine swertias, are amongst the most beautiful of late autumn flowers in Tibet, but not one is in cultivation so far as I know. *L. oreocharis* is probably the finest. At least three species of Cremanthodium and two species of rosette-like lactucas, their flat spirals of violet florets wound inside a spreading collar of green leaves, grew on the scree. Just over the pass I found a colony of the cotton-headed *Bolocephalus saussuroides*, the saussurea-like genus I had discovered at Tsogar in July.

From the pass a precipitous track led down to a deeply scoured valley, and we halted at the village of Yutö which is on the pilgrim road round Takpa Shiri. We had descended the north side of the range twice the altitude we had ascended on the south side, so Yutö could not have been much over 12,000 feet. It was also exceedingly damp and chilly, and when about dusk thick cloud came rolling up, I felt that Tsari was no place to be in in the autumn.

To call Yutö a village is perhaps to abuse words. It is a rest-house for pilgrims. There was no cultivation. One inhabited hut, two uninhabited, and three in ruins, surrounded by bleak mountains and wet meadow was all there was to it. Half a mile down the valley there was fir forest.

I might have crossed the pass above Chickchar — the Drölma La, and followed the pilgrims' road round Takpa Shiri, crossing in turn the Shagam La, over 16,000 feet, Tama La, Go La, Tapgyu La (all these over 15,000 feet), and several other passes. Yutö is the eleventh stage from Chickchar, on the short pilgrimage called *Kingkor* in Tibetan. F. M. Bailey made the pilgrimage in 1913, and George Sherriff, the botanical explorer, followed him in 1936, and made a magnificent collection of plants in Tsari, where occur many species not as yet recorded for any other part of Tibet.

September 13th was my unlucky day. We were enveloped in a thick, wet blanket of cloud throughout the grinding eight mile ascent to the Takar La, and consequently saw nothing. It took us nearly five hours to reach the pass. Above Yutö was a lot of scrub, including two dwarf honeysuckles with fat soft glaucous blue berries in paper collars — one was *Lonicera cyanocarpa* (probably var. *porphyrantha*), the other *L. coerulea*; with them was a common species abundantly covered with small scarlet berries, *L. setifera*. Above the last thickets endless drifts of pale dwarf *Primula sikkimensis* and the milky-white-flowered cut-leafed variety, *subpinnatifida*, were in bloom, so there was no hope of getting ripe seed of this latter for another six weeks. There were also great numbers of Bolocephalus, even more beautifully fluffy in fruit than in flower, shining like lambent fairy lights through the clammy mist. Other plants which grew in colonies were a Caltha-leafed Cremanthodium, and yellow Corydalis with delicate almost seaweed-like foliage. Finally we reached dirty black screes of pulverized slate, where few plants lodged — the long tap-rooted Saussurea (*S. tridactyla*) alone wallowed in the glutinous mess. But by this time the mist was so opaque and I was so chilled that it was hard to see anything.

The Takar La is 16,700 feet high, steep on both sides. There is an easy path down into the alpine valley below the Cha La, and the yak took this path. But we ourselves followed a more direct track, fit only for goats and humans, and reached the bottom where we had camped on June 30th an hour before the yak arrived.

Just over the pass I found crusted mats of the charming little *Gentiana Sherriffii*, which looks like blue bubbles frothing out from under the stones to crystallize in glassy mats; as we got down from the windswept screes, more and more alpines appeared.

We found the herds not yet departed, and rested in their tents till the yak arrived. We could have reached Sanga Chöling that evening, but I was content to camp a few miles lower down the valley. The coolies were in a hurry to get back because the whole population of the Tsari valley had been ordered to appear before the Jongpen of Guru Namgye Dzong, to account for their actions. About a month previously, some person or persons unknown had slain five ponies in Tsari, and the horse coopers were worried.

There were few ripe seeds in the valley, *Cyananthus microphyllus*, studded with periwinkle-blue flowers, trailed over the grassy slopes as though good for months, and lower down there was *C. lobatus* again. There were even flowers on *Primula pulchelloides*, and at the higher levels *Dracocephalum Hemsleyanum* was magnificent. We camped at the spot where I had first seen it in flower on June 30th. The plants had grown enormously, filling out into little bushes, and here I collected plenty of seed. As I have said before this plant might well be grown as an annual, and one of its charms is the long flowering period, which in England is only cut short by the first frosts. If it is grown as a perennial, it should be cut back after flowering, to encourage basal growth and ensure a bushy habit.

A very slow-growing composite, probably a species of Lactuca, was in flower in the tough soil. My attention had been drawn to its thin pale green leaves, in June. I expected that by now it would have grown up into a big plant. Not a bit of it! So far as the visible head of palest violet flowers was concerned, they grew flush with the ground, contrasting pleasantly with the Nile-green leaves. But the early promise of something exotic was not confirmed.

On September 14th we reached Sanga Chöling in a little over two hours, to find it almost evacuated. It is a curious fact that the population of even the most settled parts of Tibet is nomadic. Returning to a village after an absence of three months, one often meets quite a different set of people. Old friends are scattered in all directions; some have gone to Lhasa, others on pilgrimage round one of the sacred mountains, still others to China or India, to trade.

Staying at the inn, if one could call it that, was a young Chinese trader, named Hen Shung K'ung. He represented a large firm which has branches or agents in Shanghai, Likiang, Rangoon, Bhamo, and elsewhere. I could not help regretting that international finance or Big Business, was getting a hold upon even so poor a country as Tibet, and would wring it dry. For Tibet is desperately poor. It has no raw materials, except wool and borax from the salt lakes, and a little gold dust. It cannot afford to import great quantities of manufactured goods – certainly not European manufactured goods, and so raise the standard of comfort for the inhabitants. On the other hand, the crops and herds of Tibet assure a pleasant livelihood for the people under prevailing conditions. If the west must interfere in the economy of Tibet, the kindest thing it can do is to improve gradually those services which the country is suited to render mankind: better pastoral returns.

In the evening, the Jongpen, who had been absent for the day, returned, and invited me round to his rooms, in the same block where Hen Shung K'ung and I resided. The Chinaman came too, and we drank spirit which was absolute – alcohol. The Jongpen himself did not drink, but I think that was because he was feeling too coy to drink with strangers; he seemed to me to have had one over the eight before we arrived. He was very friendly. I learnt that he had not received the letters I had sent him through the Jongpen of Kyimdong, in July. Possibly these had been sent to Lhasa, and thence to India, but of that I could not be certain; alternatively, they had been lost, or thrown away, between Kyimdong and Sanga Chöling.

Hen Shung K'ung spoke Chinese in a cultivated voice, with clear enunciation, but after our visit to the Jongpen, and a tot of brandy in my room on the way back, I could not understand a word he said; whether owing to a thickening of his speech, or to a lapse in my hearing, I do not know. I gathered that there was a black tiger — or possibly leopard — in Tibet, and a unicorn — or possibly a one-horned rhinoceros, and that he was very interested in a mica mine on the road between Sanga Chöling and Lhasa, and that the Tashi Lama was returning to Tibet in November. But as I say, I may have misunderstood him.

During the three days I spent here I enjoyed pleasant company, and had enough work to keep me from being idle. Indeed I have seen no village in Tibet which attracts me so much as Sanga Chöling. It had a well-kept air.

I spent the morning of September 15th with the black lizards down the valley. It had rained in the night, but the sun came out, and the midday warmth tempted scores of these ugly creatures, known to science as *Agama himalayana sacra*. They can run very swiftly, and when frightened betray their presence instead of keeping quiet. Their usual tactics, as one approaches, are to make a dash, then stop, run again, then stop once more. Only when they believe themselves in imminent peril do they bolt into a hole. When running they carry the tail erect. They can climb a vertical rock face, and are not afraid to plunge into a bush which overhangs a cliff; sometimes they will risk a long leap. They love to lie flat on a slab of rock warming their cold blood in the sunshine. When out of one eye they see anything move, they become alert. Up goes the head, and starts to nod like a mandarin. I found it possible to frighten them suddenly into a cul-de-sac, and capture them alive. Stalking them, I would often see the ugly head of one in front of me cautiously raised, to peer over the top of a rock; flat and vicious looking like an adder's as the head is, and repulsive the black skin, this reptile has a beautiful golden-orange eye. It was now changing its skin, and looked even more repulsive than usual. I could not discover exactly what their food consists of, but they are certainly carnivorous.

I wanted sunshine now, to ripen seeds; there was really

nothing ripe in the valley, nor were there any flowers worth mentioning. The red-berried *Polygonatum cirrifolium* and the common *Paeonia lutea* were two plants I noticed; but as already remarked the valley is arid, and one must ascend to a more rarified atmosphere, and more constant precipitation, to find plants in variety. The houses made up for the barren appearance of the hillsides; the window frames were gay with China asters, marigolds, tropaeolum, dahlias, Paul Crampon geraniums, and hollyhocks, adding a fine flush of colour to the already splendid colours of the monastery.

The river reflected the uncertainty and violence of the weather which see-sawed at the change of the monsoon; one hour the water was yellow with mud, the next it had turned green again. Local storms caused a sudden rise, but the excess water quickly flowed away.

A brick-red and coal-black redstart with a circular white cap on the crown of its head flew up and down the river, and a fan-tailed grey laughing thrush with a red patch on the rump, *Trochalopteron henrici* probably, was common. But apart from these two, and a number of crows, there were few birds.

One day a great Lama called on me, and I gave him some brandy, which he thought extremely good. Later he sent me a huge present of groceries, consisting of eggs (not in the first flush of youth), dried meat, flour, potatoes, and turnips. The Jongpen, not to be backward, sent me some rice and peaches, thick-skinned but otherwise excellent. I do not think that any of the food plants which have found their way into Tibet have found their way out again to America; nor can I help thinking that the wonderful organization known as the Bureau of Plant Industry (Division of Plant Exploration and Introduction), United States Department of Agriculture, might turn its attention to Tibet and try out certain fruits, such as peach and walnut, and certain grains, in parts of the United States.

After I had bought a little fresh mutton, I felt we were well set up for a month. Moreover, I sent a small cash present to the monastery, and so grateful were the monks they sent me in return a chunk of butter weighing several pounds, with a scarf.

One person I recognized in Sanga Chöling was the old beggar man. He still tapped his way across the flagged courtyard, and basked in the sun. He must, I thought, surely perish of cold in the winter.

There were several riding ponies stalled below, and I was surprised to see their owners giving them beer to drink — out of a horn. Even racehorses are rarely given champagne to drink in England; and for a Tibetan to give a horse beer is not very different.

On September 18th, we started westwards up the valley of the Char Chu. A crowd collected in the great courtyard to see us start; the idle or the unemployed, the curious of both sexes, old and young; a buffoon, whom I had nicknamed Jingle, performed antics, and kept the spectators amused.

Before I left Sanga Chöling the Jongpen begged me to take his photograph, and I willingly consented. His household, consisting of wife and daughter, both good-looking, especially the girl with her rosy cheeks and merry bright eyes and her glossy hair, and a serving maid were all present in the flatlet, and the Jongpen insisted on my sitting down and having a drink before I started work. This meant more than it sounds, because he and his wife and his daughter all pressed me to drink and I had to pledge each in turn.

The Jongpen was a middle-sized man with close-cropped black hair and a long white scar on one cheek. His complexion was darker than it should have been without frequent recourse to stimulants. His expression was kindly, but there was a firmness in the line of mouth and chin, a thinning of the lips, which boded no good to the trifler. On the whole, a fine, strong face, I thought.

He received me like an emperor, resplendent in his official robes of purple and Imperial Heavenly gold. Two collars, one of purple, and inside it a second of rich orange silk, clasped his

neck, a mandarin's hat covered his head, and his long boots were of the finest leather. Nor was this all; around him as he sat cross-legged on his dais were cups of exquisite workmanship, set on scarlet lacquer tables, and on his lap lay the tiniest, most cantankerous and saucy Tibetan dog imaginable.

While I was setting up the camera, the Jongpen chatted affably, arranging himself to suit his fancy, not at all self-conscious, while his amiable wife and daughter offered criticisms. I should have liked to take their photographs too, but was short of plates.

When I had finished I would have said good-bye then and there, but the whole family insisted on coming down to the gate with me. Then I took a friendly farewell of the handsome Tibetan and rode away, sad to leave this exquisite medieval city-state. Just before turning the corner at the end of the long mendong, I looked back; mother and daughter still stood at the gate, waving to me. I kissed my fingers to them, then turned resolutely westwards.

In two hours we reached Shé, a village which is mainly on the right bank. There is a bridge across the river, and we had to change transport. From here to Bung took us nearly four hours, though the path was not difficult. We passed many ruined watch-towers and empty villages. I cannot help thinking that a hundred or possibly two hundred years ago, all this country between Lhasa and Tsela Dzong on both sides of the Tsangpo was more thickly populated than it is to-day. The ruined watch-towers may be the result of war, as the people say; but even without war, there is an equally good reason for depopulation in the amount of land which has gone out of cultivation, due either to the difficulty of irrigation as the water-table sinks, or to a change of climate. The Tibetan lakes are shrinking, the glaciers vanishing; it would seem therefore that the climate of Tibet is becoming drier. If so, rivers like the Loro Chu are necessarily growing smaller, which would help to account for the increasing difficulty of irrigation.

A close study of the vegetation also suggests that the Tibetan climate may have changed more than once. Dry region plants are found in comparatively moist regions, and moist region plants like *Primula Florindae* and *Lilium Wardii* in comparatively dry regions; such relic plants are not rare.

Travelling westwards up the Char Chu, the vegetation became more varied, and it was evident that there was either a heavier rainfall here, or less wind. On the steep hill-sides, whose surface was rubble, unstratified, unsorted, and unrolled, there were the usual small shrubs, sometimes thorny as Sophora and Rosa, but often not, as Cotoneaster, Ceratostigma, and Buddleia; common too on these hostile slopes was a rosette composite, *Jurinea Wardii*. Masses of fleshly-leafed cream-flowered sedum, *Didissandra lanuginosa*, and a solitary plant of *Onosma Waddellii* with purple-pink flowers, and a great many foot-long black lizards, were other sights along the road. A bushy Euonymus was in ripe fruit.

The Tibetans are beginning to build better houses, with plaster floors and walls; the former are far from level, the latter not plumb, but one must not expect too much. Bung, the estate of a rich country squire, is 12,000 feet above sea level, set amidst fields and wooded hills. It rained monotonously after we arrived, and the wet valley looked forlorn in the gathering dusk.

Between Sanga Chöling and Bung I had been on a known route, but the Mo La over the range to the south had not yet been explored by a European traveller.

On September 19th, after crossing to the right bank of the Char Chu by a cantilever bridge, we turned south up a wooded ravine, and presently heard and saw Harman's pheasants again. Tashi ran off with my .410 and five minutes later I heard a shot. He returned grinning, with *two* pheasants, male and female. The male weighed 4½lb. This happened where there were trees, so the altitude was not much more than 13,000 feet. A thousand feet higher I shot a hare; several were running about amongst the rocks in the lower alpine region. At this point the valley forks, one branch leading to the Dongyu La, the other to the Mo La. Both roads lead to the Nye Chu.

Ascending steeply towards the Mo La, we noticed a number of Tibetan snow-cock (*Tetragallus himalayensis*) on the screes. The indefatigable Tashi took the gun and went off to stalk them. These birds when alarmed run up-hill, uttering a shrill note of warning, then suddenly rise and nose-dive very fast down into the valley below. In summer at least they are never found below 15,000 feet, keeping to the barren screes and jagged ridges.

I lost sight of Tashi, but heard him fire twice, and saw the birds planing down, so I thought he had missed. However, he joined me on the pass with a fine snow-cock, weighing 2¾lb. Tashi, devout Buddhist though he was, enjoyed going after game birds, and bringing one down after a successful stalk.

Just as we reached the Mo La, after a hard climb, the last thousand feet exceedingly rough and steep, a sudden snow squall blinded us for several minutes. Then the storm cleared off. The view to the north was blocked by the nearness of the fold range across the Char Chu, but far away in the south-west the snow peaks of the Assam Himalaya stood out clearly. In the immediate foreground a snow-bed nestled against a dark rock pyramid, but I could see no glaciers. The slate rocks were highly contorted.

The Mo La is about the same height as the Drichung La, twenty miles to the south-east, which we had crossed on the outward journey, that is about 17,000 feet. The summit was rather bare.

It was 3.30 when we reached the top, and we hurried down the other side as quickly as possible A long troublesome march down the valley brought us after dark to a large village, not before most of us had fallen at least once into the torrent. I could see numerous cultivated terraces on both banks, but the village itself was invisible, until at seven o'clock we suddenly came to a large house belonging to a rich man. People came bringing torches, and showed us in. My bed was set up in the private chapel, the walls of which were painted rather garishly with designs depicting highly improbable incidents in the lives of quite impossible people, and hung with *tankas*. These *tankas*, or religious banners, are brightly coloured (when new), and represent Buddhas and lesser luminaries of the Buddhist theocracy, in conventional attitudes. They are hung in every monastery in Tibet, and in every rich man's chapel. There must be tens of thousands of such paintings in the country, and new ones are continually being added. The old ones are no better than the modern, and are always faded, and generally cracked.

If the decor of the walls was crude, the colour scheme of the furniture was painful. A series of cabinets, striped red, yellow and blue like a Central American Republic's ensign, startled me at every turn. The room was new and clean, and it was obvious that a good deal of money had been spent on it, and more particularly on the ecclesiastical vessels which lined the shelves. Some of these were works of art, real treasures. I was enchanted with a copper and silver water jug of almost Grecian design so delicately proportioned was it; the silver-lidded cups, too, were charming.

The lady of the house came in bringing a metal brazier of charcoal, for which I was very grateful; and I am sorry to have to say that in spite of pleasant features, she looked a slut, and her children were in rags, and extremely dirty in a cleanly sort of way.

At first sight it appears odd that wealth should be so lavished on the inanimate object, and denied to the humans. But religion rules the life of the Tibetan, and he considers it more reasonable to spend money on the symbols which represent his religion than on individuals, who in any case will benefit in proportion to the religious investment. Few people hanker less after great possessions than the average Tibetan; so long as he has enough food, warmth, and clothing, his physical wants are modest. But he likes to know that his spiritual needs are being catered for.

Before going to bed, I skinned the snow-cock. The following morning, I skinned the cock Crossoptilon; the hare we ate.

It was nearly eleven o'clock before we started again. Daylight and a bright sunny morning showed Dikiling to be a scattered prosperous looking village, situated in the midst of irrigated cultivation, at an altitude of about 13,000 feet. We soon reached the broader Nye Chu valley, which is well cultivated here, in spite of its extreme dryness. A few miles to the east is Lhontso Dzong, a place of some importance. We turned west down the Nye Chu, a swift muddy river, passing several small villages on gravel terraces, each of which boasted a monastery, or at least a *chorten*. Notable was Shangtze Gompa perched half way up a cliff. Above Shangtze Gompa the district is called Nye, below it is Chayul. Three or four miles below the junction of the Dikiling stream, we crossed to the right bank at the village of Gyana. There were whole meadows of *Iris lactea* in the flat moist sandy wastes, its leaves yellow and its seeds ripe.

After changing transport we went on for another four miles to where a bold monastery, like a fortress, straddled a chisel-edged rock ridge. It appeared, however, to be deserted. On the other side of the high slab, a large torrent leaped down from the mountains, and up the valley almost due east, I could see a snow peak and several small glaciers. I had seen the same peak previously from the valley above Sanga Chöling. Up this valley is the path to the Dongyu La, already mentioned.

By the torrent stood a row of enormous poplars heavy with years, their heads broken by the fierce winds which sweep across this barren land.

A common plant on screes and cliffs from Dikiling to Potung Yangze was *Dicranostigma lactucoides*, now in ripe seed. It does not descend much below 13,000 feet. Adenophora and Onosma were in bloom, and along the irrigation channels was a handsome blue delphinium.

Beyond Nyerong, where the Nye Chu turns abruptly south, the valley completely changes its appearance. Now the river is cutting its way across the strike of the strata, and also across the southern fold range. The path became more difficult and the last march was long and tiresome. Towards evening, having descended many hundred feet, we reached the Loro Chu, and twenty minutes later were back in Chayul Dzong, after an absence of ninety days.

In these three months I had covered more than eight hundred miles, mostly through unexplored country, and in regions botanically even more unknown.

CHAPTER XXIII

WINTER COMES TO TIBET

NEXT morning I unpacked my other stores box, and enjoyed such modest luxuries as Indian tea, jam, and biscuits again. The weather was set fair and in the middle of the day the temperature rose to nearly 70°. Only one guilty thought disturbed my slumber. Already there were rumours – slightly conflicting rumours it is true – of official displeasure over my escapade. But Tashi reassured me; it was nothing, he said.

Anyhow, what did it matter now!

The Jongpen was away. Two days after my arrival he returned, and the first thing he did was to pay me a visit. He was not the same man I met here in June, and in his wine-red robe with yellow silk lining, he looked royal. He wore the inevitable Homburg hat; and his manner was frank and friendly.

Five days I spent at Chayul Dzong, packing specimens and preparing for the return journey over the Himalayas. Each day I wandered through the thorn thickets by the river, to see what life was stirring. I trapped more voles, shot doves for the pot, and a laughing thrush (*Trochalopteron*), collected seed of *Iris lactea* and of *Sophora Moorcroftiana*, and found several bog plants in flower. The vegetation as a whole was even more dead than in June; but the ponds were full of tadpoles, as though it were spring.

One day a smart looking man in clean clothes called. His face seemed vaguely familiar; some important official I thought. But Tashi almost winked aloud at me and said in a reverberating aside: '*Chor*' (thief)! It was our local jailbird! He had served his sentence and been set at liberty. His financial position must have been a strong one.

Next door to our house was a carpet factory, or more exactly a carpet weaving cottage industry. Four people, all women, were engaged on the job. Two were actually weaving rugs; a third was combing out the raw wool and a fourth was twisting it on a spindle, drawing out the thread. Somewhere the twine was dyed yellow, red, blue, brown, or green -- curiously assorted tints -- and dried in the sun before being wound into balls.

On September 27th we started for home and halting at a village called Yara, where there are a lot of ruins, reached Trashi Tongme Gompa the second night. I saw more black lizards here, so this creature ascends to at least 12,000 feet. The Assam Himalayas seen through this crystal atmosphere looked sublime.

On the 29th we reached Karta. Halting at Sho for lunch, I lay on the grass in a pleasant garden, surrounded by beds of marigolds, cosmos, and China asters. The Mexican cosmos did not get here on its own legs; man brought it.

At Karta the poplars were still green, but the corn was reaped. Transport was hard to get, and after waiting one day, it seemed I might have to wait a second. The Jongpen was making difficulties. But towards noon on October 1st men, women and ponies appeared, and we travelled four miles up the valley to Cha, where we halted another day; and a very cold day it was too! The yak were still up in the high pastures, and a messenger had to be sent to bring them in. We were lucky to get away on the 3rd.

It was harvest time in Cha, and huge yak loads of barley were being brought in.

As already noted there is a serious lack of fuel in dry Tibet, and the underground rootstocks of Ephedra are supplemented by yak dung; a little Hippophäe wood is also burnt. Ephedra reaches a great age, and grows much more underground in the hard rocky soil than above in the thin sharp air, producing knobby rhizomes as big as a football, which make excellent fuel. Dicranostigma is another plant with big subterranean growth, and not much in the air; but it is too spongy for fuel.

The crossing of the main range by the two passes, Pen La and Tulung La, took three days (October 3-5) and at this season offered no difficulty. The nights were cold, but the sparkling sunny days were delicious; there was not enough wind to be troublesome. In our camp between the two passes, at about 15,000 feet, the temperature inside my tent dropped to 16°. Outside on the grass the gentians were frozen stiff as parchment, but the corollas seemed to protect the ripening seeds.

From the Tulung La I had a close-up view of the snow peaks on the south side, but as we got down towards Mago, the sky became more overcast as though the monsoon were still raging over India. But no rain was getting through to Tibet; the plateau was fast drying up, after the short summer deluge.

South of the Tulung La, the large vermilion berries of *Cotoneaster microphylla* studding the rocks made a gorgeous coverlet, and as soon as we reached scrub level, patches of the brilliant blue *Gentiana amoena* appeared. Common in fruit on the hillsides was *Morina popyphylla*, its prickly flower spikes sometimes eight inches long. If all the flowers opened at the same time it would be quite a handsome plant; but they do not, and most morinas are rather disappointing. I had not seen this in June on the way up, because it is a summer plant.

In twenty-four hours we exchanged the bare arid rocky plateau north of the great snow range for the well-wooded valleys of Mago, brilliant with autumn fruit and foliage. The air had lost that flint hard edge which high altitude gives to it in Tibet; and the abundant vegetation was white with the dawn frost.

On October 5th we left the herds rounding up their cattle at Chunak, and continuing down the valley of the Goshu Chu reached Mago early in the afternoon.

In the clearings late meadow flowers bloomed. In the forest, robust species of Senecio, Polygonum and a few other plants lingered on. A tall Allium (*A. Wallichii*), with big umbellate heads of flimsy-paper capsules containing jet black seeds was rather a rarity.

How welcoming and mild was Mago after the deadness of the Tibetan plateau! The grassy slope above the village was chequered with the periwinkle-blue of *Cyananthus microphyllus* and the more brilliant blue of gentians. The few broad-leafed trees in the dark fir forest shone like red and yellow flames.

I went back to my garret, and sun-bathed for two days while waiting for the yak to come down. Meanwhile the village was filling up as day by day parties of herds returned from the high alpine valleys. Some Lopas arrived on their way to Tibet to buy salt. In the cold weather these naked savages lose much of their swagger, and take on the helpless appearance of wet kittens.

There were ground frosts at night, but so dry was the air that only a sparkling film formed. Most of the rhododendron seeds were ripe now, but the capsules, which take some time to dry up, remained closed. I collected *R. Baileyi*, *R. campanulatum*, and other species. The lovely rose-pink form of *R. lanatum* which had had all its flower buds so badly frosted in the spring that they had never opened, bore a fine crop of new flower buds. This was partly due to the fact that this year's flowers had failed, thus relieving the plants from the drain of food which ripening seed entails.

On October 6th I walked up to the hot spring and had a bath. Several plants were flowering amongst the rocks and in the nearby streams, but none of them were of any horticultural value whatsoever. In one stream I collected *Potamogeton panormitanus*, *Epilobium alpinium*, *Cyanotis barbata*, and *Eriophorum comosum*.

The villainous coarse weed *Scopolia lurida*, which scavenges in the sea of mud round the houses, was being cut down and tied into bundles. It is used for fodder.

On October 8th the yak were ready, and we set out for

Dirang Dzong. As we neared the top of the Chera La, I kept looking back, and there rose gradually into view the lofty peak of Gori Chen. Descending to the Gorjo Chu, we turned upstream. Soon the forest was left behind. We were in a bleak alpine valley; winter had come to Mönyul too, and the upper valley might have been on the Tibetan plateau. We passed two groups of stone huts (empty) marked on the map as villages, though they are only occupied for a few months in the summer, and presently camped on a sandspit covered with short turf. A few huddled shrubs grew in sheltered hollows; the herbaceous plants had died down and disappeared.

We had gone only a few miles eastwards the next day when we turned south again and after a short gentle climb reached a country of rolling grassy hills. We were crossing the Tse La, 15,500 feet high. Two small glacier lakes came into view. It began to snow, then to rain hard. After the previous night's frost (27° inside my tent) and the primrose dawn sky, I had expected better weather. Descending from the grassland, we came to a valley, where small shrubs grew sparsely at first, then more thickly. As the stream increased in size, so did the bushes. Silver firs appeared and when late in the afternoon we camped in a clearing called Chutong, we were already on the edge of the forest.

That night it froze hard, and when I awoke on the morning of October 10th, the grass was crisp with hoar frost, and the rhododendron leaves, rolled like cigars, hung stiffly down. For a thousand feet up either side, the valley was solid with the interlacing branches of rhododendrons, and I vowed that one day I would come back and see them when they were all in flower; the clear daffodil-yellow of *R. Wightii* shot with the glowing crimson of *R. fulgens*, and the rose-pink of *R. lanatum* mingled with the variable purples of *R. praestans*.

We were over the Zela range, but not yet over the last pass. Ahead of us towered the rocky Poshing La, 11,950 feet, and towards this we toiled. The sky, clear at dawn, had clouded over rapidly and we approached the pass in a freezing mist, which seemed to corrode the skin like powerful alkali.

The Poshing La proved to be more of a barrier than a pass; at least it was a barrier for the stream which had cut a deep valley for itself round the foot of the spur. Yet once upon a time the glacier from the Tse La had flowed *over* the Poshing La, and retreating slowly had left its mark in the form of a dry rocky stream-bed — at least, it was dry now — on the south side. As the glacier retreated up the valley, the stream found an easier exit by doing a little digging on its own account; it went round the spur instead of over it.

Men had used some of the big rocks to make a rough stairway down the south side, and in a thick congealing mist we scrambled over the pass. The yak, on their billiard-table legs, lurched heavily from rock to rock. At times they seemed to be standing on their beam-ends; every minute I expected to see one capsize. We passed under a high butte, climbed a second stairway, and found ourselves on the crest of a ridge, which dropped steeply on either side into unfathomable forested valleys.

Three years later, in May 1938, I returned to the Poshing La to see the rhododendrons in flower; paying another visit in July, to find out what were the alpine plants whose almost empty seed capsules I discovered now shaking as with an ague in the wind. Of rock plants, the most interesting were *Meconopsis sinuata*, scattered among the boulders, a gaunt and skinny stem covered with yellow prickles, and bearing a few flimsy aquamarine flowers; *Nomocharis nana* on the grassy cliffs; and a species of Omphalogramma, possibly *O. Elwesiana*, a rare Sikkim plant. It has softly downy leaves and large deep violet gloxinia-like flowers borne singly on stems hardly six inches high; though as the fruit ripens they lengthen out to a foot. All the other species of this strange genus, including the very similar *O. Delavayi*, grow farther east, in the mountains of north Burma and western China.

In May 1938 I found plants in flower here of which I had no

inkling in the thick wintry mist during my first crossing of the pass. Notable amongst these was a charming 'Nivales' primula bearing at the top of the stem large rounded heads of violet or white flowers, each on a pedicel long enough to avoid crowding its neighbour. The effect is that of a loose mop, springing from a rosette of sleek strap-shaped leaves. This plant was so common amongst the boulders, that I rather wondered how I had missed it in fruit in 1935, even in the mist. I never met with it anywhere but on the Poshing La.

Another unexpected plant was the delicate grape-hyacinth-like *Primula Wattii*, of which hundreds of plants grew almost like moss on the slabs. In July 1938, a fine yellow-flowered Cremanthodium, a foot tall, formed part of the lush herbaceous growth which surged over the boulder slope concealing the rocks.

But to return to that wintry October day in 1935, when the only living plant I could see cowering down amongst the cold stones was the dwarf *Aconitum Hookeri* – dwarf in stature but capped by a relatively enormous purple flower, looking as though it was cut out of frosted glass. From the narrow ridge, where we met the silver fir forest again, we descended headlong to a grassy alp called Chala, a summer yak pasture. Here we halted for lunch. Then descending a steep groove gouged in the knife-edge ridge, where only dwarf rhododendrons such as *R. glaucum* and *R. lepidotum* could face the sweeping wind, we came to another alp, called Kadam; and here we halted for the night.

When the sun rose next morning I gasped with joy. Dawn revealed a grid of violet mountains to the south, long parallel ranges like sea waves, their tops almost level, separated by deep narrow valleys. They stretched far away to east and west and vanished out of sight amongst higher peaks. Through a gap in the last range of hills, I caught a glimpse of the grey Assam plain itself; I even thought I could see the flash of the Brahmaputra river, like a silver eel, fifty or sixty miles distant. Far below, in the deep hollows, the morning sun shone on honey-coloured fields around Dirang Dzong.

The alp on which we were camped was surrounded by a forest of silver fir and rhododendron. A dozen species, large and small, grew mixed together; their colours in May are indescribable. Most abundant was *R. praestans*, which ascends higher than any other big-leafed rhododendron, to 11,000 or 12,000 feet. Its flowers open in late May and June, and vary from crimson, to cerise and purple; the deeper colours are the finest, but all are good. Other species here are: *R. Wightii* with yellow flowers, speckled crimson; *R. campylocarpum* (pale yellow); *R. Thomsonii* (blood-red); *R. triflorum* (greenish-yellow). There are also a few dwarf species, including the epiphytic *R. megeratum* (cream), which forms large mistletoe-like masses in the fir trees.

The spur of the Zela range astride which we were descending separates the cultured civilized Mönbas to the west from the savagely civilized Daphlas and Akhas to the east; treacherous tribes living in the gloomy rain forests of the Bhareli, Subansiri and other great Himalayan river valleys. From our alp we had an uninterrupted view obliquely eastwards for a hundred miles across unexplored mountains, which stretch another hundred miles beyond the uttermost horizon, to the gorge of the Dihang. Immediately below us was a deep valley, whose lower slopes were chequered with clearings and fields like those of any hill tribe; but the Akha villages were out of sight.

So we went down the ridge — and up, mile after mile; for the southern spurs of the mid-Himalayan ranges have been cross-cut by the monsoon rains. In some places the water runs along the narrow crest of the ridge before tumbling over the side. The result has been to cut deep grooves along the ridge, with banks twelve or fifteen feet high, overhung with trees. One may walk for half a mile through a tunnel whose roof is of pleached rhododendrons; their fallen flowers in spring crimson the ground like glowing embers. In some places our laden yak could scarcely squeeze between the banks. The path was very rough, the water having torn stones of all shapes and sizes from their moorings in the sand; the forest in fact is built on sand.

Now in October, the rains had ceased, and it was easier to get along. But in May and more particularly in July, 1938, when I revisited the Poshing La, the pleached walk was filled by a furious torrent, from which there was no escape; one paddled through it ankle deep, and the rushing water washed the stones from underfoot, making it difficult to keep one's balance.

Just over the edge of the ridge grew giant rhododendron trees forty or fifty feet high, with leaves eighteen inches long. When in full bloom about April or May, the avenue is magnificent, bunches of blood-red, white, sulphur-yellow, and purple flowers rocking and swaying amongst the foliage, and illuminating the forest as with thousands of Japanese lanterns.

The species met with here are: *R. arizelum*, *R. Falconeri*, *R. grande*, *R. sidereum*, all with big leaves and yellow flowers; and *R. Hookeri*, *R. barbatum*, *R. argipeplum*, and *R. arboreum* with smaller leaves and blood-red flowers. They all grow together in the silver fir forest, or at lower altitudes in the hemlock forest, but are eager for light. So overwhelming are they, that when in flower they blind one to everything else. And yet there *are* other trees and shrubs. *Magnolia globosa*, a small deciduous tree with a spreading crown and flowers like large white billiard balls, is a fine sight in July, when most of the rhododendrons are over. So is *Clethra Delavayi*, a tree with tall, tapering spires of white flowers in red saucers; and *Enkianthus himalaicus* dangling innumerable bunches of little bell flowers, yellow striped with red. Others are birch, several kinds of oak and maple, Ilex, prunus, pyrus, Brassaiopsis, and many other species, becoming more varied as we descend to warmer regions.

In two hours we reached a third pasture called Dongri. Here we met a party of Mönbas from Tembang, who had come to repair the cattle shed and cut back the encroaching forest. They wore their thick woollen winter coats, dyed madder red, which kept their bodies warm; but their legs were bare from the knees; a few of them wore Tibetan cloth boots.

Dongri is a beautiful alp surrounded by conifer-rhododendron forest, at an altitude of about 10,000 feet. I spent several days here in the summer of 1938, and early one morning had a wonderful view of snow peaks towering above the nearer ranges to the north-east. (The bearing of the snows was from 17° to 28°, i.e. about north-north-east.) Between the farthest wooded ridge and the snows yawned a wide chasm, its position clearly indicated by the cloud beginning to rise from it. These peaks may stand on the main Himalayan range, just east of Gori Chen, which is thirty-five miles distant. But they looked to be closer than that, and may perhaps stand on the ridge crossed by the Tse La, at the source of a large river which joins the Bhareli from the north, some miles east of Tembang. If that is so they are quite unknown.

Clumps of a prickly-leafed evergreen dwarf Berberis formed impenetrable thickets at the north end of Dongri. The leaves which are separated by distinct internodes recall those of *B. insignis*, but the stems also bear spur shoots with crowded leaves. The yellow flowers are borne in large fascicles, and are followed by deep violet fruits. This handsome plant is *B. dasyclada*.

In July, the lily-like *Rhododendron polyandrum* was in full bloom all round Dongri, and colonies of the shade-loving rose-flowered *Primula Normaniana* were massed under the trees. The sturdy hemlocks are made bulkier with moss which gives anchorage to many shrubby and herbaceous epiphytes, including dwarf rhododendrons (*R. micromeres*), Gaultheria, the charming helmet-shaped orchid Pleione and others. Between Kadam and Dongri hemlock is mixed with silver fir.

From Dongri we continued down the mountain by a very steep rough path till the last hemlocks disappeared, and blue pine was the only conifer; most broad-leafed trees increased in number and variety; only rhododendrons decreased.

There is an alternative route from Dongri to Dirang Dzong, shorter but worse than that through Tembang. In May, and again in July 1938, I followed this path which, instead of descending direct to the main river, turns east below Dongri and follows a ridge to the Sangti river. We had already met the Sangti river as an infant at the Tse La.

On the open ridge outside the forest an angularly limbed Cotoneaster grew almost as tall as a tree. It was 10 or 12 feet high, with stiff gawky branches flung out like spindly arms in every upward direction. But these same branches were studded with large red berries; evidently the birds would have none of them. A bird-proof berrying shrub is invaluable.

Shortly afterwards we came to another grassy alp, called Showri. It was covered with meadow plants, except immediately round two herds' huts, where such ground as was not liquid manure was densely carpeted with the scum of the plant world—docks. The cage-like huts were made entirely of bamboo matting, and as though to make up for the slimy approach, surprisingly clean inside. Pasture was limited; the herds spend only a short time here, on their way up to a cleaner, greener land. I sat down and drank a cup of yak milk.

Below the yak camp the ridge had been partially fired, and was still charred black, the new bracken in May not having made much growth. The north face was covered with thick evergreen forest; the west face, which was precipitous and rocky, supported only scattered blue pines and oaks. Considerable areas in fact had no trees at all, or even shrubs. It was an ideal place for lilies. *Primula denticulata* was abundant, its mealy leaves growing coarse now that the flowers were over.

Precisely here in July I found a colony of the dwarf *Lilium nepalense* var. *concolor*, growing widely scattered amongst tuffets of Gaultheria, *Rhododendron lepidotum* and other plants. The trumpet-shaped flower is a pure creamy yellow with the lustre of watered silk on its recurved petals, which are finely engraved. When fully open they are about three inches long and four inches wide, borne singly on leafy stems not exceeding a foot in height; the weight of the flower causes the stem to bend over.

Though I marched through a hundred miles of similar pine

forest country in Mönyul, I never saw this lily again. There was only the one colony of a few score plants.

To come back to 1935 and our march to Tembang. A descent of about 2000 feet brought us to cultivation once more. In a clearing on the ridge stood the squalid monastery of Lagam, with one or two wretched hovels unfit for human habitation, but occupied nevertheless. Lagam, an outpost of the Lamaist church on the fringes of civilization, exists to bestow the last blessing on travellers crossing the Tse La to Mago, and to greet those arriving from Mago with a thanksgiving service. Considering the lateness of the hour, I too should have applied for a thanksgiving service, and stayed the night to see that I got it. But we could see the village of Tembang away down at the end of the valley, where the spurs flared out to the river; and I felt the urge to reach it that night. When we started, there was about two hours of daylight left.

I went inside the monastery, which was gloomy and smelt of cheese and dead mice.

Below Lagam we followed another ridge, down to the stream. Rhododendrons crowd on to the ridges because they get better illumination there. The commonest species between 7000 and 8000 feet are: *R. Lindleyi* with enormous white trumpet flowers, delicately scented: *R. bullatum*, white flushed pink, also sweet scented: *R. euchaites*, blood-red: *R. Boothii*, small chrome-yellow flowers in flattened heads: *R. pankimense*, a tree with crimson flowers: and most beautiful of all, *R. Griffithianum*, a small tree with huge porcelain-white bell flowers, faintly tinged with palest pink at the base. *R. Griffithianum*, perhaps the finest wild rhododendron in the world, has been known for three-quarters of a century, and has been one parent of a long series of magnificent hybrids. Rhododendrons were still numerous at Lagam, at least on the ridge. But they were no longer dominant; many other trees and shrubs had now appeared including laurels, Illicium, Eurya, *Eriobotrya Wardii* and Decaisnea, together with birch, hornbeam, maples, Viburnum, hollies, oaks, Michelia, and willows. A considerable undergrowth of arundinaria filled in the spaces between the tree trunks.

When we started from Lagam the afternoon sun shone brightly on the late autumn flowers which grew along the path. But as we got down into the deep valley it sank behind the ranges to the south-west, and we were left in the cold shadow.

Many hours had passed since, at dawn, we had seen the plains in the distance, and now it was growing late. There was no twilight. It was light, and then it was dark.

We plodded on, the yak dropping gradually behind. Tashi, that iron man, went ahead to warn the people; the peasants retire for the night when darkness falls, and are apt to be suspicious of those who move under cover of darkness. When it became pitch dark I had to walk warily for the path was narrow with a steep slope on one side. I tripped and stumbled, and put out my hands in front of my face, feeling my way. Monstrous forms rose up in front of me. I saw things which certainly were not there, and failed to see some which as certainly were there! The last mile I could see nothing; I seemed to be walking in my sleep. Then there were houses silhouetted against a starry sky. I heard voices; men from Tembang were coming down a long flight of steps, carrying pine torches which sizzled and were drawn out into tails of fire by the wind. I climbed the steps, passed through a stone archway, and was in Tembang. It was nearly nine o'clock; we had been ten hours on the road. The headman brought me to an empty two-roomed house, and shortly after the yak arrived.

I slept, but not for long. A full moon filled the valley with soft light, and I awoke to bask in its silvery rays. The shadowy landscape looked fantastic as a dream. At five I got up and went outside to watch the stars fading, and the sky far down the valley being slowly lit by the rising sun.

Tembang proved to be a walled village of crowded stone houses and muddy alleys. It stands on a windy spur more than a thousand feet above the river, the most easterly outpost of the Mönbas. Neither the protecting wall, pierced by two narrow gateways — without gates — and approached by steep flights of steps, nor the natural strength of the position, inspire the inhabitants to resistance. The Mönbas are too lazy to hold the fort. Possibly Tembang has withstood assault and battery in the past; clearly it was designed to that end. To-day not swords and bows and leaden bullets and the drums of war hold back the invader, but *manis* and paper bullets, and a holy smoke screen and prayer drums; reinforced of course by substantial payments to the Akhas.

The people of Tembang are far from beautiful. Inbreeding has sapped them, and there seems to be a high proportion of village idiots. One deaf and dumb dwarf was of so simian an aspect, with long trailing arms, that had he worn even a goat skin one might have mistaken him for a baboon.

Just outside the village wall stood a fine maple tree (*Acer oblongum*). The young foliage was a deep polished mahogany, and the swinging bunches of winged fruit a rich purple.

Turning westwards up the river, but high above it, we covered the remaining distance to Dirang Dzong in a long day's march. At the village of Namshi, about half way, the house roofs were blood-red where chillies had been spread out to dry in the sunshine, and the rows of maize cobs hanging from scaffolds suggested processional banners so heavily crusted with gold that no wind stirred them. It was an immense open-air harvest festival; an heraldic design.

The hot rocky slopes were bright with flowers. Thin blue spires of Adenophora like tall hairbells, yellow Sopubia, orchids, saussureas. It was growing dusk when Dirang Dzong at last came into view — on the opposite side of the river. We had to go a mile past it, descend several hundred feet to cross the Sangti river from the north (the river which rises at the Tse La) and then cross the main river. That last half mile into Dirang Dzong was exhausting. So we had come from Mago in five days, which was good travelling.

CHAPTER XXIV

THE END OF THE JOURNEY

THERE is not much more to tell. I was now back at my starting point in Mönyul, rather footsore, having walked nearly a thousand miles in the round trip which had included little retracing of my footsteps over the same ground. There remained only the few days' journey across the middle and outer ranges to the plains; but even that was not to be accomplished without a diversion.

One thing only disturbed me. I had had no news of the outside world, and no letters for four months, and naturally I expected to pick up a big mail at Dirang Dzong. But Tashi came back from his visit to the Jongpen with the disappointing information that there was not one letter for me. I heard afterwards that all my letters had been sent to Tawang. It was months before they came back; most of them I received in England, where in the summer of 1936 I read of what had been happening to my friends in England in the summer of 1935.

Dirang Dzong seemed very dry; as though the rains were long since over; as indeed they were. The inner valleys get little rain; most of it falls on the mountains.

Mirabilis, a common weed of tropical South America with lurid magenta flowers, was in bloom in the hedges, and the charming *Clematis ranunculoides*, whose nodding purple square-sided thimbles with tip-tilted points, rambled over every hedge.

On October 16th we continued our journey south, and crossing the three intervening ranges, reached Shergaon on the 18th. It took us ten hours to cross the Manda La from Dirang Dzong to Phutang; I wanted to camp near the summit, but the coolies said there was no water.

Dumkho was in the throes of a harvest festival. To the beating of drums a priest rode through the village on horseback at the head of a procession of madly dancing men and modest maidens who carried images. Women with bundles of babies on their backs, rushed up to the equestrian monk and plucked the hem of his garment. That was enough to acquire merit. But to seal the bargain, somebody carrying a beaker of water ladled it out on to the heads of the true believers. Or was it *zoo*? – maize beer. One prancing dervish, his features modestly hidden behind a mask, waved an immense wooden phallus; he represented fertility. Two more twirling figures flourished swords – to check exuberant fertility? And so to the monotonous throb of drums and the wail of conch shells, the procession moved up the valley.

No doubt it was a serious ceremony, yet there was something slightly comic about all this frantic symbolism. When the symbol becomes more important than the idea symbolized, religion begins to degenerate.

Shergaon was cold at night. It is 1500 feet higher than Dirang Dzong, and open. It froze hard.

The festive Wangia, king of Shergaon, was in sober mood. He brought me three chickens, together with the unwelcome news that it would be weeks before we could cross the Pankim La; the path on the other side was the bed of a raging, roaring torrent. I noticed that, although the sky at Shergaon was clear, we were now close to the monsoon which had not yet ceased on the plains. Three miles away, beyond the fir-fringed pass, black clouds were banked up and it was obviously raining.

I had one strange experience. Stepping outside my hut in the middle of the night to admire the marvellous moonlit landscape, I suddenly perceived a white cord moving towards me horizontally head high at what seemed a high speed; but the ends of the cord – if cord it was – were unsupported. How could a cord stay rigid and move horizontally toward me? Or was I dreaming? Maybe it was not a cord but a rod! I had little time to speculate physical problems however, and I ducked swiftly, fearing to be hanged without leaving a clue. I was scared not only at the prospect of strangulation, but still more at the reversal of nature which seemed to be taking place—an unsupported cord describing an arc in mid air. No sooner had I escaped a mysterious death as it seemed, than I turned and saw the rope coming towards me again from the other direction. I was being pursued, hunted, by this awful thing. The house was in deep shadow! But not far off, the moonlight shone on an open ploughed field, and the frost glittered like a million diamonds.

And then I ran.

In the morning the mystery was solved. A pony was tethered to the hut by a long rope, invisible in the shadow. My sudden appearance had so frightened it that it had galloped to and fro, making scarcely a sound. I complained to the owner, and that night he hung an iron bell round the beast's neck, which sounded the tocsin so successfully that I got no sleep.

We rested one day at Shergaon, then started down the valley, marching north-eastwards, that is away from instead of towards the plains.

Had we been able to cross the Pankim La we would have reached Tiger Flat in three days. By the route we were following it would take us at least six days to reach the plains. But it could not be helped.

After marching a few miles we entered a limestone gorge. At 2.30 the coolies wanted to halt in a cypress grove, saying it was the only flat ground for miles. But I was impatient to get on, and we climbed the cliff till we were 2000 feet above the stream; there was no flat ground here, for a certainty. Towards dusk we descended again to the stream, and had almost reached the bottom of the cliff when I caught sight of a charming slipper orchid, the broad standard white with a purple network of pencilled lines, the honey-coloured base of the pouch thrust out like an aggressive jaw, the wings narrow and fluttering. I dug up several plants and carried them in triumph to camp, which was pitched under some trees by the river. Although this well-known orchid, *Cypripedium Fayerianum*, has been in cultivation for a century, its discovery here was of some interest, because nobody knew where the plant came from, except that it was from somewhere in Assam.

Next day we followed the winding stream out of the limestone gorge into a broad cultivated valley, enclosed by pine-clad hills. In front of us rose the tall white fortress-like gompa of Dukpen, and fifty or sixty timber houses. By the stream were thickets of *Berberis asiatica* and Leptodermis, a handsome purple-flowered Saurauja, and fine specimens of *Cupressus torrulosa*. Hundreds of slipper orchids, with the sun shining through their delicately poised and pencil-veined flowers, flickered on the steep banks. Here and there a ripening capsule of *Lilium Wallichianum* was visible.

Dukpen, or Rupa, was like a larger Shergaon; but the towering gompa, more fort than monastery and more a godown than a fort, was impressive. I camped in a sort of annexe, and climbed belfry ladders to the top, whence through slits in the wall I enjoyed a good view of the valley. The Seven Kings of Rupa meet in solemn conclave round the base of the tower — which is mostly used to store inconvenient junk. On the top story are parked the animal and ogre-like masks used in the religious dances.

A gang of troubadors appeared the day after my arrival, and performed some very boring dances. Two young men disguised as maidens were particularly uncouth.

We stayed a day at Dukpen while coolies were collected, and on October 22nd continued eastwards down the valley. The hills were still covered with pine forest, high grass and scattered oaks (*Quercus glauca*); *Lilium Wallichianum* now near its eastern extinguishing point; and on the rocks a brilliant yellow-flowered Kalanchoe. I noticed also an equally brilliant gamboge-flowered Crotolaria.

After six hours' marching we camped in the forest; we had

reached the end of the Mönba country. Ahead lay the first Akha villages.

Although we continued to march down the same valley in the same direction at almost the same altitude next day, a swift change came over the scenery. At one moment we were in open pine forest; the next in thick jungle. It all happened within a few miles.

There are no villages between Dukpen, the last Mönba village, and Jamiri the first Akha village. As soon as I saw the long, low thatched huts, I knew I was back amongst the Assam hill tribes who can be relied on to give anybody a headache.

Jamiri was almost empty. However, the headman promised to find coolies for me in a day or two. Meanwhile, we must stay. I was impatient to get on, and resented any delay.

Next day there were no coolies, and the headman said all his people were either sick or away on government work – for the Jamiri Akhas are called 'tame', and are under 'loose political control', as it is called. Most of the Akha clans are as wild as leopards – and as unreliable.

By badgering the headman, I gradually wore him down. We must, he said, get coolies from another village. He himself would be charmed to supply them, but unfortunately . . . so what could he do?

'I have five men,' he said pathetically, 'five men; but what is the good of that? You want fifteen! Of course, you can have five men, but . . .!' He was most urbane. Oh, yes! He would help get the coolies from a neighbouring village, but it really was their turn to earn some money. He was quite solicitous for their welfare.

'All right,' I said, 'I'll start to-morrow with five coolies. I can just manage. Send the other loads on as soon as possible.'

The headman coughed and scratched his head. This was not at all what he wanted. The five miraculously became seven, the seven became nine – men in buckram. They will carry double loads, if I will pay by the load, instead of by the coolie.

I agree. They want an extra present on arrival at Charduar. I agree. They demand their wages in advance. I agree. I feel certain that by next morning there will be fifteen coolies, even if they spring out of the ground — in buckram.

There are. It is just Akha tactics. I congratulate myself that I am only compelled to deal with 'tame' Akhas who are under 'loose political control', even if it is more loose than political. I feel that wild Akhas might be the undoing of me.

On October 25th, after endless wrangling, we started; three coolies had decamped, and now there were twelve. Three loads were left behind with Pemba, who had picked up sufficient Assamese to talk to the Akhas — Assamese being the *lingua franca* of those who go down to the plains. I told Pemba to follow the next day, and catch us up. I was eager to be moving.

It was high noon when we got off, and after climbing the opposite slope, where I noticed some beautiful specimens of *Engelhardtia spicata*, from which a thousand green fox brush tails of winged fruits swished, reached the forest and camped far short of the regular stage.

Two days later we reached the top of the range and saw the Bhareli river below. Many striking begonias with white, yellow and pink flowers grew here. The crinkly leaves of one species, moulded against the rock were immense. Other species had variegated leaves of curious shape. In the forest I noticed *Podocarpus latifolia*, and other interesting trees.

We were just starting on the third morning when Pemba caught us up. After a descent of several thousand feet we came down to the broad Bhareli river, slinking out of the hills.

It began to rain, and brushing through the wet undergrowth on the river bank we got covered with leeches; the blood trickled from us in streams.

Hour after hour we trudged on. It began to grow dark, so we camped on a sandbank by the river; and next day resumed our march through the jungle. Every minute I expected to see

some wild animal; elephant, tiger, or even a buffalo, for the country teems with game; but I saw nothing.

We were back in the dense tropical evergreen rain forest of eastern India; the trees were magnificent, no two alike. Lush undergrowth surged waist high between the trunks, and a tangle of vines zigzagged and twisted upwards to be lost in the dark canopy amongst a wealth of epiphytes. It was a garden suspended between earth and sky; every now and then a flower fluttered down from some invisible blossom to remind us that it was there, though we could not see it. We crossed a torrent of ill repute. It was neither broad, nor deep now, but it flowed in a ravine whose sides were vertical. I learnt later that two Akha coolies from Charduar were bringing a month's mail up to me in July by this route. When they came to this stream, they found it in furious flood, so they constructed a raft, and tried to cross on that. Unhappily the raft upset, and the Akhas were almost drowned. They just succeeded in scrambling out before the torrent swept them out into the raging Bhareli. Everything was a total loss – the crew's clothes, their knives, their food, and of course the mail bag containing my letters. What winged words were lost evermore in the mail, I do not know, and never shall.

About twenty miles from Charduar, on the bank of the Bhareli, is a sort of summer house where the European planters from the neighbouring tea gardens come out to picnic and fish on Sunday afternoon. The next day was Sunday – or at any rate I thought it was; and the idea struck me, it would be pleasant to drop in on a party of planters picnicking at Balipung, and join them for tea. I would blow in unexpectedly, a spirit from across the ever mysterious 'inner line', the bourne from which no traveller returns because none is allowed to go there.

I therefore speeded up the coolies, urging them on long after they wanted to stop, till they seemed ready to drop. But darkness came on before we reached Balipung and we were compelled to camp, much to my disappointment.

Next morning we reached the summer house in an hour, only to find it deserted. Suddenly the overgrown and almost invisible path became a wide sandy road, and there was a stout timber bridge over a stream. By the bridge stood a large notice board: 'Trespassers will be prosecuted'? 'Rubbish not to be shot here'? 'Keep off the grass'? Or a pedestrian crossing? No! It marked the 'inner line' and announced, though illegibly, that the most dire penalties awaited anyone who dared to cross it without first obtaining a pass from the Political Officer. I was certainly back in civilization.

Presently I picked up the fresh tracks of a car; so somebody had been to Balipung the previous day, and I had probably missed an enjoyable tea party. Or hadn't I? However, it turned out later I was a day out in my reckoning and this was Tuesday, not Monday.

Walking along a wide and level road was a fresh experience. To walk upright, like a man, to stride and swing one's arms was wonderful. Liberty! I felt free as air. Even the coolies tripped along gaily at two and a half miles an hour. The road ran very straight, and was lined with trees which towered up into the soft blue sky. We covered another ten miles, then in an open space where the ground rose slightly, and a stream gurgled, camped for the night. There was another hour of daylight yet, but I had worked the Akha coolies hard the last two days, and they deserved some consideration.

There was open savannah here instead of jungle, and it was delicious to sit outside my tent after supper and watch the brilliant stars wheel in majestic procession across a gun-metal sky.

It was still dark when I rose a little after four o'clock, but the faintest flush was beginning to paint the eastern sky. Everything was drenched with dew. A bird began to sing. Ten miles to go!

I told Tashi to start directly after breakfast and warn the Political Officer of our arrival. But he walked so slowly that, although he started an hour before me, I arrived in Charduar almost as soon as he did, to meet the Political Officer just starting off in his car to pick me up.

So at last I heard the news of the world; I had felt just as happy without it.

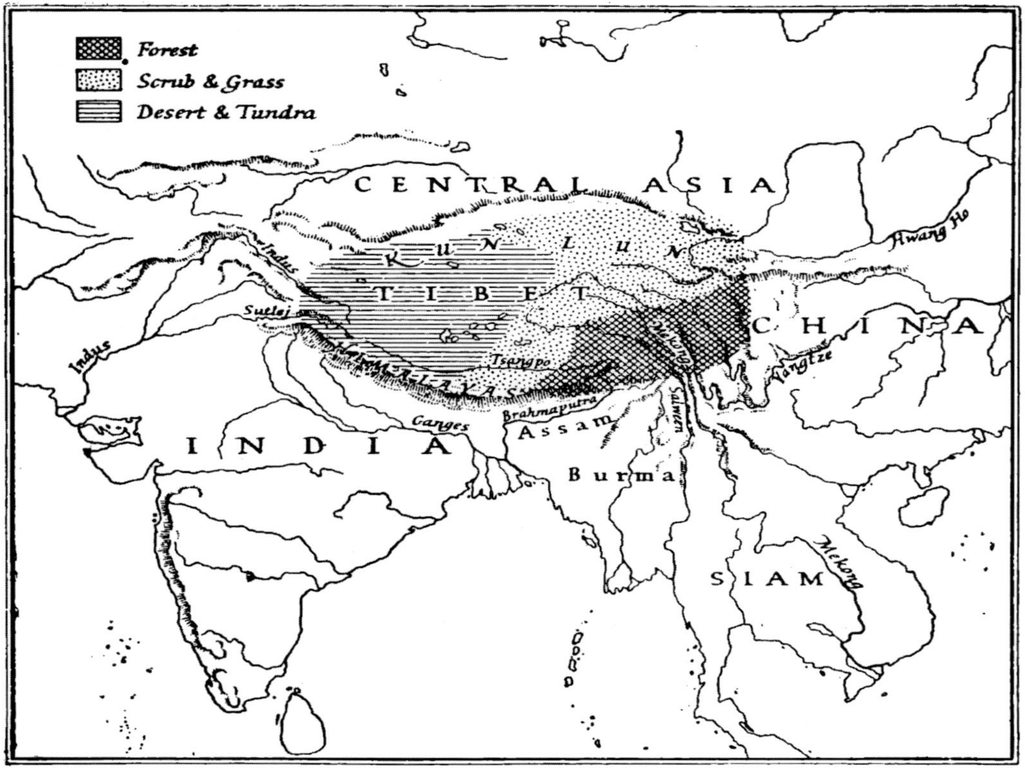

Forest
Scrub & Grass
Desert & Tundra
CENTRAL ASIA
KUNLUN
TIBET
CHINA
INDIA
Assam
Burma
SIAM
Hwang Ho
Yangtze
Mekong
Salween
Brahmaputra
Tsangpo
Ganges
Sutlej
Indus
HIMALAYAS

CHAPTER XXV

THE BOTANY AND GEOGRAPHY OF TIBET

Tibet and the Himalayas are geologically new. They were raised up during the great Tertiary mountain building epoch, and previous to Eocene times, 80 to 100 million years ago were still at the bottom of the Mesozoic sea called the Tethys.

The entire Tibetan plateau, covering six hundred thousand square miles, was originally a basin, dotted with huge lakes which, having no outlet to the sea, were brackish or salt. To-day, owing to gradual disintegration, less than half the plateau is included in the Tibet lake basin; but much of the remainder, while draining slowly outwards, is so elevated that it hardly differs from the interior plateau in appearance, climate, or vegetation.

The gradual crumbling of the rim of the basin occurred both during and after the ice age. First glaciers ploughed wide troughs in the plateau. At a later stage streams, rising from the great glaciers on the outer slopes of the Himalayas, cut their way back into the rim, and beheaded the short interior rivers, whose valleys lay east and west. Thus the lake basin began to be linked up with the outside world, and to shrink.

The Himalaya is not a single range. Viewed from the plains of India, it is seen to consist of a series of more or less parallel ranges, gradually increasing in height, and finally culminating in the great snowy range at a distance of a hundred miles or more from the base of the foothills. It is convenient to divide the eastern Himalaya into three zones:

(*i*) Foothills, rising gradually from the plains to a height of 6000 to 10,000 feet. Covered, at least on their outer slopes, with dense sub-tropical evergreen rain forests below, and with semi-evergreen temperate rain forests at higher altitudes.

(*ii*) Middle or inner ranges, up to 15,000 feet, with intervening valleys as low as 5000 feet. The inner valleys are much drier than those of the foothills, and are filled with pine forest. The inner ranges are forested up to 12,000 or 13,000 feet with warm temperate, cool temperate, and finally conifer forest, according to altitude. Deciduous trees are common in the cool temperate zone, but even here the forest is semi-evergreen.

(*iii*) The crest line or great snowy range, from 15,000 to 25,000 feet. The crest line itself is often double. The valleys between the culminating ranges may be as low as 11,000 to 12,000 feet, and are filled with conifer forest; but the flora is mainly alpine.

The valleys of the middle Himalayas, like those of the main range, are glaciated. Their alpine courses are wide and stoney, the gradient gentle; from here they plunge into impassable gorges at the tree line, so that there is no direct route from the herd villages and pastures to the lower villages and cultivation. The river pattern of Mönyul appears complicated, but is in reality simple; it is the routes which are roundabout. The river system may be briefly described as follows:

(*i*) The Zela range, an offshoot of the main Himalayan range, trends north-east—south-west and forms the water-parting between the eastward flowing and westward flowing rivers of Mönyul.

(*ii*) The eastward flowing rivers rise south of the Zela range, and flow to the Bhareli, which joins the Brahmaputra above Tezpur. The westward flowing rivers rise north of the Zela range, and flow to the Manas, which flows through Bhutan to join the Brahmaputra above Goalpara.

(*iii*) The westward flowing rivers, as soon as they reach the forest, plunge into impassable gorges, because they have still to cross the Zela range which blocks their way southward. The eastward flowing rivers having no such obstacle to cross, continue to flow in open valleys.

(*iv*) This drainage pattern is a result of the glaciation of the eastern Himalayas.

As the glaciers retreated the rivers carved for themselves V-shaped channels in the wide U-shaped valleys, which they could easily do, being charged with glacial grit. These eastern Himalayan valleys are *longitudinal* valleys; that is to say, the streams flow parallel to the main range, in their upper courses, and not as one might expect, transverse to it. Eventually they must turn southwards, in order to reach the plains at all. This is true of all the rivers which drain the Assam Himalayas, from the mighty Tsangpo and the Subansiri, to the little Bhareli. Only when they have followed this course for many — perhaps for hundreds of miles, do they turn south and force their way through the Himalayas.

North of the great snowy range lies the Tibet plateau.

The water parting rarely coincides with the crest line, and often lies far behind it. But the streams which flow down the northern flanks of the Himalayas without exception flow to the Indian Ocean. In spite of its huge extent and importance the Himalaya is not a continental divide.

Beyond the Himalayas are other high parallel ranges rising from the plateau; these ranges appear to converge eastwards. Unlike the Himalayas, the plateau ranges do not consist of many ranges; they are at most double or treble, hence their bases are narrower. This may be due to the fact that they start, not from a few hundred feet, but from 10,000 or 12,000 feet above sea level. They are separated from one another by wide troughs.

It is important to recognize that the Himalayan ranges form one mountain system, and that each of the Tibetan ranges forms a separate system, although all of them are geologically of the same age.

The Tibet plateau, ever since it was first uplifted above the surface of the Tethys, has been subjected to the usual processes of disintegration common to all land surfaces; that is to say weathering. Being well protected from rain by the great rampart of the Himalayas, however, the disintegration has been comparatively slow.

Formerly the entire plateau drained inwards, and comprised one enormous lake basin with innumerable lakes. Then inevitably a breach was forced in the rim of the plateau, and drainage outwards towards the plains and the distant seas began.

During many thousands of years, the outward flowing rivers – following the great glaciers of the ice age and improving on their work – have worn down and dissected the south-eastern quarter of Tibet until to-day it is possible to recognize three distinct regions, each of which marks a stage in the disintegration of the plateau.

The three regions are:

(*i*) The interior plateau, or Tibet lake basin. The short rivers flow inwards and end in salt or brackish lakes. There is no external drainage. The average altitude is about 16,000 feet.

(*ii*) The outer plateau. This has, over a considerable area in the north and west, many of the characteristic features of the interior plateau, but the water is beginning to flow away, and the streams eventually unite to form the great Tibetan rivers which break through the mountains and reach the sea. In the south and east the outer plateau merges into

(*iii*) The river gorge region where the now big rivers have worn deep gorges through the containing rim of the plateau to reach the plains. Here the country has lost all outward likeness to a plateau. It consists of close-set parallel or perhaps converging ranges of mountains separated from one another by terrific gorges which in the south-east are forested.

East of the Tsangpo bend, owing to the meridional arrangement of the gorges, the mountain ranges also appear to be meridional. But it seems probable that the underlying structure is that of a series of ranges which are prolonged eastwards, perhaps right across China to the Pacific coast; and that the apparent meridional arrangement over a brief distance is a superficial feature, due to the very recent cutting of the gorges.

A great mountain range has breadth as well as length and height. If two deep meridional rifts are made close together across an east to west mountain range which is a hundred miles wide, the effect is to isolate a meridional ridge a hundred miles long from north to south. If several such rifts are made, the result must be to give an appearance of meridional ranges in that region.

Admittedly the Chinese ranges to the east are far older than the Tibetan ranges. They were an ancient land surface when Tibet still lay at the bottom of the Tethys. But that does not invalidate the probability that the Tertiary uplift of Tibet gave a new orientation to the Chinese mountains – then very much the worse for wear – rejuvenating and welding them in with the new alignments.

The distribution of plants between eastern China and Tibet, and between Tibet and the south, as well as the raw newness of the Tsangpo, Salween, and Mekong gorges, suggests that this is the true explanation. In geography, things are not always what they seem.

Thus it is probable that the extensions of the Tibetan ranges, which east of the Tsangpo bend seem to turn south through 90° should really be sought eastwards, in China. And this may be equally true of the Himalayas, although a southern loop of the same age can be traced through Assam south of the Brahmaputra valley.[1]

During the last ice age, and before the cutting of the gorges which let in the moist winds and let out the rivers, Tibet was almost completely sterilized of vegetation.

Thus its present flora is derived from surrounding regions, and at so recent a date that few endemics have been evolved.[2]

[1] The Naga, Lushai, and other hill ranges, forming the southern boundary of the Assam valley.

[2] Endemic genera are: Notholirion, Nomocharis, Berneuxia, Chionocharis, Paraquilegia, Oreosolen, Cyananthus, Pegaeophyton, Cremanthodium, Ligularia, Salweenia, Kingdon-Wardia, Lomatogonium, Asteropyrum, Kingdonia, Wardaster, Omphalogramma, Bryocarpum, etc.

For the above reasons, it seems best to regard the flora of Tibet and of the surrounding mountainous regions, the Himalayas, and the mountains of western China, as a major *Floral Region* of Asia comparable with the Central Asian, East Asiatic, and Indo-Malayan regions. This Tibetan region may be called Sino-Himalaya.

Here, however, we are concerned only with the Tibet plateau.

The division of the plateau into three parts in accordance with the physiography, corresponds with the appearance of the country, with the climate, and with the types of vegetation.

The outer plateau, being the link between two extremes, the inner plateau to north and west, and the river gorge region to the south and east, has features in common with both. In the west, the outer plateau is indistinguishable from the inner plateau; in the east, from the river gorge country. Elsewhere it has an individuality of its own.

As regards their flora and vegetation:

(*i*) The interior plateau (Chang Tang) is a desert with an extremely scanty flora, comprising about fifty-three species of flowering plants.

(*ii*) The outer plateau includes the most habitable parts of Tibet, although the average elevation is 12,000 to 15,000 feet. There is a considerable flora, amounting to several hundred species of flowering plants. The plateau nature of the country is obvious; but towards the south-east, the gradual dissection of the plateau as the rivers cut deeper, and the intervening snow-clad ranges converge, becomes the most prominent feature.

(*iii*) The river gorge region. Here the streams which rise on the outer rim of the Chang Tang and flow for hundreds of miles across the outer plateau in comparatively broad shallow valleys, are cutting deep grooves for themselves through the lofty containing wall in order to reach the plains below. The contrast of altitudes and climates is extreme. All the main types of vegetation are met with, and the flora probably amounts to several thousand species.

Whereas the wide valleys of the outer plateau are ice worn, the gorges are entirely the work of rivers.

Thus the geography of Tibet, which at first sight appears complicated, is in its essential features, simple; and the vegetation conforms to the physiography.

To the geographical botanist the river gorge region is by far the most interesting. It consists of converging or parallel ranges of mountains crowned by peaks 25,000 feet high and pierced by gorges 10,000 feet deep. This physical diversity gives rise to a corresponding diversity of climate and vegetation. The flora of the river gorge region is very rich. Here are found the only forests in Tibet; and the vegetation varies from sub-tropical moist evergreen forest to alpine in the space of a few miles. More than a thousand species of flowering plants and ferns are already known from this comparatively small region. But great areas are still completely unknown.

Broadly speaking, the vegetation of the interior plateau is a tundra climax, that of the outer plateau an alpine climax, and that of the river gorge region a forest climax.

The first part of Tibet to become known to scientific men was, curiously enough, the Chang Tang, or Tibet lake basin – the most repellent part of the country. Small wonder that this cold wilderness with its fifty odd species of flowering plants gave a distorted idea of the flora of Tibet as a whole! For the sake of convenience it was lumped in with the Central Asian flora although it had very little in common with that region.[1]

During the present century, much botanical exploration has been carried out in southern and eastern Tibet, particularly in the river gorge region, as a result of which it is necessary to modify considerably our views of the Tibetan flora.[2] Having

[1] 'A Sketch of the Botany and Geography of Tibet', *Journal of the Linnean Society* (Botany), vol. I, No. 333 (1934).

[2] The explorations of Mr. F. Ludlow, Captain George Sherriff and Dr. George Taylor deserve special mention.

regard to the flora of Tibet as a whole — and at least 2000 species are now recorded — it is found that the relationship is with eastern Asia and to a lesser degree with Indo-Malaya, rather than with Central Asia.

The following is a list of the climax formations of Tibet, with their distribution. Future workers in this field may reduce the number; but for the present it seems best to label all major formations as climax formations.

Climax Formation	*Locality*	*Characteristic Plants*
Tundra	Interior plateau (Tibet lake basin). Outer plateau adjacent, including head-waters of the great rivers	*Thermopsis inflata, Draba alpina, Tanacetum tibeticum, Astragalus Malcomii*
Alpine Climaxes Grassland	N.E. Tibet, and eastwards to Kansu; Koko Nor, Chamdo	*Meconopsis quintuplinervia*
Gravel	South - central Tibet; Lhasa, Gyantse; Shigatse	*Meconopsis horridula, Iris lactea, Clematis orientalis*
High alpine turf and scree	Great ranges of S.E. Tibet, 16,000-18,000 feet	*Primula macrophylla, Allium calcophengos*
Alpine thorn scrub	South - central Tibet. Tsangpo valley. Sources of Subansiri	*Hippophäe rhamnoides; Lonicera spinosa, Iris goniocarpa, Incarvillea lutea*
Alpine scrub	Great ranges of S.E. Tibet, 12,000-15,000 feet	*Rhododendron lanatum; Lonicera cyanocarpa*
Woodland Climaxes Betula-Quercus Formation	Upper Gyamda valley; Tsangpo valley above the gorge; sources of the Subansiri	*Betula utilis; Quercus Ilex; Rosa sericea; Spiraea canescens*
Forest Climaxes (A) 'Moist' Forest (*i*) Deciduous Type Acer-Magnolia Formation	Zayul; Tsangpo gorge, 6000-8000 feet	*Magnolia rostrata; Acer Campbellii; Michelia lanuginosa*

Climax Formation	*Locality*	*Characteristic Plants*
(*ii*) Semi-deciduous Type		
Quercus-Rhododendron Formation	Tsangpo gorge; Po-Yigrong gorge, 7000-9000 feet	*Cedrela; Rhododendron; Iris Milesii*
(*iii*) Evergreen Type		
Tsuga-Rhododendron Formation	Zayul; Mönyul; Pemako, 8000-10,000 feet	*Rhododendron; Cotoneaster Wardii; Lonicera; Magnolia globosa*
(*iv*) Sub-alpine Type		
Abies-Juniperus Formation	Tsari; Eastern Tibet, 10,000-12,000 feet	
Abies-Picea-Larix Formation	Mönyul; Shugden Gompa; Kongbo; Zayul; Tsari; Pome; and S.E. Tibet generally	*Rhododendron cerasinum; Acer stachyophyllum*
(B) 'Dry' Forest		
(*i*) Sub-alpine Type		
Picea-Betula Formation	Shugden Gompa 12,000-13,000 feet	*Picea likiangensis; Betula utilis; Caragana jubata; Rhododendron vellereum*
(*ii*) Montane Type		
Pinus-Quercus Formation	Lower Zayul; Mönyul	*Pinus insularis; Quercus glauca; Pieris ovalifolia; Symplocos; Myrsine semiserrata; Ailanthus*
(*iii*) Evergreen Type		
Mixed Pine Formation P. insularis; P. excelsa	Middle Tsangpo gorge; Po-Yigrong gorge	*Syringa villosa; Rhododendron niphargum; Taxus Wallichiana; Iris Milesii; Lilium Wardii*

The topographical results of the journey and the conclusions I arrived at, may be summarized as follows:

1. Between the crest line of the Assam Himalayas and the Tsangpo are two lesser ranges of fold mountains which may bear the same relation to the main range on its north flank that the ranges of Mönyul do on the south flank. These ranges, composed mainly of sedimentary rocks, can be traced from the 92nd to the 94th meridian, east of which they disappear, or merge into the main range. Both ranges are intermittently elevated above the snow line, although the peaks probably nowhere exceed 20,000 feet. Most of the glaciers have disappeared, but there is abundant evidence of former glaciation.

Takpa Shiri stands on the southernmost of these two ranges, not on the Himalayan crest line.

II. These fold ranges are composed of slates, phyllites, schists and limestone, with numerous quartz veins, and are highly contorted. Good examples of this contortion are seen immediately north of the Rip La, north of the Mo La, and in the gorge of the Char Chu below Sanga Chöling. Their crest lines are usually of the sierra type, and the sharp saw-edged spurs present one fractured precipitous and one sloping face.

III. The Loro Chu and the Char Chu both flow along cracked anticlines, as is shown by the rocks dipping away from the river on either side. The strike of the rocks is approximately east and west. These valleys show no signs of glaciation, although all the short tributary valleys, such as the Karta valley, are glaciated in their upper courses.

IV. North of the Tsangpo, between the meridians 91°-94°, extends a single range separating the Tsangpo valley from the valleys of the Kyi Chu and Gyamda Chu to the north. There are a few snow peaks, not exceeding about 20,000 feet, and small glaciers on this range also; it has been extensively glaciated in the past. In its structure, however, it is very different from the fold ranges just described, for it is composed mainly of igneous, not of sedimentary rock; on the Ashang Kang La the rock is arkose, derived directly from the disintegration of igneous rock.

The general trend of this range appears to be south-west to north-east, parallel to the Great Himalyan range. Possibly it is an extension of the range which is crossed by travellers on the main road to Lhasa, north of Gyantse; this range was called by Burrard the Ladhak range.[1]

The Tsangpo may cut through this Ladhak range in longitude 93°.

East of Tsetang four passes, the Kumba La, Gechi La, Ashang Kang La, and Sho La, connect the Tsangpo valley

[1] Op. cit.

with the Gyalam (China road), and are used by traders between Takpo and the north, and by pilgrims visiting Tsari. I crossed the Kumba La in 1925, and the Ashang Kang La in 1935.

v. South of the Salween river the evidence of former glaciation in Tibet decreases steadily from east to west, and from south to north. As far west as the 90th meridian there is abundant evidence of glaciation; but beyond that, on the plateau itself, there seems to be little or none. The shrinkage of the lakes, however, suggests that the Tibet plateau is drying up, and that it formerly enjoyed a moister climate. One would therefore expect glaciers to have existed here during the ice age.

vi. The following areas of southern Tibet crossed in 1935 show intense glaciation. The whole of Tsari; both the fold ranges referred to in paragraph I above; the upper Po-Yigrong; the mountains between the Tsangpo and the Gyamda river. It is clear that the whole of south-eastern Tibet between the meridians 90° to 100° and the parallels 28° to 32° was once covered by an ice sheet, so large and numerous were the glaciers. This represents an area of about 110,000 square miles and it was probably the largest continuous ice sheet north of the Himalayas.

vii. One result of the shrinkage of the glaciers has been a diminution in the volume of the rivers which they feed. Thus the vast accumulation of gravel in the valley of the Loro Chu below Karta was laid down by a much larger stream than the present one, as the size of the boulders moved indicates.

viii. The following six passes south of the Tsangpo were crossed for the first time: Over the southern fold range, the Drichung La and Mo La. In Tsari, the Rip La and Ja La. Between Tsari and the Tsangpo, the Bimbi La and Lang La.

ix. Beyond Migyitun and the Tsari river, the sacred lake Tsogar and the snow peaks and glaciers overhanging it were discovered. These peaks are on the main Himalayan range, as also are those seen from the Lang La.[1]

[1] This fact, suspected by me, was established by Ludlow and Sherriff in 1936.

x. North of the Tsangpo and at a distance varying between thirty-five miles in the neighbourhood of the 95th meridian and fifty miles or more farther west, stretches a magnificent range of snow peaks. Between Gyamda and Tongkyuk this range trends approximately east and west. Beyond Tongkyuk it converges towards the Great Himalayan range. I propose to call it the Po-Yigrong range.

xi. This snow range is composed mainly of igneous rocks. Its westward extension may be the range I crossed by the Ashang Kang La, between the Tsangpo and the Gyamda river; but more probably the westward extension lies north of the Gyamda Chu. In about longitude 93° it appears to be identical with the Salween-Tsangpo divide.

xii. Its glaciers give birth to the following rivers: Yigrong and Tongkyuk rivers, entirely; Gyamda river (eastern branch) entirely or mainly; several tributaries of the Gyamda Chu.

xiii. The main crest line of the Po-Yigrong range lies south of the river gorge, and the highest peaks are situated just north of the Pasum Tso. The snow crest line north of the Po-Yigrong may also belong to the Po-Yigrong range, giving it a double crest line with the river between them.

xiv. The following passes, in order from east to west, cross the southern crest line of the Po-Yigrong range: Sobhé La; Ba La; Lochen La; Tse La; Pasum Kye La. I discovered and crossed the Sobhé La, Lochen La and Tso La in 1935, and the Pasum Kye La in 1924. The Nambu La above Tongkyuk which Cawdor and I crossed in 1924 and 1925 is not on the main Po-Yigrong range, but on a spur.

xv. The high peaks of the southern crest line occur in groups. There is a group of very high peaks a little north of the Sobhé La; another group stands almost opposite Ragoonka; a third group is the source of the large glacier blocking the Po-Yigrong valley at Nyotö; a fourth commands the source of the river and blocks the head of the valley. No heights are known. From the size of the glaciers and the levels to which they descend, I should judge there are several peaks over 23,000 feet high, and possibly one or two over 25,000 feet. All the glaciers seen are, and have long been, retreating; nevertheless they are amongst the largest known north of the Tsangpo.

XVI. I followed the Po-Yigrong river from the lake westwards to its source, a distance of nearly a hundred miles, discovered the villages of Temo Chamna, Tagé, Ragoonka, Nyöme, and Nyotö, all in the gorge, and found the source of the river in a group of glaciers south-east of Atsa. Between the Sobhé La and the Lochen La, I counted over forty transverse glaciers descending from the northern and southern crest lines to the river. Only two *longitudinal* glaciers still survive, both at the source of the river above Nyotö.

XVII. In the *Geographical Journal*, February 1926, I suggested that the stream which flows eastwards from the Atsa Tso might prove to be the source of the Po-Yigrong. This has been shown to be incorrect; but probably the Atsa Tso does empty into the Po-Yigrong lower down. It may enter the Po-Yigrong at Nye.

XVIII. The gorge of the Po-Yigrong is comparable with that of the Kongbo-Tsangpo itself in depth, though not in length. Like the Tsangpo gorge, it is forested throughout, but being colder and less moist, the forest is everywhere poorer in species. Conifers form a large proportion of the trees; there is no subtropical evergreen rain forest as there is at the lower end of the Tsangpo gorge.

XIX. The eastward and westward extensions of the Po-Yigrong range are unexplored. Eastwards it probably extends through Pome to the neighbourhood of Shugden Gompa, north of the Po-Tsangpo. Westwards it extends beyond the Giamda-Atsa road (which crosses it by the Tro La), and probably becomes the Salween-Tsangpo divide in about latitude 30° to 31°, longitude 92° to 93°. Otherwise it may fork and one branch trend south-westwards from the source of the Po-Yigrong to continue as the range between the Tsangpo and Gyamda rivers which I crossed by the Ashang Kang La.

XX. Coming to the mountains of Pome, Gyala Peri and Markandro appear to be off the alignment of the Po-Yigrong range. Their position suggests that they stand on one of the fold ranges between the Great Himalayan range and the Tsangpo, referred to in paragraph I. But these ranges disappear east of 94°, where the distance between the Himalayan crest line and the Tsangpo is sometimes less than ten miles. If Gyala Peri does stand on this alignment, then the Tsangpo must cut across one or both of these fold ranges between Tsela Dzong and Kyikar. The appearance of the river here is entirely in harmony with its cutting across a mountain axis.

Alternatively Gyala Peri and Markandro may stand on the Great Himalayan range, which then shows a double crest line, with the Tsangpo flowing between, exactly as the Po-Yigrong flows between parallel ranges of snow peaks.

Gyala Peri is almost due north of Namcha Barwa, and sixteen miles distant; and Namcha Barwa itself is about twenty-five miles north of the foot of the Himalayas as measured from the Dihang valley, a few thousand feet above sea level. Allowing an equal distance north of Namcha Barwa for the breadth of the Himalayas at this point – and the range is here at its narrowest – this would include both Gyala Peri and Markandro in a total breadth of less than fifty miles! Elsewhere the breadth of the Himalayas is as much as a hundred and twenty miles.

XXI. The Po-Yigrong range is not, in the region explored, the Salween-Tsangpo divide, which lies farther north. But as pointed out in paragraph XIX, it may merge into or become the Salween-Tsangpo divide farther west. The region bounded by the meridians 93° to 96° and the parallels 29° to 31° with a superficial area of 25,000 square miles, is a region of maximum elevation.

XXII. Crossing the Tibetan plateau are a number of great mountain ranges separated by wide shallow troughs. More ranges emerge from eastern Tibet than are known to enter western Tibet, they are closer together, and less parallel than the central Tibetan ranges. A possible explanation is that the original ranges bifurcate eastwards and so give rise to more ranges.

XXIII. The Po-Yigrong range defines the boundary between the forests to the south and the dry grazing plateau country to the north. It acts to some extent as a rain screen, just as farther west the Great Himalayan range acts as a rain screen.

XXIV. The Gyalam nowhere touches the Po-Yigrong river but on the contrary avoids it by turning north from Gyamda and crossing the snow range west of its source.

In the most recent map of this part of Tibet published by the Survey of India corrected to 1929 (Sheet 82 1/M), two streams are shown between the meridians 94° and 95°, meeting at Alado (or Alando), the Sya Chu from the east, the Nok Chu from the west; these are represented as the sources of the Po-Yigrong. But this Alado Chu is only a small tributary; the main stream has its source fifty miles south-west of Alado.

Between Nyöme and Alado three passes must be crossed. The Alado Chu, as described in chap. XXIII, flows in a deep gorge which would account for the passes, since it is unlikely that the path keeps close to the river.

XXV. There remains the possibility that the Po-Yigrong range is the continuation of the Ninchinthangla range, which Burrard suggests, reasonably enough, continues eastwards.

But in longitude 93°, the Ninchinthangla range is a hundred and twenty miles north of the Tsangpo, whereas the Po-Yigrong range is nowhere more than fifty miles north. The Littledales[1] crossed the Ninchinthangla range north of Lhasa; but Nain Singh, who traced it for a hundred and fifty miles beyond that point, found that it trended north-east and formed the watershed between the Tsangpo and the interior plateau. Thus in longitude 94°, it lies far north of where I crossed the Po-Yigrong range. It is impossible to identify the one with the other.

Thus a lot more work remains to be done before we shall have a correct picture of Tibetan geography.

[1] *Geographical Journal*, 1896.

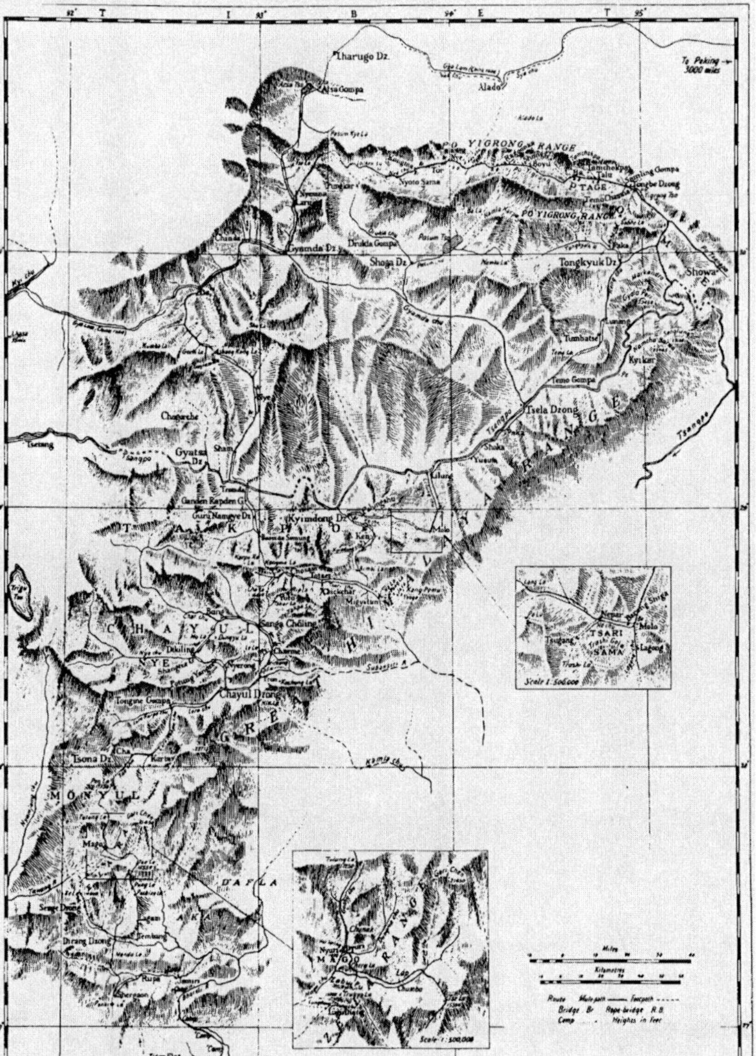

T I B E T
Tharugo Dz.
Atsa Gompa
Alado
To Peking 3000 miles
PO YIGRONG RANGE
Gyamda Dz.
Drukla Gompa
Shoga Dz.
Tongkyuk Dz.
Showa
Tumbatse
Temo Gompa
Tsela Dzong
Tsangpo
Chagarche
Tsetang
Gyatsa Dz.
Gandem Rapden G.
Guru Namgye Dz.
Kyimdong Dz.
Molo
TSARI
SAMA
Lagung
Scale 1:500,000
Sanga Chöling
Chayul Dzong
Tsona Dz.
MONYUL
DAFLA
Senge Dzong
Dirang Dzong
Rupa
Tiger Flat
Charduar
Tezpur
Brahmaputra
Miles
Kilometres
A S S A M

APPENDIX I

SUMMARY of Marches from Tezpur in Assam, over the Great Himalayan Range, across Southern Tibet, and back to Tezpur. (The more important places are printed in italics.)

Date	*Name of Stage*	*Approximate Distance (in miles)* *Inter-mediate*	*Total*	*Remarks on road, villages, passes and transport*
25 April	*Tezpur*	0	0	On the Brahmaputra; reached by river steamer or rail or both.
26 ,,	*Charduar: Lokra*	21	21	Outpost, Balipara Frontier Tract; by motor.
29 ,,	Tiger Flat: Camp	24	45	Dry weather motor road to the Belsiri river, wade across, walk five miles.
30 ,,	Doimara: Camp	11	56	Up the stream bed, jungle and savannah; swampy in places. Coolies only.
1 May	Jungle Camp	9	65	Up narrow valley, following torrent. Camp under high cliff.
2 ,,	Jungle Camp	11	76	Stiff climb, camp in clearing just below pass.
3 ,,	*Shergaon*	8	84	Crossing Pankim La, 9000 feet; village.
6 ,,	Dumkho	10	94	Village; crossing pass, about 8000 feet. From Shergaon onwards, ponies and mules can be used.
14 ,,	Phutang	9	103	Village; crossing pass, about 8000 feet.
19 ,,	*Dirang Dzong* (5700 ft.)	12	115	Crossing the Manda La, about 11,000 feet. Large village.
26 ,,	Liu	5	120	Large village; some rice cultivated.
27 ,,	Nyukmadong	7	127	Large village.
28 ,,	*Senge Dzong* (9900 ft.)	5	132	A stiff climb; small village and monastery.
3 June	Alpine Camp	12	144	Crossing the Ze La, 14,000 feet.

APPENDIX I

Date	Name of Stage	Approximate Distance (in miles)		Remarks on road, villages, passes and transport
		Inter-mediate	Total	
4 June	Alpine Camp	7	151	Alpine valley; crossing two passes, about 14,000 feet.
5 ,,	Lugathang	8	159	Crossing the Kya La, about 14,000 feet; Drokpa village.
7 ,,	Alpine Camp	7	166	Crossing the Trukya La, about 15,000 feet.
8 ,,	*Mago* (Dyuri: 11,800 ft.)	10	176	Crossing the Chera La, 14,100 feet; Drokpa village by the Dungma Chu.
12 ,,	Alpine Camp	8	184	Passing Chunak, temporary herds' camp; Yak transport from Mago.
13 ,,	Alpine Camp (Chupda)	12	196	Crossing the Tulung La, 17,250 feet; no fuel (Main Himalayan chain)
14 ,,	Alpine Camp	12	208	Crossing the Pen La, 17,320 feet; no fuel (Main Himalayan chain)
15 ,,	*Karta*	10	218	Large village; on the Tibet plateau, ponies and mules.
17 ,,	*Tongme Gompa* (12,400 ft.)	13	231	Village by the Loro Chu; monastery.
18 ,,	Hordoryu	14	245	A large house.
19 ,,	*Chayul Dzong* or Chadze (11,450 ft.)	7	252	Small village and monastery.
24 ,,	Trön	17	269	Village: cliff climbing by ladders, coolies only, from Chayul.
26 ,,	Alpine Camp	8	277	On a spur overlooking the Loro Chu.
27 ,,	Charme	11	288	Crossing the Drichung La, about 17,000 feet; small village.
28 ,,	*Sanga Chöling* (10,900 ft.)	11	299	A beautiful village, with two fine monasteries.
30 ,,	Alpine Camp	10	309	With the herds.
1 July	*Chösam* (14,200 ft.)	15	324	Crossing the Cha La, 16,610 feet; Drokpa village.
2 ,,	*Chickchar* (12,700 ft.)	15	339	Small village with several monasteries, on the pilgrim road.
6 ,,	Migyitun (9630 ft.)	12	351	Small semi-Tibetan village on the borders of tribal territory.
7 ,,	Tsogar	12	363	Long march crossing 3 passes, the highest, Ja La, about 17,000 feet. Sleep in small house.

APPENDIX I

Date	Name of Stage	Approximate Distance (in miles) Inter-mediate	Total	Remarks on road, villages, passes and transport
8 July	Alpine camp	6	369	In alpine valley, below a glacier.
9 ,,	Migyitun	6	375	Sleep in communal inn.
11 ,,	Camp	12	387	In meadow.
12 ,,	Camp	12	399	Crossing the Bimbi La, about 15,000 feet; ponies and yak can cross.
13 ,,	Ken (Sumbatse)	12	411	Small village.
14 ,,	*Kyimdong Dzong*	8	419	Very poor village.
15 ,,	Camp	8	427	Near the last house in the valley.
16 ,,	Camp	12	439	Crossing the Lang La, 16,100 feet.
17 ,,	Barong Shiga	12	451	Passing through Nepar; a small village.
18 ,,	*Lilung*	18	469	Passing Molo, a large village; Lilung, 3 houses on the Tsangpo.
19 ,,	Yusum	10	479	Village.
20 ,,	Tokar	15	494	Village.
21 ,,	Paka	8	502	Village.
22 ,,	*Tsela Dzong* (9700 ft.)	6	508	Ferry across the Tsangpo. Small village.
26 ,,	Temo Gompa	13	521	By coracle across the Gyamda river confluence; large monastery.
27 ,,	Tumbatse	15	536	Crossing the Temo La, 14,600 feet. Village.
28 ,,	Chunyima	13	549	Passing through Lunang; small village.
29 ,,	*Tongkyuk Dzong* (8500 ft.)	10	559	Village.
31 ,,	Camp	5	564	By the Tongkyuk river.
1 Aug.	Camp	9	573	In alpine valley; ponies returned from here.
2 ,,	Camp	12	585	Crossing the Sobhé La, about 17,000 feet. Coolies only.
3 ,,	Temo Chamna (7500 ft.)	10	595	Small village by the Po-Yigrong lake; most easterly point reached.
4 ,,	Camp	6	601	In the Yigrong gorge, by torrent in forest. Coolies only.
5 ,,	Camp	5	606	In the forest.
6 ,,	Talu	4	610	Crossing the Po-Yigrong by rope bridge; village.
8 ,,	Camp	9	619	Yigrong gorge
,,	Tongdü	7	626	Small village.

APPENDIX I

Date	*Name of Stage*	*Approximate Distance (in miles)* *Inter-mediate*	*Total*	*Remarks on road, villages, passes and transport*
10 Aug.	Camp	5	631	Passing through small villages, Boyu and Shonggyi.
11 ,,	*Ragoonka*	4	635	Big village high above the river.
13 ,,	Camp	7	642	Difficult marching in the gorge; camp in forest.
14 ,,	Camp	5	647	Cliff climbing; camp in forest.
15 ,,	Camp	3	650	Cliff climbing; camp above the gorge.
16 ,,	Nye	5	655	Cross Po-Yigrong by rope bridge; village.
17 ,,	Kongma	12	667	A few herds' houses.
18 ,,	Camp	12	679	Passing through Nyotö Sama; camp in meadow above glacier.
19 ,,	Camp	8	687	Yak camp in alpine valley.
20 ,,	Camp	6	693	Crossing the Lochen La, about 17,000 feet; yak camp.
21 ,,	Camp	7	700	Alpine camp; no fuel. Most northerly point reached.
22 ,,	Camp	9	709	Crossing the Tze La, about 16,000 feet; herds' camp.
23 ,,	Camp	8	717	Passing through Nyemna and Laru; on the Gyalam.
24 ,,	*Gyamda*	8	725	Town on the great road from Lhasa to Peking; all forms of transport except wheeled traffic. Post office.
28 ,,	Chinda	13	738	On the Gyalam.
29 ,,	Camp	14	752	On the Gyalam.
30 ,,	Camp	7	759	Passing through De; camp with herds. South of the Gyalam.
31 ,,	Camp	10	769	Herds' camp.
1 Sept.	Camp	9	778	Crossing the Ashang Kang La, about 17,000 feet; ponies and yak can cross.
2 ,,	Nye	15	793	A long march; Nye has 4 huts.
4 ,,	Shām	15	808	Village
5 ,,	*Tromda*	12	820	Cross the Tsangpo by ferry to south bank; village.
8 ,,	*Guru Namgye Dzong*	6	826	Passing Ganden Rapden Gompa.
9 ,,	Trupchuka (14,950 ft.)	14	840	Dropka village.
10 ,,	Chösam (14,200 ft.)	18	858	Crossing the Kongma La, 17,520 feet.

APPENDIX I

Date	Name of Stage	*Approximate Distance (in miles)* Intermediate	Total	*Remarks on road, villages, passes and transport*
12 Sept.	Yutö (13,200 ft.)	8	866	Crossing the Rip La, about 17,000 feet. One hut.
13 ,,	Camp	13	879	Crossing the Takar La, 16,700 feet.
14 ,,	*Sanga Chöling*	5	884	Garden city.
18 ,,	Bung	12	896	A large house and estate.
19 ,,	Dikiling	18	914	Crossing the Mo La, about 17,000 feet. A large village in arid country.
20 ,,	Potung Yangze	10	924	Village and fine monastery.
21 ,,	*Chayul Dzong*	12	936	Village and monastery.
27 ,,	Yara	10	946	Village.
28 ,,	*Tongme Gompa*	11	957	Village and monastery.
29 ,,	*Karta*	13	970	Large village, and monastery.
1 Oct.	Cha (14,300 ft.)	5	975	Small village.
2 ,,	Camp	10	985	Crossing the Pen La 17,330 feet; camp in valley just below, about 15,000 feet.
3 ,,	Camp	10	995	Crossing the Tulung La, 17,250 feet; camp when we reach brushwood.
4 ,,	*Mago* (Dyuri)	12	1007	Passing summer village of Chunak, and hot spring.
8 ,,	Camp (Lap)	12	1019	Crossing the Chera La, 14,100 feet, and ascending the Gorjo Chu, with yak transport.
9 ,,	Camp (Samjung)	10	1029	Crossing the Tse La, about 15,000 feet.
10 ,,	Camp (Dongri)	9	1038	Crossing the Poshing La, 11,950 feet.
11 ,,	*Tembang* (7600 ft.)	18	1056	Passing through Lagam.
12 ,,	*Dirang Dzong* (5700 ft.)	13	1069	Passing through Namshu.
16 ,,	Phutang	12	1081	Village.
17 ,,	Dumkho	9	1090	Village.
18 ,,	*Shergaon*	10	1100	Village.
20 ,,	Camp	14	1114	By the stream in limestone gorge.
21 ,,	Rupa (or Dukpen)	6	1120	Large Sherdukpen village.
22 ,,	Camp	12	1132	In the forest.
23 ,,	Jamiri	12	1144	Akha village.
25 ,,	Camp	6	1150	In the jungle.
26 ,,	Camp	10	1160	In the jungle.
27 ,,	Camp	10	1170	By the Bhareli river, in jungle.
28 ,,	Camp	14	1184	On the cart road.
29 ,,	Charduar	10	1194	Outpost.
2 Nov.	Tezpur	21	1215	On the Brahmaputra.

APPENDIX II

Gardeners who grow new and rare plants will be interested in the following list of Tibetan plants, most of them 'new', or not previously in cultivation, which I have introduced to the West as the result of three extensive journeys in the interior of Tibet, in 1924, 1933, and 1935. It may serve also as an aperitif to that Flora of Tibet which must some day be written. I have added from my notebooks the first field number under which the species was collected in Tibet – which is not necessarily the seed number under which it has been raised, but may refer to a herbarium specimen *only* – now lurking in the naphthalene-scented cabinets of the national herbaria at Edinburgh, Kew, or the British Museum (Natural History). In the fourth column I have added the year of the plant's finding, in southern Tibet; and if it was previously or subsequently found in adjacent regions of different political complexion, the years of such discovery also; thus indicating its known distribution in space.

A.M.=Award of Merit; A.G.M.=Award of Garden Merit; F.C.C.=First Class Certificate – all Royal Horticultural Society's blessings; Bot. Mag.=Curtis's Botanical Magazine, now after more than a century's vicissitudes, edited for the Royal Horticultural Society by Sir Arthur Hill, Director of the Royal Botanic Gardens, Kew, in which plants grown in this country are figured in colour and described.

K.W. No.	*Name*	*Bot. Mag. Tab.*	*Remarks*
5832	Acer caudatum. var.		1924
9493	„ taronense		N. Burma 1931, Tibet 1933
10368	„ tibetense		1933
10616	Ajuga ovalifolia		1933
	Androsace Wardii		
10852	„ zayulensis		1933
6308	Berberis calliantha		1924
11036	„ chrysosphaera		1933
10548	„ circumserrata		1933

APPENDIX II

K.W. No.	Name	Bot. Mag. Tab.	Remarks
11716	Berberis kartanica		1935
6244	Cassiope selaginoides		1924
6400	Cotoneaster conspicua	9554	1924
6400A	,, ,, var. decora.		1924
5949	Cyananthus lobatus var. insignis		1924
6082	,, Wardii		1924 Lost to cultivation
11992	Desmodium callianthum		1935
11841	Dracocephalum Hemsleyanum	9547	1935
10640	,, heterophyllum		1933
10994	Gaultheria codonantha	9456	Assam 1928, Tibet 1933
6071	,, Wardii	9516	Tibet 1924, N. Burma 1926, Assam 1928
10954	Gentiana laghuensis		1933
10860	,, sino-ornata dichroa		1933
10898	,, Szechenyi		1933
	,, Przewalskii		W. China 1922, Tibet 1933
	,, Waltonii		1924
11009	,, oreodoxa		
11729	Incarvillea lutea. var.		1924,1935
11712	Iris lactea		1924. A good form
10775	,, goniocarpa		1933, 1935
6034	Lilium Wardii		1924. A.M., F.C.C.
5776	Lonicera hispida. var. bracteata	9360	1924
5784	Meconopsis betonicifolia Baileyi	9185	1924. A.M., F.C.C. Gold Medal, Ghent
6115	Onosma Hookeri Wardii	9254	1924. Probably lost to cultivation
11710	Paraquilegia grandiflora		
6268	Parnassia nubicola		1924
5746	Primula alpicola luna	9276	1924
5818	,, ,, violacea	9276	1924
5985	,, Baileyana	9189	1924. Lost to cultivation
	,, bellidifolia		1924
5740	,, chungensis		China 1913, Tibet 1924
5741	,, Cawdoriana	9196	1924
5781	,, Florindae		1924. F.C.C., A.G.M.
5819	,, latisecta	9245	1924
	,, pulchelloides		W. China 1911, Tibet 1924, 1935
6221	,, vinosa	9210	In Bot. Mag. as P. sikkimensis microdonta
7101	Rheum		1926
6278	Rhododendron auritum		1924
5830	,, cerasinum		Tibet 1924, N. Burma 1926, Assam 1928
5849	,, chamaetortum		N. Burma 1919, Tibet 1924
5874	,, concatenans		1924
6311	,, Coryanum		1924
10542	,, crebreflorum		N. Burma 1926, Assam 1928, Tibet 1933

APPENDIX II

K.W. No.	Name		Bot. Mag. Tab.	Remarks
5863	Rhododendron	doshongense		1924
6313	,,	flavantherum		1924
5734	,,	fragariflorum		Tibet 1924, Assam 1935
5659	,,	hirtipes		1924
6257	,,	Keysii unicolor		1924. A.M.
5700	,,	kongboense	9492	1924
6273	,,	leucaspis		Tibet 1924, 1935, Assam 1928
6286	,,	megacalyx		N. Burma 1914, Tibet 1924, Assam 1928
6257A	,,	melinanthum		W. China 1913, Tibet 1924
5660	,,	niphargum		W. China 1913, Tibet 1924, 1935
6333	,,	Nuttallii stellatum		1924
5729	,,	paludosum		1924
5875	,,	parmulatum		1924
6381	,,	pemakoense		1924. Stoloniferous
10500	,,	pruniflorum		N. Burma 1926, Tibet 1933
5856	,,	pumilum		Tibet 1924, N. Burma 1926, Assam 1928
6284	,,	Ramsdenianum		1924
5845	,,	repens chamaedoxa		1924
5847	,,	repens chamaethauma		1924
6415	,,	rhabdotum	9447	Tibet 1924, Assam 1935
5828	,,	riparium		A.M., Tibet 1924, N. Burma 1926, Assam 1928
6325	,,	scopulorum	9399	1924
6258	,,	silvaticum		1924
5733	,,	temoense		Tibet 1924, Assam 1935
5687	,,	triflorum mahogani		1924
5844	,,	tsangpoense		1924
5876	,,	uniflorum		Not happily named; in cultivation often bears 2-3 flowers together
5656	,,	vellereum		Tibet 1924
6285	,,	venator		A.M. Tibet 1924
10952	,,	vesiculiferum		N. Burma 1926, 1931, Tibet 1933
5829	,,	viridescens		1924
5736	,,	Wardii		W. China 1913, Tibet 1924
6026	,,	xanthocodon		1924
6101	Rosa Wardii			1924
10591	Salvia Wardii			1924, 1933
10680	Salweenia Wardii			1933
5899	Thalictrum diffusiflorum			1924
10808	Trollius			1933
10377	Vaccinium glauco-album			